HOUSING, 'RACE' AND COMMUNITY COHESION

Malcolm Harrison, Deborah Phillips, Kusminder Chahal, Lisa Hunt, and John Perry

Chartered Institute of Housing
Policy and Practice Series
in collaboration with the
Housing Studies Association

Coventry: CIH, 2005   1903208211

The Chartered Institute of Housing

The Chartered Institute of Housing is the professional organisation for people who work in housing. Its purpose is to maximise the contribution housing professionals make to the well-being of communities. The Institute has 19,000 members across the UK and the Asian Pacific working in a range of organisations, including housing associations, local authorities, the private sector and educational institutions.

Chartered Institute of Housing
Octavia House, Westwood Way
Coventry CV4 8JP
Telephone: 024 7685 1700
Fax: 024 7669 5110
Website: www.cih.org

The Housing Studies Association

The Housing Studies Association promotes the study of housing by bringing together housing researchers with others interested in housing research in the housing policy and practitioner communities. It acts as a voice for housing research by organising conferences and seminars, lobbying government and other agencies and providing services to members.

The CIH Housing Policy and Practice Series is published in collaboration with the Housing Studies Association and aims to provide important and valuable material and insights for housing managers, staff, students, trainers and policy-makers. Books in the series are designed to promote debate, but the contents do not necessarily reflect the views of the CIH or the HSA. The Editorial Team for the series is: General Editors: Dr. Peter Williams, John Perry and Professor Peter Malpass, and Production Editor: Alan Dearling.

Cover photographs provided by the William Sutton Group

This publication has been sponsored by the William Sutton Group

ISBN 1 903208 21 1

Housing, 'race' and community cohesion
Malcolm Harrison, Deborah Phillips, Kusminder Chahal, Lisa Hunt, and John Perry
Published by the Chartered Institute of Housing © 2005

Printed by Alden Press, Oxford

Contents

Chartered Institute of Housing

Foreword

The William Sutton Group – one of the largest housing association groups in England – is pleased to sponsor this important book.

The relevance of this book for housing associations is clear. The Regulatory Code, published by our statutory regulator, the Housing Corporation, requires all housing associations to demonstrate their commitment to equality of opportunity. Similar obligations apply to associations in Scotland and Wales.

That demonstration must include adoption of an equality and diversity policy which should incorporate targets for meeting the needs of black and minority ethnic communities, who often form a significant proportion of our residents and applicants for housing.

This is important work for us but is also easy to get wrong: by pursuing a 'box-ticking' culture at one extreme. By being too distracted by current media headlines that are serious, but untypical, at another.

Proper consideration by housing associations has to start from good research, information and awareness of the issues so that we can better understand the needs of our clients from the ethnic minority communities. They deserve nothing less from us.

This book contains a variety of thought-provoking contributions and should be required reading by all housing associations – and others – seeking a better understanding of the challenges and issues we face in the field of housing, race and diversity.

Mike Morris
Group Chief Executive
William Sutton Group

Preface and acknowledgements

This book arose out of an invitation from the Chartered Institute of Housing with the Housing Studies Association to provide a volume covering key issues in the field of housing, ethnicity and racism. The aim was to offer something accessible that would be useful for practitioners and policy-makers, as well as for researchers, scholars and students. The project has taken a long time to complete, not least because so much has been changing in the national politics of ethnic relations. One of the biggest shifts has been the move of people seeking asylum to the top of the political and media agenda, and two of our chapters are therefore devoted to them. There has also been a political backlash against multi-culturalism and 'difference', with Islam in particular coming under attack from early in the new decade, because of events in the USA and Middle East. In this climate, happenings within the UK in 2001 stimulated a national debate about 'community cohesion', and we touch on this from a housing perspective in the book. Although one might have strong reservations about aspects of this community cohesion debate, it is worth noting not only its flaws but also the positive potential that specific strategies may have 'on the ground'. Here the book builds on recent investigative and good practice work with which the CIH has been involved. Given the impact of community cohesion ideas on public policy, Chapter 1 suggests that we can usefully add an *inclusion and co-operation agenda* to the *equality agenda* and *diversity agenda* to which we have become accustomed in recent years in UK ethnic relations policy domains.

Several people have assisted this project. We would particularly like to thank Mike Morris, Chief Executive of the William Sutton Group, for support generously given to assist publication. Thanks are of course due to my co-authors for their chapters. In addition, Deborah Phillips has effectively acted as second editor for most of the work, and Lisa Hunt has checked the websites, acronyms, and parts of the referencing. John Perry has maintained his constructive support for the enterprise consistently and very patiently, and thanks are owed to Peter Williams for contributing to the initial exchanges of ideas that led to the book. Paul Bagguley, Sarah Blandy, David Brown, Stuart Cameron, Pete Dwyer, Ian Law, David Mullins, David Robinson and Duncan Sim have provided valuable insights, advice, or material for specific chapters. Further individuals have given much appreciated help to my co-authors. Finally, we should thank the series review panel for constructive comments. Force of circumstance has meant that I have authored more parts of the book than originally planned, as well as editing the whole text. I alert readers to this now in case it has meant more mistakes than usual, or tempted me into being less cautious than has been my custom as a social scientist. For errors within particular chapters, individual authors take responsibility, and we do not all share the same opinions on every matter. Views expressed in the book do not necessarily reflect the perspective or carry the endorsement of the CIH.

For practical reasons some parts of the book do not refer to much new evidence after late 2004, so readers may wish to up-date for themselves on specific topics. Given the rapid pace of change and the benefits of illustrative material, our text cites press reports from time to time, although clearly these might not always prove reliable.

A postscript; the London bombings of July 2005

The manuscript for this book had been finalised for posting to the publisher when news came of the London explosions, and then of the involvement of people from Leeds. Our book has a bearing upon several topics that have figured in the national debates about these tragedies, including integration and exclusion. One feature that surprised many people was the origin of the terrorists themselves, although there may later turn out to be links with others outside the UK. It is generally felt that people willing to engage in such activities are a tiny minority in Britain, and many Muslims here are deeply angered as well as saddened by what has happened. It seems that there have been reactions already from people hostile to Islam, through attacks on individuals and religious buildings, and this has extended to some other Asian faith groups too. Our book's comments on the dangers of racism and stereotyping seem even more appropriate now than when we drafted them. Everyone must hope that hostilities will diminish as the trauma becomes more distant. The laws and regulations referred to in Chapter 3 offer some defence against any deterioration of the climate in public and voluntary sector institutions (although cities with substantial minority populations desperately need more minority ethnic personnel employed in policing). Nonetheless, if there are subsequent bombings in Britain in future months, there may be a profoundly negative impact for community relations.

Governmental approaches to community cohesion appear unlikely to have much effect in inhibiting terrorism, or the environments in which it might take root. The bombers were in many ways well assimilated into UK society, and might have scored high in any 'measuring' of integration. As Chapter 5 intimates, it is through engagement in specific constructive enterprises and activities that people will be brought together effectively, not through top-down attempts to control residential clustering or downgrade service providers that reflect the neglected needs of particular groups. There should be better and more extensive ways of learning, communicating, and collaborating, perhaps especially for younger people, and youth work and anti-racist initiatives need to be revisited and reinforced. Vigilance is required over the performance of organisations involved in education and training.

Much has been said immediately following the bombings about the role of religious commitment amongst terrorists. We should keep in mind that over the years terrorism has often been inspired primarily by political events, even though religion may have been taken to provide justification for some violent actions. Several politicians have keenly denied the importance of British military support for the USA in Iraq, as a causative political factor in the development of a UK environment where anger has grown and terrorism might emerge. Such denials seem to be unrealistic or disingenuous. Furthermore, inequalities and uneven economic development both within and beyond the UK may play a role in reducing grass roots confidence in positive change and mainstream politics. Nonetheless, religion is important, and Chapter 11 attempts a balanced commentary when discussing the limits of multi-culturalism in the public sphere. Muslims are not in any sense collectively responsible for the violent actions of individuals claiming the same religion as themselves. Adherents are diverse, religion is only a part of their identities, and (as Chapter 10 indicates) many daily concerns of households are similar to those of indigenous white people. Nonetheless, there is an imperative that the bombings reinforce. It will be crucial to keep open debates about faiths, behaviours, and equalities in UK society, rather than allowing discussion to be closed down (either because a government wants to manipulate religious constituencies, or because someone feels it disrespectful to question what is written in important texts or proclaimed by powerful traditionalists). One of the best protections against dangerous fundamentalisms may be an open-ness to challenge, and acceptance that no-one of any religion should expect that a claim to possess true knowledge will in itself be treated with respect by other people. Achieving a degree of solidarity across differing segments of UK society in the face of present challenges means all of us accepting that there are genuine political and economic discontents to be addressed, while also acknowledging that any of our cherished beliefs may be open to disagreement.

Malcolm Harrison
Leeds, 15th July 2005

The contributors

Kusminder Chahal is a Senior Research Fellow in the Housing and Urban Studies Unit, University of Salford, and at the Ahmed Iqbal Ullah Race Relations Resource Centre, University of Manchester. He has a wide range of experience in policy-relevant research and analysis, especially in the arena of ethnic relations and housing. Commissioned work has included overviews of this field for the Joseph Rowntree Foundation, and (with Louis Julienne) the high profile study *'We can't all be white!': racist victimisation in the UK* (1999).

Malcolm Harrison is Reader in Housing and Social Policy at the University of Leeds. His previous books and reports include: *Housing, 'race', social policy and empowerment* (1995); *Constructing equality: housing associations and minority ethnic contractors* (with Davies, 1995); and *Housing, social policy and difference: disability, ethnicity, gender and housing* (with Davis, 2001). In 2003 he reported for the ODPM (with Phillips) on the evidence base and national priorities for research on housing and BME communities.

Lisa Hunt is a Research Officer at the University of Leeds. She recently completed work for a PhD thesis, dealing with asylum seekers and women's 'agency'. Her research study has been based in West Yorkshire, and involved contact with women from a variety of refugee backgrounds.

John Perry is Policy Adviser at the Chartered Institute of Housing, and a regular contributor to national debates and policy analysis relating to housing and allied concerns. He has written, co-authored or facilitated the production of numerous reports with a practice orientation, and has been closely involved with recent work on community cohesion, BME housing associations, and asylum seekers.

Deborah Phillips is a Senior Lecturer in Geography at the University of Leeds. She has written and researched on housing and ethnicity since the 1980s, and acted as an advisor to numerous bodies in the governmental and voluntary sectors. Her studies have included contributions to the early 'classic' UK analyses of discrimination in council house allocation processes (including *What price equality?*, 1986). Most recently she has investigated minority ethnic household preferences and bounded choices, issues of outward movement away from traditional areas of settlement, and questions of segregation.

Abbreviations

ADP   Approved Development Programme

BME   black and minority ethnic

BNP   British National Party

CARF   Campaign Against Racism and Fascism

CBL   choice-based lettings

CEHR   Commission for Equality and Human Rights

CIH   Chartered Institute of Housing

CORE   COntinuous REcording System (for monitoring housing association and local authority lettings and sales in England)

CRC   Community Relations Commission

CRE   Commission for Racial Equality

CRER   Centre for Research in Ethnic Relations (Warwick University)

CRESR   Centre for Regional, Economic and Social Research (Sheffield Hallam University)

DETR   Department of the Environment, Transport and the Regions

DFG   Disabled Facilities Grant

DPs   displaced persons

DTLR   Department for Transport, Local Government and the Regions

ESRC   Economic and Social Research Council

ELR   Exceptional Leave to Remain

EMF   Ethnic Minority Foundation

FAIR   Forum Against Islamophobia and Racism

FBHO   Federation of Black Housing Organisations

hact	housing associations charitable trust
HSA	Housing Studies Association
ICAR	Information Centre about Asylum and Refugees
JWCI	Joint Council for the Welfare of Immigrants
JRF	Joseph Rowntree Foundation
LGA	Local Government Association
MFT	'Mixed and Flexible Tenure'
NASS	National Asylum Support Service
NDC	New Deal for Communities
NHF	National Housing Federation
ODPM	Office of the Deputy Prime Minister
ONS	Office for National Statistics
PATH	Positive Action Training in Housing
RCOs	Refugee Community Organisations
RHA	Refugee Housing Association
RSLs	registered social landlords
SEU	Social Exclusion Unit
SRB	Single Regeneration Budget
TMG	The Monitoring Group

Chapter 1:
Introduction

Malcolm Harrison

Racism and ethnicity pose demanding challenges for public policy, and for people working in fields such as housing. Today's practitioner environments in the UK are complicated not only by increasing awareness of diverse cultures and backgrounds, but also by the ongoing need to confront persisting racist outlooks and incidents, despite genuine progress that has been made towards fairness and good practice. The British situation, furthermore, is not unique although it is distinctive, for racism continues to threaten social order and relationships between groups in many apparently 'advanced' societies. This may seem surprising at first glance. We might agree with a view attributed to Mahatma Gandhi, voiced after he and a companion had been forced to step into the gutter to allow two white men to walk along a South African pavement. He expressed amazement '... *that men should think themselves honoured by the humiliation of their fellow human beings*' (cited in Hill, 1967, before preface).

Yet perhaps we should not be surprised to discover extensive racism in Western countries, since public debate – as we have seen recently on asylum seekers – can exacerbate as well as dampen tensions, while divisions between groups connect not only with identities but with concerns about access to resources and opportunities. Furthermore, although the increasing importance of cultural issues on the policy agenda reflects the richness of a multi-ethnic society, it also poses new tasks and presents new areas of knowledge and potential conflict for those delivering services. Neither frontline housing practitioners nor policy analysts can turn their backs on 'race' or ethnicity if they wish to come to terms with urban society's needs, or with related issues of organisational performance and service delivery.

This book provides an account of current issues in the housing and 'race' field, set against the backcloth of recent history. We hope it will prove of interest for housing practitioners and others involved with policy formulation and implementation, as well as for researchers, undergraduates, and postgraduate students. Although the volume is not a practice manual, we nonetheless highlight various key points in summary form as arguments proceed. The book goes well beyond a descriptive overview when engaging with the issue of community cohesion as well as with more longstanding concerns. In sketching the housing picture, we acknowledge failures and policy problems, but also draw attention to positive trends, achievements, and ways forward. Minority ethnic groups are not portrayed here as if they were passive victims of disadvantage and exclusion. People's ethnicity is often a source of strength and solidarity for them, providing cultural resources and personal networks that may help towards successful pathways through urban life.

The present chapter sets the scene, commenting on policy concerns in the context of diversity, racism, and migration, and on key challenges in housing. *Chapter 2* gives an overview of demographic and locality dimensions of change, focusing particularly on housing outcomes, and reviews patterns of divergence, continuities and similarities in experiences. *Chapter 3* discusses governmental responses, through an account of regulatory practices. *Chapter 4* reviews urban policy history affecting minority communities, and *Chapter 5* complements this with comments on the emergence, problems and potential of community cohesion strategies. *Chapters 6* and *7* explain issues surrounding asylum seekers and refugees, *Chapter 8* reviews housing need, while *Chapter 9* addresses racist harassment and prospects for better practice. *Chapter 10* uses a case study from a northern city to illuminate preferences and needs. A brief conclusion is then provided in *Chapter 11*.

No book covers everything, and readers must look elsewhere for more detail on contemporary urban regeneration policies, social support services linked into housing, or theoretical analysis (see Harrison with Davis, 2001). We do not deal separately with gender, disability, age or sexual orientation, although we try to take account of these. Furthermore, our materials relate primarily to the UK, and we only provide brief links to a wider cross-national context. Nonetheless, some parallels may be evident to researchers from other Western countries, not only in terms of discriminatory practices, but also in relation to the kinds of assumptions that have informed thinking about segregation and cohesion. Perhaps our critical review of the UK community cohesion debate may hold interest as a case study for some urban analysts from other countries. In addition, readers from other parts of Europe may be interested in Chapter 3, given that UK regulatory systems and practices now seem comparatively advanced and complex. For UK readers seeking an excellent text that explains and comments on racism and ethnicity more broadly than this volume, we recommend *Race, ethnicity and difference*, by Ratcliffe (2004).

'Race' and ethnicity: a note on terms used in this book

Terminologies used in ethnic relations are sometimes confusing and often disputed. This book adopts a flexible approach, using a range of terms in hopes that they will readily be understood. We are doubtful about the idea that racial categories can be usefully designated in the UK on the basis of supposed physical or biological groupings linked to skin colour or bodily features. Consequently, the word race often appears as 'race', reminding readers of its limitations as a descriptor. At the same time, however, being *perceived* as a member of a supposed racial group, or as black, white or non-white, can be significant for people's opportunities and interactions. Thus, we acknowledge the significance of ideas of race and colour in daily life, and therefore refer to black and white, as well as non-white, particularly when considering the differentiation of experiences patterned by ongoing attitudes and demarcations.

Ethnicity is often a more useful lens than 'race' through which to examine differences between groups. Everyone has an ethnic location. Whatever our origins we all have a setting in terms of culture, kin and up-bringing, and our personal histories give us part of our identities. In many contexts in this book we use the terms black minority ethnic (BME), or black and minority ethnic (or sometimes minority ethnic), following current practice in the housing field, for reasons of brevity and effective communication. This usage refers mainly to a range of groups who are perceived as non-white minorities, but should not be taken in any way to imply that white people do not have ethnicities. Irish or Eastern European people are sometimes included as minority ethnic groups in housing discussions and reports, so that black and minority ethnic is used in some situations in a way that embraces them too. We usually say minority ethnic when discussing a group, rather then the reverse, because this avoids implying that there is an 'ethnic' minority group and a white ('non-ethnic') majority group.

Some writers use the word black inclusively, and we may do this to vary our text (or when this is how people describe themselves). Less inclusive use is also made of black by people referring to themselves, or of Black in line with categories within official data. The terms African/Caribbean and Asian (or South Asian) may be used, following a distinction drawn in current UK practice, although there is overlap in reality, and smaller groupings are aggregated here despite their distinctiveness.

Recent debates about 'race' and ethnicity in Britain

'Race' and ethnicity were much in the news in the late 1990s, and have retained their high profile into the present century. One reason for concern is the continuing pattern of relative disadvantage and social exclusion, affecting employment, housing, income levels, and health. As the government's Social Exclusion Unit has pointed out, in comparison to their representation in the population, people from minority ethnic communities are more likely than others to live in deprived areas, to be poor, to be unemployed compared with white people having similar qualifications, to suffer ill-health, and to live in over-crowded and unpopular housing (Cabinet Office, 2000, p. 17). This is despite considerable economic successes achieved by many households from specific groups or communities. Furthermore, after more than four decades of UK debate and dispute over 'race relations', there is evidently still significant discrimination, and racist activity seeking to harm individuals. Indeed, the report from the Stephen Lawrence Inquiry (the Macpherson Report of 1999) pointed to the existence of a '… *sub-culture of obsessive violence*', fuelled by racist prejudice and '… *hatred against black people*', while recent reporting reflects what seems to have been a rise in the incidence of 'race hate' crimes. Although it is hard to be sure about trends in active discrimination, one recent research study found that two in every five respondents felt that there was more 'racial' prejudice in Britain today than five years ago, while one in six felt there was less, and one in three about the same amount (Attwood *et al.*, 2003, pp. xiv, 27-53). While confined to specific situations and probably having only limited numbers of adherents, extreme and active racism is the tip of a larger iceberg of suspicion that still operates against black minority ethnic people.

The Stephen Lawrence Report also provided a reminder of how easily things can go badly wrong in public services, and made clear the ongoing significance of 'institutional racism' (see Macpherson, 1999, pp. 5, 20-35). Although many forms of discrimination are illegal in Britain today, groups may still be disadvantaged indirectly by particular rules or policy priorities. An organisation may operate in ways that have negative effects for black and minority ethnic people, even though its formal policies aim at equal treatment. The Stephen Lawrence Report refers to the collective failure of an organisation to provide '... *an appropriate and professional service to people because of their colour, culture, or ethnic origin*' (1999, p. 28). While charges of institutional racism should not be made against an organisation as a substitute for detailed analyses of specific practices, there is nonetheless a crucial challenge here for all public sector, private sector, and voluntary bodies genuinely interested in better performance. Central government strengthened the law through the Race Relations (Amendment) Act of 2000, but some disconcerting signals nonetheless continue to be given by senior politicians, especially when discussing asylum seekers.

Diversity and the community cohesion debate

Debate has been influenced increasingly by recognition that the UK is a multi-ethnic society. The 2001 Census gave an overall figure for non-white minority ethnic people of 7.9 per cent for the UK (although the percentage now will be higher), and inner London has the largest minority ethnic population (see Community Cohesion Panel, 2004). Within this broad category there is a rich diversity of cultures, lifestyles, and household characteristics. Each community or grouping and the way it is developing is distinctive. A considerable amount of information on communities has been made available by writers, community representatives and researchers, but there are small groups (including some newer arrivals) about whom much less is known. Divisions or boundaries between minority ethnic groups, and between them and white households, are not clear cut. Half of the present minority ethnic population were born in the UK, and Britain has growing numbers of households with mixed ethnic heritages.

Although public policy has responded positively to the multi-cultural environment that has developed in urban areas, this response has been overlaid recently by fears about geographical segregation and separatism in lifestyles and social organisation, and by the potential for new manifestations of conflict. Interest in integration and community relations is an old concern that was evident especially in some earlier phases of 'race relations' work in Britain, but has now been given something of a 'makeover'. In particular, a high profile debate has taken place about an apparent lack of community cohesion, following disturbances on the streets of northern England at the start of this decade. (The *Cantle Report* is a key document here: see Community Cohesion Independent Review Team, Home Office, 2001.) On the one hand we hear continuing praise for the role of 'faith groups' and the richness of minority cultures, with expectations that public services should become more culturally-sensitive as well as meeting equal opportunities requirements. On the other hand, warnings are voiced about dangers of separation along lines of religion, culture or ethnicity, and about supposed 'self-segregation' of minority communities. International alarm about terrorism and religious fundamentalism has increased reservations in some circles about separatist tendencies linked to religious affiliations within Western societies, tendencies apparently reflected in geographical and institutional segregation. At the same time, heightened preoccupations about asylum seekers and other migrants have added to complexities and tensions locally and nationally.

A degree of voluntary geographical segregation amongst households need not necessarily be problematic in itself, and we would counsel firmly against any kind of 'moral panic' about that issue. On the other hand, there remains real concern about material disadvantages and barriers being encountered by residents in particular geographical areas. Central government acknowledges the situation, endorsing the view that 67 per cent of people from black minority ethnic communities live in the 88 most deprived districts in England, compared to 37 per cent of the white population (see Home Office, 2004). Furthermore, there are genuine issues to consider about developing a more inclusive and collaborative society, even if the agenda of the community cohesion debate should be viewed with a degree of scepticism.

Bearing these things in mind, we can characterise today's policy agenda in terms of three overlapping dimensions necessary for good practice (see Box 1).

Box 1: Three aspects of the policy agenda

The equality agenda
Key targets: protecting equality of rights for individuals, and challenging direct and indirect negative discrimination.

The diversity agenda
Key targets: making more space in services and planning for differing cultures, religions, preferences and community priorities.

The inclusion and co-operation agenda
Key targets: building collective capacities to handle tensions and conflicts of interest, and developing co-operative, collaborative and inclusive approaches and mechanisms.

The context for today's policy agenda

To complement what has been said so far, we now summarise some key information about minorities, and add a commentary on migration experiences. Variations between minority ethnic groups occur along lines of religion, socio-economic circumstances, settlement patterns and histories, household composition, or culture. In some contexts it is no longer adequate to discuss an 'Asian/African-Caribbean divide', or to refer to 'UK South Asians', but desirable instead to disaggregate. For instance, we may try to discuss Pakistanis, Bangladeshis, Indian households, or religious groupings. Even so, there may be further divisions within such broader categories. Additionally, people may belong to more than one group, have complicated connections which cross ethnic boundaries (as in the case of multi-ethnic households), or have uncertain affiliations. Some may see themselves as bi-national or transnational, while others emphasise the distinctive but British form of their ethnic identity. We cannot be certain, in advance of knowing individuals, exactly what their ethnicity means to them. Ethnic positioning may provide people with ways of interpreting the world, based on shared cultural resources, and a sense of collective social location; or ethnicities may offer some choices of lifestyle and values. Ethnicity has to be set alongside other variations relating to gender, age, sexuality, and so forth.

Chapter 2 includes fuller information related to housing in particular, drawn from recent data sets, so Box 2 highlights now some features arising from the more general published analyses about black and minority ethnic groups (see Harrison with Phillips, 2003; and ONS website, http://www.statistics.gov.uk/focuson/ethnicity).

Box 2: Britain's black and minority ethnic population

- The overwhelming majority of Britain's black minority ethnic population live in England, and about half are of Indian subcontinent origins (Indian, Pakistani and Bangladeshi).

- Minority ethnic groups are concentrated in certain regions (in large urban centres), and 45 per cent of the total minority ethnic population live in the London region. Other regions with substantial concentrations are the West Midlands, the South East, the North West, Yorkshire and Humberside, and the East Midlands. Substantial percentages of Black African (78 per cent), Black-Caribbean (61 per cent) and Bangladeshi (54 per cent) households live in London, but other large minority groups are more dispersed nationally.

- Data from national surveys have indicated considerable diversity between ethnic groups. This has shown up in measures such as average household size, which is largest for Indian subcontinent groups (particularly Bangladeshis and Pakistanis) and smaller for white people and Black-Caribbeans, and is affected by differing age structures (with effects from old people living in small units or in extended families, and dependent children in large households). Asians are least likely to live in lone-parent households. There have been higher proportions of female-headed lone-parent families among African/Caribbean people and more extended household structures among the South Asian groups. None of the black minority ethnic groups has a very high representation of 'pensioner only' households (although the figure is 13 per cent for Black-Caribbeans), and this reflects a youthful age structure as well as the greater tendency for Asian elders to live within extended family households.

→

> • Unemployment and low incomes affect groups to differing degrees. In general terms, though, people from minority ethnic groups are more likely than white people to live in low-income households. Higher percentages of white people are retired than in other groups, and white and Indian households have the lowest percentages of unemployed heads of households. Pakistani and Bangladeshi households tend to be found relatively often amongst the heads of households and partners in the lowest income category. Almost 60 per cent of the million people in the Pakistani and Bangladeshi category have been found to be living in low-income households before housing costs were deducted (and the figure increased to 68 per cent after housing costs). While the white and Indian groups are well represented in the higher income ranges, the reverse has been true for Pakistanis and Bangladeshis.

National data have shown diversity amongst the major categories that are referred to, as well as the continuing significance of overall disadvantage. When looking at large data sets we should not forget that caution is needed in interpretation, because figures sometimes aggregate in a potentially insensitive way, and groupings may embrace great diversity (as is the case for UK Chinese people; see Chan *et al.*, 2004). It should also be borne in mind that the white population itself is fragmented. A categorisation of groupings within it might produce a picture in which some relatively excluded white groups were found to have much in common materially with the poorest black minority ethnic categories.

Two features have become increasingly apparent as far as change for minority ethnic households in the UK is concerned. First, somewhat differing trajectories are evident for different minority communities, with some apparently faring significantly better than others. This can be kept in mind alongside differences in age structures and family composition which may be seen for broad ethnic categories, as well as differences in settlement histories. Second, divisions along lines of gender or socio-economic status may cross-cut ethnic categories. For example, Nazroo has demonstrated the salience of class as a variable linked with poor health across ethnic divides, Ratcliffe has noted the emergence in data of a *'familiar'* social class gradient in relation to specific housing disadvantages amongst minorities, whilst Phillips and others have indicated the ongoing disadvantages of women in housing terms across specific ethnic categories (see Nazroo, 2001; Ratcliffe, 1997; Phillips, 1996; Peach and Byron, 1993). We do not yet have anything comparable to tell us whether impairment is a variable that also systematically cuts across or reinforces ethnicity as an indicator of relative disadvantage, although it is probably significant in view of the general adverse impact of disability. In any event, while ethnicity remains very important, it has not superseded other divisions. Unfortunately, government policies sometimes seem to reinforce rather than modify market forces and economic trends that sustain inequalities for large numbers of people across ethnic divides. Additionally, the differing treatment of established migrants, various newer arrivals, and asylum seekers generates disparities between the rights, security and opportunities of different cohorts and groups, depending on their settled, temporary or insecure status.

For some communities there is a combination of weak labour market positions and low socio-economic status on the one hand, with experiences of negative discrimination related to racist labelling on the other. This combination of problems is exacerbated further if there are high levels of chronic illness and impairment, and may have specific manifestations both for women and men. For children the outcome is that large numbers in particular communities are growing up in relatively extreme poverty in UK terms. A study by Platt and Noble produced bleak findings from Birmingham, confirming impressions of severe poverty for Bangladeshi, Pakistani, and Black African/Caribbean-Black Other groups, and observed that '... *we can calculate that 56% of all Bangladeshi children under the age of 16 are living in poverty'* (1999, pp. 20-23). Recent data on Muslim housing experiences reveal the extent of disadvantage faced by children, in terms of over-crowding, lack of central heating, and residence on a second floor or higher (Housing Corporation, 2004a). Since consequences for children provide important tests of the significance of inequalities and low incomes, such evidence ought to be a cause for much concern.

Migration and minorities in the UK, USA and Europe

Migration and the growth of specific minority ethnic communities have been important in helping shape parts of cities in recent decades, and we need to place UK experiences here in a wider setting. This section therefore notes some important features, commenting where useful on the USA and European Union along with Britain.

Migrants vary considerably, from people escaping poverty or ill-treatment, to elite personnel recruited from overseas by employers. In specific periods, skilled immigrants have been encouraged by Western governments to fill gaps in the labour force. Recruitment has come onto the agenda again recently, in the context of skills shortages, and worries about a developing demographic profile in which the proportion in older age groups has grown. In countries with low birth rates and concerns about ageing populations, governments may be tempted to seek a youthful labour supply elsewhere, although perhaps hoping to filter the inward flow of people in favour of the most skilled and educated. It seems that within the UK there is some divergence of governmental attitudes, with Scottish leaders keener to welcome migrants because of population decline. Meanwhile, numerous people in older age retire from the UK to enjoy cheaper living or more comfortable climates abroad.

It has often been men who have been the first to move to a new country, and initial labour market migration has tended to be selective, involving active young workers, some of whom hoped to return eventually to their countries of birth. In the early stages such migrants may have encountered very difficult environments. For instance, some migrant men in Britain lived at first in 'bachelor hostels' or similar accommodation, experiencing considerable deprivations while taking on tough jobs and un-social hours. Given the relatively youthful profile of many migrations, it has been suggested that an average immigrant household tends to pay more in taxes in relation to income, and draw less in services and benefits, than does an average 'native' or longer-settled household of a host country (see for instance Parrillo, 1998, pp. 58-60). As time passes, populations become more complex as families are established, and as further migrants join existing households and communities. To some degree traditional marriage practices and family reunification patterns have strengthened communities and confirmed kinship networks. On the other hand, households with mixed ethnic heritages are increasingly important. In the UK there has been a rapid increase in numbers of children of 'inter-ethnic unions' (Scott, Pearce and Goldblatt, 2001).

It is important to note that internationally there have been flows of migrant women, perhaps hastened in some places by demand for casualised labour in services such as cleaning, catering and domestic work, with traditions of having predominantly female workforces. Although we do not know as much as we should about the circumstances of female migrants, there is said to have been some degree of 'feminisation' of migration in more recent decades (see Castles and Miller, 1998, p. 9; cf Morris, 2002, pp. 124-131).

Although migrations have long and complex histories in continental Western Europe, the period since World War Two is distinctive. Several nations that had previously ruled extensive colonial territories (or had had other strong links with particular countries) began to receive significant numbers of migrants from them. As the remnants of the imperial political systems faded, continuing economic dependencies and labour market pressures encouraged people to move to particular Western European countries (France, The Netherlands, Britain, etc.) with which their places of origin had had strong ties. Some migrants also came from other parts of Europe, or from relatively near at hand as in the case of Turkish people. Germany has been the main Western European destination for Turkish migrants (Van Kempen and Özüekren, 1997, p. 3), as well as drawing on the 'repatriation' of 'ethnic Germans' from within Europe (see Kvistad,1998; Morris, 2002, p. 26). In several countries, economic migrants sought work or were deliberately recruited from abroad in order to fill jobs. In the 1960s, for instance, a shrinking labour force and growing labour shortage in Austria encouraged the signing of 'recruitment contracts' with Spain, Turkey and Yugoslavia (see Giffinger and Reeger, 1997, p. 43). Post-war Britain called on migrant labour from the European continent ('European voluntary workers'), Ireland, and the colonies and so-called 'New Commonwealth' countries. Men from Asia and the West Indies came to get work and achieve a better standard of living. There were also 'push factors', such as political persecution (from the mid-1960s) of Asians in some parts of Africa. As the migrations from the 'New Commonwealth' developed, however, British governments took steps to impede the flow, through legislation on immigration that was passed from 1962 onwards.

Britain's experiences with ethnic relations are often compared with those of the USA, the suggestion being offered that Britain has much to learn about social divisions and policies from the history of migration and ethnic differentiation in North America. In that continent, however, there are still ongoing consequences for the original indigenous populations from the devastation created by settlers from Europe, while the additional impact of slavery for African-Americans created a persisting and distinctive US legacy of social divisions and oppressive practices. Later waves of in-migration created increasingly complex patterns of ethnicity. As racist outlooks and practices persisted and developed down the generations, successive cohorts of non-European migrants were frequently treated as non-white, and as possessors of a second class status. Two American scholars remind us, for instance, that the California Supreme Court ruled in the 1850s that the then new Chinese immigrants were to be classified officially as 'Indians', and would thus be ineligible for rights of citizenship (Smith and Feagin, 1995, p. 7). National legislation at various moments also endorsed discriminatory practices (such as entry quotas and exclusion of people with particular origins), reflecting prevailing negative views of those immigrants who were not from Europe.

As time passed, the USA nonetheless drew in large numbers from less favoured countries, a process facilitated by reforms in immigration law in the 1960s (Winant, 1995, p. 42). US political, military and economic connections in specific parts of the world helped shape in-migration patterns, as did geography. The needs of employers played substantial roles, and one feasible interpretation is that ethnicity and discrimination are factors which employers have used to their own advantage, seeking out cheap labour forces that would be weakly organised and lacking in rights. In any event, while the relative status enjoyed by differing settled migrant groups has varied, some hostility against non-European migrants has persisted. Mexicans in the USA, for instance, are apparently targeted with assertions about their involvement with drugs, laziness, and criminality. Meanwhile, economic progress for African-Americans has been far less than might have been expected in such a wealthy country, with high unemployment levels and suggestions that improvements after World War Two were concentrated in a relatively short time-span between the late 1960s and mid-1970s, when federal anti-discrimination laws were being strictly enforced, and when there was a substantial increase in numbers employed by employers subject to affirmative action requirements (Clayton and Watson, 1996, p. xxv). These action requirements – representing an effort to discriminate positively so as to begin to offset entrenched patterns of exclusion – have come under attack in more recent years.

In any event, the erosion of formal barriers to equality (which has been a feature of public policy in recent decades in several Western societies) eliminated neither the patterns of discrimination or segregation, nor inter-group violence, nor the disproportionately significant negative encounters experienced by black people with US criminal justice systems. As far as housing is concerned, there appears to have been extensive illegal discrimination against both black and Hispanic people, through private sector institutions such as financial organisations and mortgage market intermediaries (see for instance Yinger, 1995; although the incidence of discrimination may have declined somewhat since then). There is evidence too that the presence of African-Americans in a neighbourhood matters significantly for white people, often making it unlikely that they will buy homes in places where the percentage of black people exceeds 15 per cent (Emerson *et al.*, 2001). Measures of segregation show rates to be high in many metropolitan areas, although there is increasing suburbanisation of Asians, Latinos and African-Americans. If there is anything more than a token presence from non-whites in an area, some white people may move elsewhere. None of this is to deny, however, the presence of a very influential tradition in the USA of accommodating cultural diversity and accepting migrants, which contrasts with attitudes in parts of continental Europe. Furthermore, the electoral and economic importance of US minority ethnic communities means that politicians there may be much more responsive on some immigration issues today than their European counterparts.

One trend associated with migration and ongoing population change in some Western countries has been a gradual transformation of cultural patterns and political or religious landscapes, reflected in changes within specific housing areas of towns and cities. In the USA there have been clear spatial or locality outcomes, especially when discriminatory barriers to integration have been strong, with physical enclaves providing the residential bases for communities that are somewhat independent of European-American cultures. Such processes have also been observed in Europe. In Britain, numerous districts now have substantial populations drawn from minority ethnic communities, so that today it is impossible to have a competent discussion of a topic such as housing need in Bradford, Leicester, Inner London, or Birmingham without taking ethnicity into account. A more general effect for cities in the USA has been that some have become increasingly less dominated by cultural and linguistic groups of European origin. This process developed earlier and more extensively than in Europe. US data have shown that already, by 1990, Miami had a foreign-born rate of nearly 60 per cent, and Los Angeles over 38 per cent (Rodriguez, 1995, p. 213). Across the Canadian border, Toronto is today very firmly multi-cultural, with a large Chinese community and other well-established minority groups. The process of change remains less developed in Britain than in today's USA, but some cities have begun to move in the US direction. Birth rates for newer migrant communities in Britain tend to be higher than for mainstream white groups or for earlier settled black minority ethnic migrants, so that population growth amongst the relative newcomers can have a significant impact on certain neighbourhoods. As time passes, fertility rates and family structures may tend to move closer to those of the host population.

Box 3: Migrants, settlement and cities

Although migrant groups tend to be absorbed gradually into host societies, migration into Western countries has contributed to some transformation of cultural patterns and political or religious landscapes in cities. This may be especially marked in the USA, but also affects Europe. Although minorities have lived in European cities for hundreds of years, their presence today often has greater potential impact.

In Britain, while many rural areas, small towns, or outer or suburban parts of cities have predominantly white populations, some urban neighbourhoods are more multi-cultural or multi-ethnic, providing homes for well-established minority ethnic groups.

Most minority ethnic residents in UK cities cannot be described as 'migrants', as they have been settled in Britain for many years, or been born or grown up in the UK. It is usually misleading to think in terms of urban divisions based around a sharp ethnic differentiation separating white and 'non-white' along lines of culture or outlook. Settled minorities tend to take on over time many of the attributes of the host society, although cultural allegiances and personal identities may remain complex and often distinctive.

Earlier migrant cohorts may be in a better position than newcomers through having assembled resources and 'put down roots', and because they have by now often secured a fuller measure of citizenship rights or acknowledged status as members of the nation.

The differing treatment of established migrants, various newer arrivals, and asylum seekers itself generates disparities between the rights, security and opportunities of different cohorts and groups, depending on their settled, temporary or insecure status. Illegal migrants may not be entitled to state support and services, live in fear of discovery, and may be open to exploitation by employers. More generally, immigration policies and practices may conflict with notions of equality, and there is some alignment between immigration controls and restrictions on access to welfare entitlements (see Cohen, 2001, pp. 11-12, 17).

Racisms, discrimination and citizenship rights

In many countries there are 'outsider' groups seen as distinct from the supposedly 'traditional' or indigenous populations. People can be positioned not simply by the differing affiliations and beliefs they have, but by the perceptions and strategies of others. In Western countries the word 'racism' is often used to refer to conduct, practices, ideas or words which adversely affect or disadvantage particular categories of persons. We associate racism with individuals or groups holding a view that another set of people is 'different' in some way, generally relating to their origins, nationality, 'colour', or culture. When we talk about societal processes of racialisation and inferiorisation, we are referring to ongoing situations where such sets of people are marked out as different from those who observe them; in discussions, writings, or even laws and policies. They may be cast as 'different' and inferior in terms of appearance, speech, origins, lifestyle, dress, cultures or beliefs, or thought of as less 'pure', less intelligent, or less morally sound than the observer. In Western European history, for instance, Jewish people were not only often presented as having apparently distinctive 'racial' characteristics, but were associated with money-lending or 'usury' (a frowned-upon activity for pre-capitalistic Christians then, as it can be for Muslims today). In any event, a consistent feature of racism is the drawing of boundaries between people, through which some are cast as outsiders and moral inferiors (see Box 4).

Box 4: How boundaries are drawn between groups

Racist or 'racialised' practices help construct distinctions between people, and may pick out supposedly important characteristics such as skin colour as a means of so doing.

Distinguishing between groups of people is generally a process of 'social construction', rather than something based scientifically on major human differences. That is to say, the distinguishing of one group from another involves drawing boundaries on the basis of a set of variables selected in accordance with specific preferences in particular societal settings.

One person's beliefs may lead him or her to perceive Irish people as being very distinct from English people, while another may think that a line must be drawn between a Caribbean and a white person speaking the same language and brought up in the same society, simply because of 'colour'.

Since 'colour' or origin certainly may not be the most significant things about any person, there can be as many similarities between individuals in supposedly different 'colour' or 'origin' categories as there are within a category. The drawing of 'racial' boundaries is an arbitrary business, and it may reflect a wish to associate inferiority with the group or groups being designated as different.

Effects from policies on migrants and minorities

Key factors affecting integration and discrimination are the stance of governments and the development of legal rights. There is a view that the post-war period witnessed some general liberalisation of approaches across countries to migrants and minorities. Hollifield and Zuk refer, for instance, to a, '... *new, more expansive type of citizenship'* and a new sensitivity to the rights of minorities and refugees which '... *grew out of the experiences of World War II and the cold war'*. They argue that – notwithstanding political backlash against immigration – civil and social rights for foreign and ethnic minorities became entrenched in the jurisprudence, institutions, and political processes of the USA and Western European states (1998, pp. 70-71). To a degree this may be true, but there have also been tendencies in specific periods towards increased controls over new migration which have had side-effects for those minorities already within Western countries. Thus liberalisation has been overlaid with fears about the scale and impact of immigration, giving rise in particular to the concept of 'Fortress Europe' in recent years (implying high barriers against outsiders but relative freedom of movement within the Union for its full citizens), paralleled perhaps at some

---

moments by concerns about reducing access to welfare benefits for migrants in the USA. Within the European Community, southern region states once perceived as traditional countries of emigration have joined the north and west as the focus for 'new' or 'late' immigration, perhaps being seen as a 'weak link' in terms of controlling entry to the Union (Sales, 2002). A partly harmonised or integrated EU immigration regime is developing (for the European Union see Morris, 2002, pp. 10-27).

Despite positive innovations and equal opportunities laws in specific countries (and for the European Union as a whole), approaches to asylum and migration issues have cut across notions of equality, sometimes leading to a resurgence of defensive or punitive practices (for the UK record in relation to housing law see Cohen, 2001, chapter 13). Sales (2002), suggests that the trend across Europe has been to reduce the rights of asylum seekers in relation to welfare and security of residence, and to increase detention and deportation. Nevertheless, over the long term, refugees who stay tend to be absorbed like other migrants into the larger patterns of ethnic diversity in host countries, and will face some similar issues of need, services provision, and social exclusion, even though their initial circumstances and personal histories may be painful.

One variable affecting integration and inclusion in host countries is the extent to which people who arrive to take up work can gain access to full citizenship rights. While immigrants have sometimes been incorporated effectively into mainstream civil society, some European countries have classified people in the past as 'guest workers' or temporary migrants, not offering them citizenship, despite actively recruiting them to meet labour force needs. Van Kempen and Özüekren refer to the concept of the guest worker being *'invented'*, with migrants only being given labour and housing permits for short periods (1997, p. 5). Even where settled communities expanded, with family reunification and growth, formal status remained inferior. Morris refers to an effective resurrection of the guest worker system more recently, allowing recruitment of temporary labour through bilateral agreements with non-EU countries, *'... but limiting potential demands on the welfare state'* (Morris, 2002, pp. 17-18).

Determining formal rights to citizenship status can rest on laws of birthplace, parentage, or naturalisation. Parrillo states that determining citizenship by descent or bloodline was originally set down in the 1791 French *Code Napoleon*, and is *'... the more globally applied principle'* (Parrillo, 1998, pp. 61-62). The approach can pose difficulties for children born or brought up in a host country. The UK government in the early 1980s removed the established right to citizenship through place of birth (see for instance Bloch, 2000). Another route to citizenship – naturalisation – may be governed by very specific rules, such as requirements about minimum length of residence (see Parrillo, p. 63). Assimilation into the perceived cultural heritage and practices of the host country, a fixed job, or a 'positive attitude' towards the host state, may have been seen as tests of a person's acceptability (as in Germany or Austria), after which full citizenship might be felt appropriate.

In recent years there has been fuller acknowledgement that minorities are entitled to maintain their own cultures and languages. This is the case in the UK, although Britain in any case did not previously deploy formal tests of cultural or political assimilation. Nonetheless, there have been UK provisions perceived as constituting 'loyalty tests' (see Cohen, 2001, p. 53). Recently, an oath of allegiance, English language tests, and citizenship ceremonies have come into the mainstream UK political agenda.

Responses to gender and family can be significant within immigration policies. Migrant women coming to the UK have sometimes had restricted rights (for instance over receiving child benefits, conferring citizenship on their children, or bringing in a spouse) (see Anthias and Yuval-Davis with Cain, 1993, pp. 32, 125-6). Family rights and family unification remain complex territory today in Britain, even though there has been a '... *gender alignment of qualifying conditions for family unification in domestic law'* (Morris, 2002, pp. 84-87, 88-89).

The housing dimension

Housing has tended to be an important focus for discrimination in different countries, and British history illustrates how minorities have been treated as outsiders with inferior status. Today, however, UK practice environments are markedly different from those of earlier periods, and probably more developed in terms of equality, monitoring, and diversity practices than in some of the other large EU countries. Practices and policies in social rented housing provision in particular have undergone a considerable shift in response to criticisms and developments in law and guidelines. Some observers believe that progress in the UK housing sector has been greater than in several other fields. For instance, while equal opportunities have not yet been secured in housing employment, a Cabinet Office report claims that housing is '... *one of the best service sectors in terms of minority ethnic employment'* (2000, p. 62). Nonetheless, very few people from minority ethnic groups have as yet found their way into top housing jobs in local government or housing associations (*Housing Today*, 22nd April 2005).

In earlier decades, UK housing experiences were analysed in a group of 'classic' housing and 'race' studies, running roughly from the 1960s to the end of the 1980s. The Commission for Racial Equality (CRE) played an important investigative role, along with academic researchers (see CRE, 1984; 1984a; 1985; 1985a; 1987; 1988; 1988a; 1990a; 1990b). Research in several cities indicated that black minority ethnic households were disadvantaged through direct and indirect discrimination when encountering public sector housing allocation processes (Henderson and Karn, 1987; Phillips, 1986; Sarre *et al.*, 1989; Simpson, 1981). Minority ethnic households often ended up in inferior dwellings or areas. There was also discrimination in private sector markets, with 'gatekeepers' such as estate agents contributing to segregation by 'steering' minority households away from areas favoured by white people. Individual private landlords could simply tell a potential renter from a minority community that a flat had already been let to someone else (saying *'Sorry, it's gone'*), even though this might be untrue. Across all housing sectors it was relatively easy for direct or indirect discrimination to occur, since monitoring and equality codes were by today's standards primitive or non-existent. Given the potency of white racism, 'no-go' areas developed that minority households were reluctant to live within, or even pass through. Meanwhile, some areas with substantial minority ethnic settlement came to be treated as representing relatively high risks for mortgage lending, so that purchasers and sellers within them faced problems of delays, extra costs or even a relative 'mortgage famine'. The term 'red-lining' was borrowed from the USA to describe the negative delineation of such areas by building societies (for mortgages see Harrison and Stevens, 1981; CRE, 1985a).

Today, many overt discriminatory practices of earlier decades could not occur in UK social renting, as the decision-making environment is far more regulated (although this is not so much the case for the private sectors). Furthermore, as well as improving existing services, the UK has paralleled US affirmative action with more modest (but less contested) strategies for Positive Action. The latter have helped 'bring through' able minority ethnic personnel in the labour market, with Positive Action Training in Housing schemes being important contributors (see Julienne, 2001), along with innovations such as mentoring schemes for housing workers. Another policy (begun in the mid-1980s) has been to support the development of black and minority ethnic housing associations, a matter this book touches upon later. Of course, implementation of housing policies is not always effective, and there are many topics on which monitoring data are scarce, or where staffing and services remain inadequate. Furthermore, new forms of discrimination may have developed as organisations and tasks shift, and we should keep this in mind in case discriminatory practices might arise in fields such as the control of anti-social behaviour, or the treatment of young people in housing. In the private sectors, an emergent issue has been the performance of mortgage lenders, banks and insurers in relation to religious or cultural minorities, where particular living arrangements and religious requirements may not be well catered for. Meanwhile, there may be an absence of facilities or cover for specific low-income housing districts, so that the term 'red-lining' has reappeared in press reporting, this time being applied to insurance companies (see *The Guardian*, 14th November 1998; 30th January 1999).

Housing policy comparisons are sometimes made with the USA, and some similarities to UK approaches may be found, alongside distinct differences. US legislation has been relatively interventionist in regulating private housing market transactions (including prohibiting mortgage 'red-lining' and countering private sector disinvestment in low-income and minority ethnic neighbourhoods). The UK could benefit from the experience here in terms of data-collection, monitoring, and action. On a different front, programmes referred to as Gautreaux, Gautreaux-type or Special Mobility Programs were also established (although Gautreaux programmes have now ended), involving assistance for public sector tenants or similar households, to help them gain access to housing in areas such as suburban white-occupied localities (Yinger, 1995, pp. 152-153, 234-236). Some US housing policies have connected with the idea of enhancing mobility so as to 'deconcentrate' poverty (see Goetz, 2002), and redevelopment of public housing areas plays a part here (one aim being more socio-economic mixing). There is a major programme based on demolition of sub-standard public sector housing, while vouchers have been used to assist low-income households to enhance their housing choices. Some issues familiar in the UK may be relevant to these US interventions (for instance the potential for 'gentrification' through renewal).

Organisations and institutional racism

One issue highlighted for ethnic relations in the UK in recent years has been the question of ongoing institutional failures to confront negative habits and practices inside organisations. This was touched upon briefly early in this chapter. While much discrimination today may be unintended or hidden, minority groups can also encounter open hostility because of a 'canteen culture' amongst personnel involved in running or providing services (Macpherson, 1999, pp. 21, 25). Those who challenge these hostilities are often accused of seeking to interfere with deeply held personal values, of imposing 'political correctness' on debates and day-to-day human interactions, or of over-riding the knowledge that staff have of the 'real' characteristics of people 'out there in the community'. It is important to clarify key issues here at the outset, since there is a big difference between trying to ensure fairness, and supposedly seeking to 'sanitise' people's thoughts and interactions (which would generally be undesirable).

An important practical issue is that many of us carry in our minds judgemental stereotypes or images of those whom we think may be 'different' from ourselves, and may label or classify negatively many people that we encounter, before we know anything about them. The concern is not that stereotypes never draw on or connect with real problems, but rather that they encapsulate simplifications, assumptions and misinformation which render them potentially damaging. In Britain such stereotyping can relate to a wide range of 'targets', including young African/Caribbean men, Travellers, Asian women, single parents, people who use wheelchairs, people who live on council estates, or people with learning difficulties. In the last few years 'Muslim' and 'asylum seeker' seem to have been added to the list of 'usual suspects' classified as potentially deviant, disruptive, threatening, criminal or peculiar in their lifestyles and beliefs. From a public policy perspective, however, the problem to address is not primarily about whether people hold views that are negative about others. It is never easy for any of us to set aside our prejudices, although it is always worth trying, and achieving so-called 'political correctness' at a personal level is not an objective that serious reformers are generally the least bit interested in. Deliberately offensive behaviour is of course not acceptable, but underlying outlooks cannot necessarily be changed quickly. Few well informed observers believe that social harmony and good ethnic relations can be successfully 'engineered' in the short term by policy initiatives, although equality laws and improved knowledge help change how we live and relate to each other. What is crucial, though, is to recognise that *the presence, character and impact of negative stereotyping and labelling are proper concerns for public policy.*

When people are categorised and differentiated by the observations of others, this process often portrays them and what they do in ways that not only may be unrealistic, but may also place upon them the blame for all manner of negative events. Whether labelling people as different is conscious or unconscious, it enters into the activities of organisations, and thereby affects the chances individuals have of receiving fair and reasonable treatment. It may not matter too much if a police officer or housing manager doesn't really like Catholics, Pakistanis, Gypsies, lesbians, disabled people, or Albanians, but it matters a great deal if he or she acts while at work in a way that reflects the dislike. An office environment in which minorities are demeaned as a matter of course in casual conversation sustains negative stereotypes, paving the way for discriminatory actions or failures to act. Furthermore, it is a major issue if an organisation has routine practices that permit or encourage the pursuit of the private prejudices of staff, or reflect these systematically.

Box 5: Racist attitudes and behaviour within organisations

A person may not hold racist views in a conscious or overt way, but nonetheless may have prejudices leading him or her to pre-judge people from minority groups without any detailed knowledge of them, or to persist with a judgement about them despite evidence to the contrary. It may not be easy for us to set aside such prejudices (although deliberately offensive behaviour is of course not acceptable).

Prejudiced and judgemental attitudes take on great importance where sustained through patterns of hierarchy, power and resources. It can be a major issue if an organisation has routine practices that permit or encourage the pursuit of the private prejudices of staff, or reflect these systematically.

Diverse racisms and the issue of ethnic penalties

Some writers today refer to racisms (rather than racism), to take account of the wide variety of targets or approaches that racists may have. Hostilities may arise between as well as against minorities, while divisions amongst white groups become racialised in certain circumstances in much the same way as happens for non-whites. Despite the importance of ideas about national identity and shared norms in political and popular culture, what we may think of as 'white people' remain diverse in terms of dialect, accent, beliefs, affiliations, and lifestyles. Indeed, exactly who is to be included as a member of a 'white nation' in popular debate may shift over time and place. Today, the unpleasant English children's rhyme which began, *'Taffy was a Welshman, Taffy was a thief'*, seems little more than a relic of the past. Yet many Welsh people have concerns about English second homes in Wales, or about defending or requiring the use of the Welsh language.

In some instances exclusive barriers dividing 'white society' seem rather persistent. Irish migrants into England have long experienced disadvantage (and this has been noted in the housing context in London). A CRE report refers to evidence of inequality, and of a '... *deep sense of hurt among people of Irish origin at the way they have been treated*' (Hickman and Walter, 1997, p. 5). Conflict within Northern Ireland itself reflects a longstanding rift amongst white people. Whereas the relatively secular character of public life and services has dampened cultural conflict in England, this certainly does not apply to Northern Ireland, where division and discrimination have focused around the religious divide.

Nonetheless, for those who can successfully claim 'whiteness', perceptions of bodily difference do not usually persist as an obstacle to integration in the way that has sometimes happened for later generations of non-white people. A difference of accent or regional affiliation can lose its salience and visibility over time. Meanwhile, 'colour' may remain a visible marker which transcends generational and linguistic change. It has ongoing availability as a banner for racist mobilisation or abuse, through which people are labelled as deviant or dangerous, or as being not really 'British' or 'English'. Relatively systematic patterns of hostility and discrimination have persisted, even after a degree of integration into UK lifestyles, and apply across a wide range of black minority ethnic groups. Perceptions of the human body itself become a route to labelling and categorisation, and a basis or excuse for designating groups of people as inferior and less deserving, regardless of language or place of birth. Certainly, a 'second generation' British Asian or Caribbean person, with a perfect command of English language and mainstream cultural expectations, may still be abused as a 'Paki' or 'nigger'. For the many children born into families where there is a combination of ethnic heritages, non-white or coloured remain potential labels that might in certain settings over-ride individual backgrounds. Thus, white women with children of mixed ethnic background may experience racist harassment.

Given the continuing and consistent nature of the racist discrimination and disadvantage experienced by black minority ethnic households, some writers have deployed the concept of 'ethnic penalties'. This describes a situation where all groups perceived as non-white (regardless of their qualifications or positions in job hierarchies) suffer a disadvantage which leads them to fare less well in general than similarly qualified white people (see Modood, 1997, pp. 144-145). This idea has been applied to housing disadvantage by Karn and others (Karn, 1997, pp. 266-267, 275-281). The best way to think of it for present purposes is in terms of a tendency for people from particular kinds of backgrounds to be operating at a disadvantage, even though many will succeed in spite of the obstacles.

We need to be careful with the word 'ethnic', though, since many people derive advantages from their ethnic heritages. The penalty that they pay often relates not so much to their ethnicity, but arises from them being categorised by other people as non-white. In the USA, observers have referred to people paying a tax for being black, and research sometimes points up the implications. One US scholar has recently indicated that, regardless of socio-economic positions, '... *blacks, because of racial steering and/or discrimination, are not able to fully convert their socioeconomic status into residence in the same neighbourhoods as whites*' (Darden, 2004, p. 10). Personal economic achievement does not completely overcome racist practices or hostilities.

Box 6: Paying penalties for being perceived as non-white

The idea of *ethnic penalties* has been used to describe a situation where there is a tendency for people perceived as being from non-white groups (regardless of their qualifications or positions in job hierarchies) to suffer a disadvantage which leads them to fare less well in general than similarly qualified white people. It is a useful idea to keep in mind, although the word 'ethnic' isn't really the right one to capture what happens.

Racism and the grass roots

Racist views do not take effect in a vacuum, and racist activities may weaken or strengthen partly as a result of changes in the economy, popular culture, public policy and politics. Forceful racist or anti-racist pronouncements by politicians or journalists, for instance, might affect things ranging from the incidence of verbal racist abuse to the levels of assault in school playgrounds. Nonetheless, it would be wrong to overlook the impact of people's sense of their own material interests, their concerns about their economic difficulties, and attitudes to territory (in several forms). For example, traditional white English households might sometimes feel threatened by an unfamiliar culture and wish to protect 'turf', locality or jobs against those seen as different. Over the years this has led to varying responses ranging from moving to a 'white' estate, to pressing for local social rented dwellings to be allocated to 'sons and daughters' of existing residents, or trying to 'ring fence' jobs in a firm by emphasising personal contacts within 'white' networks. More extreme manifestations have been the frequent physical attacks that occur and form part of the persisting pattern of racist harassment that has been widely documented. There is a local as well as national politics of racism, and hostile actions are by no means always confined to the spontaneous outbursts of aggressive individuals. An instance cited in a 1990s Birmingham housing study exemplifies the premeditated and deliberate character of some racist activity. A minority ethnic householder, having moved to an outer area, reports that her door handle had been wired up to the mains electricity (Birmingham City Council Housing Department, 1998, p. 19). Such activity increases the obstacles facing families who might hope to move from inner city areas of existing minority settlement to estate locations further out. Of course, despite ongoing negative events, British society has been changing in composition and outlooks, and there are many active individuals and organisations seeking to develop constructive ways forward and combat racism.

Challenges for UK housing policy-makers and practitioners

Building on the review we have provided in this chapter, we now highlight *seven interlocking challenges*, posed for people involved today in housing policy, by racisms and the complexities of an increasingly multi-ethnic society.

First, there are pressures to confront those direct or indirect racisms that persist in the housing domain, and that undermine equality in opportunities and housing options for households. Despite an increasingly strong formal commitment by government and public bodies to equality, there is still ongoing criticism of actual performance by housing organisations, and critical comments are sometimes backed up by substantial research. One task for practitioners 'on the ground' is to turn reasonable intentions into more effective outcomes.

Second, there is a wish to make housing services and provision (including specialised provision) more sensitive to variations in preferences, needs, culture and religion. As we indicated above, there is a diversity agenda, and this has entered the repertoire of public and voluntary sector services in housing. Organisations need to be more 'culturally competent' and aware than in the past, when dealing with households and communities. Central government has shown increased awareness of the challenges associated with a multi-ethnic environment, even though developing context-specific ways forward is by no means always easy. The *Action Plan* published in 2001 by the then DTLR Housing Directorate was certainly evidence of positive commitment (Department for Transport, Local Government and the Regions, 2001). In introducing this document, the Minister of State for Housing, Planning and Regeneration noted that the Race Relations (Amendment) Act of 2000 served as an important reminder '... *that we all need to raise our game'*. The *Action Plan* underlined the commitment to ensuring '... *choice and quality in housing for people from black and minority ethnic backgrounds'*, and to designing housing policies that take account of their concerns, as well as commenting on the necessity for social landlords to be alive to the fact that different black and minority ethnic groups '... *often have very different needs in relation to housing provision and services'* (Falconer, in DTLR, 2001, p. 1. For more recent statements see ODPM [Housing Directorate] *Action Plan Update No. 2, 2002*, ODPM website. See also pp. 56-57 below).

Third, investment strategies, priorities and policies designed to secure other more general governmental housing objectives could take fuller account of the likely impact for minority ethnic households, communities and organisations, to ensure that substantial disadvantaging effects do not arise. This can be thought of in immediate ad hoc and practical ways, when investment budget priorities or bids are being prepared, but could also be handled by moving towards a set of more general evaluation principles. Thus the terms *equality testing* or *equality proofing* (or sometimes *'race proofing'*) have begun to be used to refer to systematic attempts by policy-makers to identify and eliminate effects (from policies) that might disadvantage black and minority ethnic groups. 'Equality testing' (we prefer not to use the term 'race proofing') has the potential to become a salient implement for systematically getting to grips with some of the challenges facing policy-making. Moves have begun in this direction following recent legislation, with the concept of 'Race equality impact assessment' now on the agenda for public authorities (for CRE guidelines see www.cre.gov.uk/duty/reia/index.html).

These ideas can extend in principle to various dimensions of equality as well as to almost any public policy field. For instance, a government might seek to make sure that a particular transport investment policy did not work indirectly to disadvantage disabled people, or to take account of the fact that a specific law and order tactic disproportionately adversely affected young black rather than white men. There are many aspects of housing and allied services where testing could be valuable, perhaps not just for reviewing particular policy details but some longer-term shifts too (such as the gradual decline of public funding for private sector renewal within the overall portfolio of housing renewal investment in urban England).

Of course, the use of equality testing is likely to be bounded by barriers arising from expediency, contextual factors, and the greater priority given to goals outside ethnic relations in many fields. Nonetheless, as part of a more systematic evaluation strategy before policies are finalised, equality testing is something worth emphasising in many situations, and could help develop better understandings of change.

Fourth, policy development, implementation, research and monitoring could more often reflect and to a degree directly involve the diverse communities and households whose needs policy-makers are seeking to meet. This perspective has gained ground in recent years, as user involvement has become more widely accepted. It implies an inclusive approach to disadvantaged white people as well as to black minority ethnic communities.

Fifth, a fuller agenda is needed for inclusion and co-operation, and a range of possible ways forward needs to be developed and tried out. In housing this might mean thinking about strategies for involving minority ethnic organisations in more federal or collective enterprises across cities, facilitating more minority ethnic involvement with collective ownership and management of housing, ensuring that small and newly arrived groups are not overlooked, and working hard on participation and inter- and intra-group capacity building. Chapter 5 suggests that debates on community cohesion can be built on in positive ways, by focusing on a range of targets such as reducing barriers to inclusion and choice in housing, developing capacities and mechanisms to facilitate stronger inter-relationships between groups, and more shared and collaborative planning.

Sixth, housing providers need to bear in mind other dimensions of 'difference' when considering ethnicity. This means trying to take account wherever appropriate of issues raised by age, disability, gender, and sexual orientation, as well as by socio-economic differentiation along lines of class or status (incomes, available resources, etc.).

Seventh, housing providers and analysts should review fields beyond housing, keeping in mind the effects on minorities of 'reforms' in parallel service areas, implications of shifts in labour markets, decisions on nationality and migrants, and taxation trends. This is so as to be able to contribute to debates, and make representations from a housing needs perspective whenever a window of opportunity opens into an adjacent policy territory.

There are many policy domains outside housing in which minority ethnic perspectives and needs may become displaced by other more dominant priorities. This is perhaps most often where the *Achilles' heel* of UK progress on ethnic relations is to be found, since advances in one sphere can be undermined readily by lack of awareness in another, and minority households frequently face economic disadvantages that interventions such as housing policies only touch on indirectly. Even within housing policy there may be a damaging compartmentalism, in which financial strategies (such as raising rent levels) are not systematically tested for their differentiated effects across groups.

Research and analysis: some recent examples

To properly respond to challenges, practitioners need a good information base. A systematic account of literature is given elsewhere (see Harrison with Phillips, 2003), but we highlight below a few of the reports that have had a significant impact recently.

An important example early in the decade was the *Challenge Report 2001*. This emerged from a national *Race and Housing Inquiry* created as a joint initiative of the National Housing Federation (NHF), the Commission for Racial Equality (CRE), the Federation of Black Housing Organisations (FBHO), and the Housing Corporation. The inquiry was set up to challenge registered social landlords (RSLs), and the organisations they work with, to look at where and how the sector could improve 'race equality' through accountable and measurable action (see NHF *et al.*, 2001, p. 1).

The Housing Corporation has made an impressive contribution to knowledge by supporting a large number of studies of local needs and allied topics as well as several important, tightly-focused, national investigations into social rented housing issues. The resulting reports include three containing information on the performance of RSLs in relation to (respectively): meeting the needs of black and minority ethnic communities; employment and staffing; and investment. They are entitled *A question of delivery* (Tomlins *et al.*, 2001), *A question of diversity* (Somerville *et al.*, 2000), and *A question of investment* (Robinson *et al.*, 2002).

Much of the work sponsored by the Corporation has been firmly linked to finding better practices and ways forward, as well as uncovering difficulties. The National Assembly for Wales has commissioned significant research work in recent years, also partly motivated by the wish to develop strategies.

Other sponsors of studies range from councils or RSLs to charitable foundations such as the Joseph Rowntree Foundation (for a recent account of JRF findings see *Foundations: Experiencing ethnicity: discrimination and service provision*, 2004, by Chahal). Amongst many policy-relevant studies appearing recently has been a report on Bradford, *Breaking down the barriers* (Ratcliffe *et al.*, 2001), which seems to have had a wide impact. This was published by the Chartered Institute of Housing (CIH) on behalf of Bradford Metropolitan District Council, Bradford Housing Forum, the Housing Corporation, and the FBHO. It deals particularly with improving Asian households' access to social rented housing, a matter we touch on later. To add to investigations of these kinds, there have been valuable exercises setting out guidelines for best practice and methods for finding ways forward, or commenting on progress. Excellent examples are the good practice guide to black and minority ethnic housing strategies by Blackaby and Chahal (CIH, 2000), and work from Lemos (2000) on combating racist harassment (see our Chapter 9 for the *RaceActionNet*). If anyone doubts the continuing importance of harassment, they should turn to Chahal and Julienne's key report of 1999. The specific topic of people seeking asylum is generating a variety of studies, sometimes touching on housing. Useful examples are *Between NASS and a Hard Place*, by Carter and El-Hassan (hact, 2003, covering Yorkshire and Humberside), and *Providing a Safe Haven* (CIH, 2003). A new study by Dwyer and Brown is noted in Chapter 7. For analyses on community cohesion, see items discussed in Chapter 5 (including CIH publications). Finally, readers interested in the housing pathways or 'careers' of minority ethnic groups should consult the May 2002 issue of the journal *Housing Studies*, which offers excellent insights from several countries.

Chapter 2:
Housing achievements, diversity and constraints

Deborah Phillips

After 50 years of settlement, there is now great diversity in housing experiences and outcomes for black and minority ethnic groups. These reflect ethnic, class, generation, family type and gender differences. There are also different opportunities in different localities. For example, the housing choices of black and minority ethnic people living in the northern towns of Burnley and Oldham are likely to be particularly constrained by the local tensions following the racialised disturbances of 2001 and BNP activity here. Housing opportunities are also affected by the conditions in local housing markets. Buying a decent affordable home may be easier for those living in the less over-heated housing markets of the north, but only if you have a job or you are not disadvantaged by your health, age or family type. This chapter looks at the level of choice or constraint that individual minority ethnic households experience in their housing decision-making, and the implications of this for new household formation by younger generations, as well as for meeting the housing needs of particular groups such as elders, disabled people or single parents. The chapter highlights a number of longstanding issues and obstacles to housing progress for BME households, which are relevant for debates about how to promote neighbourhood and community cohesion in line with government initiatives following the racialised disturbances in 2001. Understanding the underlying causes of social division and tensions has particular significance for the 28 'pathfinder' and 'shadow pathfinder' areas identified by the Home Office as recipients of government support for its community cohesion programme (for discussion see Chapter 5).

The earliest accounts of the experiences of black and minority ethnic groups in the housing market revealed how newly arriving immigrants had little choice but to occupy the bottom end of the market, ending up in poor private rental properties or, in the case of Asians, purchasing cheap, deteriorating inner city terraced housing abandoned by white households moving to the suburbs. Distinct ethnic clusters developed in the inner cities, the product of a number of often inter-related factors, namely: the newcomers' poverty and lack of knowledge of the housing market, the pattern of job opportunities open to them, the desire for clustering for social and cultural reasons, and the often blatant discrimination faced by black minority ethnic groups, and some white immigrants, in the early post-war years. The pattern at this time was undoubtedly one of minority ethnic deprivation, segregation and inequality.

Over time, there have been some significant changes in black and minority ethnic groups' position and experience in the housing market. These groups now have access to a wider range of housing tenures, property types, and neighbourhoods, and, on the whole, experience improved living conditions. The 2001 Census indicates that 'Black-Caribbeans' and Bangladeshis (especially those living in London) are now well represented in social housing (see Table 2.1), a sector in which black and minority ethnic groups were once acutely disadvantaged by formal and informal rules and direct discrimination. For those searching within the private housing market, access to finance and information has greatly improved in overall terms since the early days of widespread institutional exclusion, landlord hostility and vendor discrimination. The lowering of barriers by these 'gatekeepers', coupled with the greater disposable income of some households, has resulted in increasing numbers of black and minority ethnic households moving well up the property ladder.

Table 2.1: Housing tenure by ethnic group, 2001

England and Wales, percentages

	Owned outright	Owned with a mortgage or loan	Rented from council	Other social rented[1]	Rented privately[2]	Other[3]	All tenures (=100%) (millions)
White							
British	25	46	12	5	8	4	45.5
Irish	26	37	14	7	11	5	0.6
Other white	19	32	8	5	28	8	1.3
Mixed							
White and Black-Caribbean	7	34	28	16	10	5	0.2
White and Black African	7	32	22	14	18	7	0.1
White and Asian	15	47	12	7	14	6	0.2
Other mixed	12	40	15	9	16	6	0.2
Asian or Asian British							
Indian	27	52	5	3	10	3	1.0
Pakistani	27	43	9	6	12	4	0.7
Bangladeshi	9	29	33	15	10	4	0.3
Other Asian	16	43	9	7	19	7	0.2
Black or Black British							
Black-Caribbean	12	36	25	15	7	5	0.6
Black African	5	20	33	17	18	7	0.5
Other black	7	28	30	20	9	5	0.1
Chinese or other							
Chinese	21	37	8	4	18	12	0.2
Other	11	28	12	8	30	11	0.2
All people	24	45	12	5	9	4	52.0

Notes: 1. Includes rented from registered social landlord, housing association, housing co-operative and charitable trust.
2. Private rented and living rent free.
3. Includes living rent free, living in a communal establishment and shared ownership.
Source: Census 2001, Office for National Statistics.

Table 2.2: Percentage of 'disadvantaged' groups without employment and in poor housing, 1996

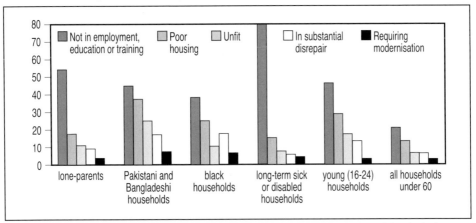

Note: 'Poor' housing is defined as that which is either unfit, in substantial disrepair or requires essential modernisation.
Source: ODPM, English House Condition Survey, 1996.

As we can see from Table 2.2, the barriers to good housing faced by minority ethnic groups will to a certain extent overlap with those experienced by other 'disadvantaged' groups. It is therefore not appropriate to explain patterns of housing advantage and disadvantage purely in terms of 'race' or ethnicity, although 'ethnic penalties' may hold back even the most economically privileged black and minority ethnic households (for this term and the care needed when using it, see Chapter 1).

The changes we have observed over the post-war years reflect the impact of 'race' relations legislation, 'race equality' initiatives (mainly within the social housing sector), changing housing demands from a socially, culturally, demographically and economically maturing population, generational differences in housing aspirations and strategies, and the role of minority ethnic creativity and empowerment in bringing advancement. Such developments have brought greater social and spatial mobility for the minority ethnic populations and resulted in loosening ties (voluntary and imposed) to particular (usually inner city) locations. One of the most obvious signs of this has been the growing number of minority ethnic households moving to the suburbs.

This pattern of change is, however, only half of the story. We can also see some worrying continuities between the early post-war years and now. The 2001 Census indicates that there are still major inequalities between white British and black minority ethnic groups when considered in terms of access to good quality housing in all tenures, levels of over-crowding, and representation within disadvantaged residential neighbourhoods. Furthermore, the *English House Condition Survey* (2001) found that black and minority ethnic households are nearly three times (27 per cent) as likely to live in 'poor' neighbourhoods as whites (10 per cent). If we add to this the finding that black minority ethnic groups are disproportionately represented amongst the homeless (representing 26 per cent of those accepted as homeless by local authorities between January and March 2004, but only 8 per cent of the general population, according to ODPM statistics) and take into account the power of racist harassment to shape housing choices, it is clear that a pattern of minority ethnic disadvantage in housing persists.

Of all the substantial minority ethnic groups identifiable in national data, Pakistanis and Bangladeshis live in the most deprived housing conditions in the worst locations. Both groups are characterised by high levels of over-crowding; 21 per cent and 39 per cent respectively have inadequate 'living space' according to the 2001 Census compared with only 4 per cent of white British. Many also live in homes without central heating: for example 18 per cent of Pakistani compared with 8 per cent of white British households. According to figures from the Office for National Statistics for 2000, about a quarter of Pakistani and Bangladeshi households were living in 'unfit' housing compared with 6 per cent of white households (see Table 2.3). Indians in contrast are generally faring better, with increasing numbers getting access to good quality, semi-detached housing in the suburbs. However, even amongst this group, there are still disproportionately high numbers living in poor, over-crowded conditions in the inner city (17 per cent of Indian households live in housing with inadequate living space).

The position at the beginning of the twenty-first century is therefore one of muted optimism. There is evidence of widening choices for some groups, notably those of Indian origin and those in middle class occupations. This not only brings access to better housing, but to better living environments, schools and other neighbourhood amenities (such as health and leisure facilities). These provide increased opportunities for social mobility across the generations. However, there are still many challenges to meeting the housing needs and aspirations of the black and minority ethnic population and many obstacles to achieving greater equality of opportunity and outcome. Four of the longstanding key issues of concern are highlighted in Box 7. In trying to meet needs, there are important potential choices for public policy, perhaps especially in finding a balance between supporting minority ethnic clustering (in inner city areas, for example) and policies for assisting movement to new neighbourhoods.

Table 2.3: Households in unfit dwellings, 2000

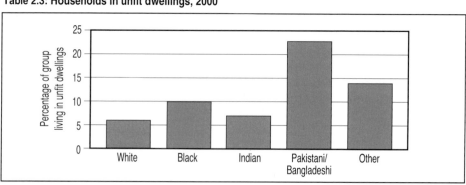

Source: ONS, *Social Trends* 30, p. 169.

**Box 7: Longstanding issues and obstacles affecting
housing progress for BME households**

- Differential and unequal treatment of minority ethnic groups by some housing market institutions.
- Poverty, unemployment and problems with housing affordability.
- The impact of racist harassment and/or fear of harassment on housing choices.
- The challenges of meeting diverse religious and cultural needs.

The rest of this chapter examines the main areas of housing achievement and concern in the different housing tenures. It then goes on to highlight the key issues that cut across the tenures to consider evidence for growing minority ethnic empowerment, widening choices and continuing constraint.

Home ownership

There are highly variable levels of home ownership between different minority ethnic groups. Owner-occupation is greatest for the Indians (79 per cent), Pakistanis (70 per cent), white British households (71 per cent) and Chinese (58 per cent), but falls to 48 per cent for the Black-Caribbean and 38 per cent for the Bangladeshi groups (Table 2.1). Large though these differences are, they are diminishing. After decades of fairly static home ownership rates amongst Indians and Pakistanis, the levels have now fallen slightly as more of the younger generation opts for renting for economic reasons. Bangladeshi ownership has also declined in line with other Asian groups, and Chinese ownership levels have dipped slightly. Meanwhile, after a rise in home ownership in the 1980s, Black-Caribbean levels of ownership have stayed the same over the last decade or so. Unfortunately we do not have equivalent data for some of the other smaller minority groups, including 'newer' ones.

Once one starts to consider variations within the black and minority ethnic groups in terms of gender, class, household type and regional location, the differences in ownership levels become less straightforward. Gender, for example, has a marked effect on tenure within black and minority ethnic groups, in that women heads of households are far less likely to own, even taking into account their socio-economic status. These gender differences undoubtedly reflect the problems faced by women in raising finance to purchase property and the option that women with children have of access to social rented housing. The high number of female heads of household (and single parents) in the Black-Caribbean group, together with their over-representation in London, where ownership is least affordable, helps to explain the high level of social renting amongst this group.

We know from earlier research that home ownership amongst minority ethnic groups is by no means always associated with higher incomes or good quality

---

29

housing. Amongst South Asians in particular, low-income home ownership has been common since the earliest days of settlement in the UK. The association between home ownership and occupational/employment category has always been much stronger for white British, Chinese and African/Caribbean households, with more working class households finding their way into housing in the social or privately rented sector. The most recent figures suggest, however, that housing choices pursued by younger Asians are now more in line with their socio-economic status than for previous generations. Many find it difficult to get a foothold on the home ownership ladder in the way that their parents or grandparents did in the 1960s and 1970s. Unimproved inner city housing could be bought cheaply for cash in the early post-war years, as whites abandoned the inner terraces for the fast developing suburbs. Now, even relatively cheap housing in the northern cities may not be affordable for many, particularly given the high levels of minority ethnic unemployment in these areas. Some Asian parents may help out by buying properties for their children, perhaps in advance of their marriage. The properties purchased are likely to be located close to the family home, thus sustaining patterns of ethnic clustering, usually within the inner city.

Hence, it seems that traditional patterns of minority ethnic ownership are beginning to change as more UK-born minority ethnic households enter the housing market. We are now beginning to see some convergence of ownership patterns in terms of *level* of ownership and the *quality* of property purchased between the later generations of minority ethnic group buyers and the white British population. Increasing numbers of young middle class people from all minority ethnic groups, but particularly those of Indian origin, are pursuing suburban ideals of good housing, spacious and low crime neighbourhoods, and access to good schools. However, some over-crowding is often still evident amongst Indian suburban home owners because of their family size. Quality measures available to us through the census are limited, but the indications are that those owners most likely to live in higher quality homes (such as those in good areas with semi-detached/detached housing with central heating) are the white British, Chinese and Indians, whilst the least likely are those of Pakistani or Bangladeshi origin. The quality and status of the housing owned by women tends to be worse than that of men, and this difference holds across classes and ethnic groups.

Box 8: Some important features of owner-occupation

The quality of housing owned by minority ethnic households is still often relatively low, but increasing numbers of young middle class people from all communities are pursuing suburban ideals of better dwellings and more spacious environments. This is especially marked for those of Indian origin.

There are significant differences between minority ethnic groups in levels of ownership, but this is changing in specific ways.

→

> The younger generations face housing markets that differ from those of earlier years, and social renting may now have increasing importance for lower income households because of problems of affordability in owner-occupation. This might be part of a gradual shift whereby the association between socio-economic status and tenure moves closer to that seen within the white population.
>
> Gender has a marked effect on tenure within black minority ethnic groups, in that women heads of households are far less likely to own. When they do own, the quality of their housing is likely to be poorer than that owned by men.

Despite some real improvements in the quality of homes owned by black and minority ethnic households over time, the overall disparity in housing standards for minority ethnic and white owners is still a cause for concern. The *English House Condition Survey* (1996) found that twice as many minority ethnic people own 'poor' housing compared with whites. This pattern is closely associated with inner city living, where neighbourhoods are often characterised by high levels of physical deprivation and social problems. Studies have shown that owners (and renters) living in these poorer inner city neighbourhoods hold both positive and negative views about their quality of life there. Understandably, most black and minority ethnic residents dislike the physical decline of many inner areas and worry about growing crime, vandalism, drug abuse and anti-social behaviour. They nevertheless value the sense of community, social support and cultural amenities of these areas, and many have no desire to move. This is particularly true of elders, but a recent study of the Asian population living in Leeds and Bradford also found some younger middle class households buying into the minority ethnic areas of the inner city in order to be part of the day-to-day life of the community there (Phillips *et al.*, 2003).

Some black and minority ethnic owners undoubtedly feel trapped in poorer housing and areas by their poverty and their fears about moving out (particularly fears of cultural isolation and harassment). Fear of racist harassment continues to limit black and minority ethnic people's choice of neighbourhood (see Chapter 9). Some may make the move to better housing in the suburbs only to return to the relative safety of the inner city community following abuse. Fear of victimisation may also constrain mobility and socialisation if a move is made to the suburbs, particularly for women.

We have plenty of evidence to show that black and minority ethnic patterns of home ownership have, in the past, also been shaped by the discriminatory activity of housing market institutions, such as estate agents and lending institutions (see Chapter 1). One aspect of this included the 'steering' of purchasers to particular neighbourhoods on the basis of their 'race' and ethnicity. Black and minority ethnic purchasers were most likely to be advised to buy in multi-ethnic areas of the inner city. A case well publicised in the 1990s was that of Norman Lester and Co, an estate agent operating in Oldham (CRE, 1990). Following complaints, actor tests were undertaken. These involved sending prospective Asian and white buyers, with similar characteristics other than their visible ethnic differences, to search for and arrange finance to buy particular properties in Oldham. The tests revealed that the agency was discriminating against people selling in Asian areas, segregating purchasers on 'racial' grounds, accepting discriminatory instructions from vendors, and discriminating against Asians in mortgage lending. Norman Lester argued that the practice ensured that people bought houses in areas where they would be 'happy to live' and that houses in Asian areas were a 'bad investment'.

Evidence of institutional discrimination in terms of mortgage lending has been hard to obtain. There were several pieces of research in the 1970s and 1980s, which pointed to discriminatory behaviour and concluded that there was a strong case for much greater scrutiny of buying and selling practices, and in particular the terms of mortgage lending to minority ethnic groups. Available information suggested that although the harsh practice of 'red-lining' (where inner city areas were designated as too risky for mortgage lending) was dropped by many lenders in the 1980s, BME home owners nonetheless were offered mortgages on less favourable terms than whites (Sarre *et al.*, 1989). However, the major institutions, the building societies and banks, have resisted record-keeping, thus making it very difficult for the Commission for Racial Equality (CRE) to undertake or justify formal investigations. A rare opportunity for substantial data analysis via administrative records arose in the late 1970s, when there was a scheme for positive collaboration with local authorities. Findings suggested mixed outcomes from lending decisions, and highlighted some localities of minority ethnic settlement with continuing difficulties of access to funds (see Harrison and Stevens, 1981; cf CRE, 1985a). Unfortunately, no similar city-scale data sets are available today.

The CRE has not undertaken any investigations of discrimination in the owner-occupied sector for over a decade. We therefore have to look to academic research to track the more recent policies and practices of private housing institutions. One of the very few studies to have examined the activity of estate agents in the twenty-first century has been undertaken by Phillips *et al.* (2003). This research, which looked at the housing markets of Leeds and Bradford, indicates that although there has been much improvement over the decades, inequalities in the treatment of ethnic groups still occur. Greater competition amongst lenders and agencies means that lending institutions and estate agents now take a less 'exclusionary' attitude to borrowers, buyers, localities and property characteristics than in the past. However, estate agents can still shape the housing opportunities of black and minority ethnic and white purchasers through a process of steering. While agents are well aware of the law and thus unlikely to engage in overt discrimination, many still use racialised stereotypes about where people might like to live (this applies to both black minority and white buyers) and hold a racialised view of the housing market. This helps to sustain existing patterns of ethnic segregation as clients are directed to particular areas based on their 'race' or ethnicity. Agents also acknowledged that, as in the past, some vendors try to discriminate.

Interviews with South Asian households in Leeds and Bradford revealed continuing suspicion of estate agents by this group and surprisingly high levels of avoidance of institutions. Only one third of purchasers in the last ten years (47 out of 138) had registered with an agent, although others had contact with an agent at some stage in the search process. As in the past, the use of 'for sale' signs or community information was the preferred method, and was seen to give more control over the purchase process. This inevitably restricts the range of search. Most of those using estate agents were satisfied with the outcome, but there were perceptions of unequal treatment amongst some and a suspicion of vendor discrimination.

Conventional lending institutions are more widely used by South Asian households now than in the past, although some still turn to community resources. Three-quarters of recent purchasers (buying in the last ten years) interviewed in the Leeds and Bradford survey had taken out a mortgage and were generally satisfied with the service received. Islamic restrictions on mortgage debt had not produced any significant difference in the use of conventional mortgages by Muslim families, mainly because of the lack of alternatives. Some had, however, used 'interest-free' community loans to minimise their debts. A number of Pakistanis and Bangladeshis said they would prefer an Islamic mortgage, if available. This highlights the need for culturally-sensitive institutional lending policies, and some development nationally has begun towards these (see also Chapter 4).

The strategies adopted by households to provide themselves with housing in the private sector, despite poverty and discrimination, have been most impressive. Although facing considerable constraints, black and minority ethnic people have shown considerable ingenuity and creativity in pursuit of their housing choices. Home ownership appears to be providing a route to the suburbs for at least the more affluent minority groups. Inner city home ownership has been a mixed blessing for black and minority ethnic groups. On the one hand, a combination of deteriorating physical environments and unemployment may make owning more of a liability than an asset for some. On the other hand, home ownership has given communities a degree of autonomy and identity which it might have been more difficult to create in social rented housing, the success of the black minority ethnic voluntary housing movement not withstanding.

Social rented housing

Debates about black and minority ethnic groups and social rented housing have centred on issues of differential access to housing, the differentiated quality of housing allocated and the minority ethnic experience of living in the social rented sector in terms of service delivery, tenant participation and neighbour relations. The restructuring of the social rented sector, which began in earnest in the 1980s, has also raised new ethnic equality issues; first, in terms of the impact of the right to buy policy, and, more recently, in relation to stock transfers and choice-based lettings systems. The variable response of local authorities to the need to house growing numbers of asylum seekers and refugees has presented additional challenges.

The social rented sector plays an important role in the housing of particular minority ethnic households. Nationally, Bangladeshi and Black-Caribbean households (48 per cent and 40 per cent of whom respectively are housed by local authorities or housing associations according to the 2001 Census) are especially well represented in this sector compared with white British households (17 per cent). Housing associations, and in particular the black and minority ethnic associations, have been an important route into affordable housing. RSLs (those housing associations and allied bodies that are formally registered social landlords) house a disproportionately high number of Black-Caribbean and Bangladeshi tenants. For example, according to the 2001 Census, 15 per cent of Black-Caribbean households and 15 per cent of those of Bangladeshi origin lived in this sector, compared with 5 per cent of white households. It is worth noting that 60 per cent of RSL tenancies are held by women, often single parents, which brings particular housing and support needs (Housing Corporation, 2003). The consequences of policy changes in this sector thus rest most heavily on these groups.

The South Asian and Chinese populations have traditionally found social renting less attractive than low cost home ownership; for example, only 8 per cent of Indian and 12 per cent of Chinese households live in this housing sector. Recent research, however, suggests that, while not necessarily a tenure of first choice, social housing may become an increasingly important housing alternative for young, newly forming Asian households in the next decade (Ratcliffe 1996; Phillips and Harrison 2000). Bradford city council, for example, has forecast that 3,500 new households will need affordable rented housing by 2010. Many of these will be Asian.

The social housing experience has been highly variable for the minority ethnic population over the post-war years. A wealth of studies has pointed to the differential treatment of minority ethnic when compared with white housing applicants, leading to a restricted range of housing options for the former (Karn and Phillips, 1998). This resulted in over-representation of African/Caribbean and Asian tenants in poorer quality and types of housing and in unpopular, deteriorating (often inner city) neighbourhoods. Even though many discriminatory policies and practices are now a thing of the past, black and minority ethnic people often lack confidence in this sector serving their needs. The *Race and Housing Inquiry: Challenge Report* (NHF *et al.*, 2001) revealed that black and minority ethnic communities thought it was difficult to access RSL accommodation and that minority ethnic tenants were more likely to be dissatisfied with their RSL as a landlord than were white tenants. In addition, the ethnic clusters produced by past discrimination are now sustained in the poorest areas by a sense of community and security. The opportunity to transfer within the social rented sector and thus escape the worst areas has also decreased for all tenants over time. The marginalisation of black and minority ethnic tenants in this sector, along with other socially excluded white groups, has been exacerbated by the so-called 'residualisation' or down-grading of social rented housing over the last two decades.

The absence of information on current state of repair is a particular handicap in assessing the quality of housing occupied by minority ethnic groups. However, we know that the squeeze on local authority resources produced a decline in maintenance standards and a reduction in resources for upgrading poor quality estates, such as the high density, flatted estates in which many African/Caribbean and Bangladeshi tenants are concentrated. Targeted regeneration through the New Deal for Communities (NDC) programme may in the end bring some measurable improvements. At the time of writing, a NDC programme of social support, selective housing demolition and re-building, and stock transfers was underway on the Ocean estate in Stepney, Tower Hamlets. This may have the potential to bring much needed housing and welfare improvements to the Bengali community, who have long lived in squalid conditions on this estate. A successful programme of community and housing regeneration has also accompanied stock transfer in nearby Poplar, where about 50 per cent of residents are from a minority ethnic background (see HACAS Chapman Hendy, 2002). A fear, however, as with some regeneration elsewhere, is that the new accommodation will no longer be affordable and may indeed attract more affluent white tenants, who wish to live close to the heart of London.

Lack of housing choice and issues of vulnerability within the social rented sector take on new meaning when considered in relation to asylum seekers and refugees. Coming from different backgrounds and with different needs from the more established black and minority ethnic communities, they pose additional challenges for the sector. This new diversity may not be adequately reflected in ethnic monitoring data, which often rely on ethnic categories which can only group them under the heading 'other' ethnic group. Yet these newcomers often need more support because of the trauma they have experienced, public hostility towards them, and because they have not had time to develop the community support networks evident in other more established groups.

We deal with refugees and asylum seekers in two later chapters, but some preliminary points may be useful now. A report produced by the Housing Corporation at the end of the last decade concluded that the social rented sector's record with respect to housing refugees was often 'mediocre', or 'bad', and that there were some cases of institutional racism (see Chapter 7). Practices vary across the country in terms of the way that refugees are treated under the homelessness legislation and there are significant variations in the extent to which (if at all) the needs of asylum seekers and refugees are considered as part of wider 'race equality' policies. Back in 1993, a Joseph Rowntree Foundation study warned of the potential dangers of allocating homeless refugees and asylum seekers to large social housing estates with impoverished populations without careful plans for supporting the new arrivals (Page, 1993). A decade later, a CIH report (2003) again identified the same urgent need for well supported housing services, not only directly to meet the needs of the asylum seekers and refugees, but also to facilitate community cohesion. All too often, these vulnerable people have been placed in areas of difficult-to-let social housing with little support for either the newcomers or the existing tenants, who may resent the influx of 'outsiders'. Myths about priority treatment and government benefits for asylum seekers and refugees have fuelled tensions in deprived areas as far apart as Wrexham (North Wales), Hull and Plymouth, as well as public outbursts against the establishment of 'induction centres' in places such as Sittingbourne, Kent. (For further comment see Chapters 6 and 7.)

In fact the record of housing asylum seekers and refugees is mixed. There are examples of good practice, which have not only provided support for the newcomers but also helped with the integration of these new groups into local communities. Leicester City Council, for example, has made an explicit commitment to supporting asylum seekers and refugees as part of its black and minority ethnic housing strategy, and has devised positive action strategies to assist integration (see Chapter 7).

Empowerment within the social rented sector: minority ethnic housing associations

A major achievement for black and minority ethnic groups has been the emergence of a flourishing black housing movement in the form of black and minority ethnic-led housing associations. The fundamental contribution of these organisations stems from the fact that the social and cultural needs of minority ethnic groups are their primary concern, not just an after-thought or one duty among many, as for some established white-run associations. This has had a profound effect on their development and management activities. Although these organisations only house ten per cent of the total of black and minority ethnic tenants in RSL stock, they can impact on other social housing organisations and act as a catalyst for change in terms of the black and minority ethnic housing strategies adopted in this sector. Chapter 4 summarises their key contributions to progress.

Importantly, black and minority ethnic-led RSLs have often provided the main access points into the social rented sector for the South Asian population. They have also addressed the needs of vulnerable households through outreach and 'Housing Plus' work, and supported housing services, including provisions for various groups such as people with mental health problems and victims of domestic violence. Black and minority ethnic people have often found it difficult to access advice and support through 'mainstream' organisations because of the lack of attention to cultural diversity and language needs, and there are 'gateway' functions that the associations may play for clients.

Black-led housing associations are still relatively small in number and in size (more than half of them own or manage less than 200 housing units). In 2004, there were 64 black and minority ethnic social landlords registered with the Housing Corporation. They account for around 1.3 per cent of the RSL stock (Housing Corporation, 2001). There are other black and minority ethnic housing bodies, which may be harder to track, that are not registered with the Corporation. The Housing Corporation's funding regime has tended to favour the largest black and minority ethnic associations at the expense of some of the smaller ones. For example, Approved Development Programme (ADP) allocations from the Housing Corporation for 2003-2004 gave substantial support to large black-led RSLs, including Ujima, Presentation and ASRA Greater London, whilst many smaller ones remained under-resourced. There were also large regional disparities in the allocation of Approved Development Programme funds, with London receiving the lion's share whilst nothing was given to the Merseyside and the North East regions.

Although a small part of the social rented sector, black and minority ethnic organisations have a political significance far beyond their size, and provide the opportunity for black and minority ethnic people to become agents, not just objects of public policy. Their development is a unique example of government support for the empowerment of minority ethnic communities. Their future roles will probably to some degree depend on enhancing their financial security and achieving a measure of diversification in activities, while retaining good grass roots links. Further explanation may be found in Chapter 4, and in the CIH report on these associations (Lupton and Perry, 2004).

The accompanying box summarises some key features of social renting before we consider the policy challenges.

Box 9: Some important features of social renting

Debates about black and minority ethnic groups and social rented housing have centred on issues of differential access, the quality of housing allocated, and the experiences of living in the social rented sector in terms of service delivery, cultural sensitivity, tenant participation and neighbour relations. Performance by housing providers still appears patchy. The restructuring of the social rented sector since the 1980s has raised new ethnic equality issues.

The social rented sector plays a very important role in the housing of particular minority ethnic households. Housing associations (and particularly black and minority ethnic associations) have provided an important route into affordable housing.

The South Asian and Chinese populations traditionally found social renting less attractive than low cost home ownership, but social housing may be becoming an increasingly important potential housing alternative for young, newly forming Asian households.

A major achievement for black and minority ethnic groups has been the emergence of a flourishing black housing movement in the form of black and minority ethnic-led housing associations.

Lack of housing choice and issues of vulnerability within the social rented sector take on new meaning when considered in relation to asylum seekers and refugees. Coming from different backgrounds and with different needs from the more established black and minority ethnic communities, they pose additional challenges for the sector.

Current challenges for the sector

The concentration of black minority ethnic tenants that may still occur within some less desirable parts of the social rented sector presents housing providers with some important challenges. First, as the number of minority ethnic households grows, it is likely to prove difficult to satisfy the demand for housing in inner city areas close to established ethnic communities. There will therefore be increasing pressure to rethink policies in order to provide minority ethnic applicants with attractive housing opportunities outside established ethnic neighbourhoods. Second, the changing housing aspirations of younger minority ethnic households will, evidence suggests, lead to a growing demand for housing in the ethnically mixed areas near to the ethnic cores as well as beyond. A report from Birmingham City Council (1998) concluded that there was a strong desire amongst Birmingham's black and minority ethnic communities to move to outer city areas (p. 1). The relatively poor environment of the inner city was thought to be the significant push factor; the potential for improving living conditions was the chief pull. Similarly, focus group research amongst Bradford's African/ Caribbean and South Asian populations conducted in 1999-2000 found that some younger members of these groups are prepared to consider living in a much wider range of areas than their parents. We deal with the Bradford case more fully in Chapter 10, but can note now that many informants displayed ambivalent attitudes towards remaining within the traditional areas of settlement for their group, seeing both advantages and disadvantages associated with living there. The young residents of central Bradford were well aware of the stigma and the wider disadvantages associated with living in deprived, multi-ethnic inner city areas. Exclusion from job opportunities and the problems of 'post-code labelling' were uppermost in their minds. Many were keen to move into slightly better neighbourhoods on the edge of the established areas of community living, giving them a degree of physical distance without too much social isolation.

Housing policy would certainly seem, at least on the face of it, to be moving in the direction of opening up 'choice' for social tenants. The move towards choice-based lettings (CBL) systems heralds the introduction of a less prescriptive social housing allocations system, which should give tenants a greater say in their housing outcomes (cf Fotheringham and Perry, 2003). In a pilot CBL scheme, Bradford Council reported (via its website) a doubling of lettings to Asians in 2002-2003. The overall impact of these schemes on black and minority ethnic options has, however, yet to be evaluated. Rather ironically, given the widespread exclusionary allocation policies of the past, some northern authorities facing problems of low demand (often on peripheral estates) now see the growing interest in social housing from minority ethnic groups as a possible solution to their lettings problems.

The aspiration for black and minority ethnic groups, however, is not only to be given more choice, but also to move towards greater empowerment within mainstream organisations. This would imply greater black and minority ethnic consultation and management involvement, as well as the development of locally based housing strategies to promote 'race equality' and respond to cultural diversity. Examples of shifting frameworks of thinking about black and minority ethnic issues are evident in the Housing Corporation's *Black and Minority Ethnic Housing Policy* (1998) and the DTLR's (now ODPM) *Action Plan* (2001) for addressing the housing needs of black and minority ethnic people (which is also touched on in Chapter 3; see also Lupton and Perry, 2004).

We nevertheless have to ask to what extent well intentioned policies will be able to overcome the institutional cultures and inertia of the present and the discrimination of the past. A national survey of social housing institutions conducted in 1999 found a number of examples of good practice for widening black and minority ethnic choices (Phillips and Unsworth, 2002). However, more commonly, the survey found that neither the resources nor the political will to devise and implement such initiatives were present. Most RSLs and local authorities in areas with significant black and minority ethnic populations recognised that outward movement into different neighbourhoods was beginning in the private sector. However, there was little commitment to widening choices or assisting movement into new locations in the social housing sector; most organisations had other more pressing concerns at the top of their agenda.

Those attempting to encourage minority ethnic group mobility within the social rented sector (mainly as an attempt to redress inequalities arising from past discrimination) have undoubtedly encountered difficulties associated with disrupting the traditional patterns of ethnic settlement. For example, in the 1990s, the London Borough of Lewisham found it hard to persuade its black (mainly African/Caribbean) tenants to move into better quality estates beyond the relatively deprived and over-crowded areas in Deptford because of established community links and the fear of harassment (Phillips, 1993). Surveys of black and minority ethnic populations in a range of localities across Britain have highlighted the very real barriers to social housing choice posed by the fear of racist violence in particular. Large 'white' estates on the edges of cities are often perceived as 'rough' and prone to drugs and crime as well as racism, and are thus commonly avoided (see Chapter 10). Tensions between minority ethnic groups, as well as between black and white tenants, can restrict housing choices if not dealt with by the social housing provider. A recent study in Leeds, for example, uncovered a reluctance by Asian people to consider parts of the housing association stock close to one of their main areas of settlement, apparently because of worries about harassment from African/Caribbean tenants living there.

These findings point to a need for sensitive and well-tuned policies to support minority ethnic households in the social rented sector. Consultation and involvement of black and minority ethnic people in the review, development and management processes will not only help to meet housing needs, but will also build a climate of trust and confidence in the responsiveness of social landlords. Despite a stated commitment to tenant consultation and involvement enshrined in local authority 'Tenant Compacts', many tenants (both minority ethnic and white) may well still feel that their social landlords do not understand their needs, aspirations or problems. Like estate agents, many local authorities and housing associations can still hold stereotyped views of black and minority ethnic housing and neighbourhood preferences, and this may sometimes underpin allocation and policy processes. A responsive housing service needs to acknowledge the importance of ethnic clustering for many black and minority ethnic people, without assuming this means a continuing pattern of inner city living. The preference for living near to other families in the same ethnic group is often as true for younger as for older people. Issues related to a sense of well-being, security and identity are commonly important, as material in Chapter 10 indicates.

Several housing associations (both 'mainstream' and black-led) have implemented initiatives to develop new settlement clusters in order to widen housing and area choices for black and minority ethnic people. For example, the Canalside Community Induction Project, involving a consortium of BME and mainstream social housing providers, has responded to the problems posed by a shortage of land in inner Rochdale by creating 'settlement nodes' of South Asian families in more outlying areas (see Blackaby, 2004, p. 45). Access to cultural facilities, schools and health services is given careful consideration before families are offered the chance to settle. The success of such schemes rests on a significant investment in terms of inter-agency initiatives and tenant support. The introduction of specialist training for wardens for the new clusters has been an important feature of this initiative and has served to provide employment, skills and sustained support for the newly settling families.

Innovative schemes such as this require the acquisition or construction of new homes. Properties owned or managed by black and minority ethnic-led housing associations tend to be located within the main inner areas of ethnic settlement, and as yet there is no strong trend of acquiring property in outer areas. It is also true that much of the property owned or managed by 'mainstream' or white-run RSLs is located within the inner urban areas, although there is more potential for mobility in some of these associations. Nonetheless, as significant stock transfers look certain to continue, both from local authorities to housing associations, and from white-run to black and minority ethnic-led associations, the potential for presenting minority ethnic groups with wider housing choices should grow.

Guidance on good practice for promoting 'race equality' in the social rented sector is now widely available, and the Race Relations (Amendment) Act 2000 has brought further legislative pressure to bear (see Chapter 3). There is an expectation that mainstream RSLs and councils will engage in a process of self-monitoring and undertake 'equality testing' or impact assessment of housing policies. However, there is still a long way to go. According to the Audit Commission, the record for local authorities in particular on 'race equality' is still poor. For example, in 2002, about 40 per cent of councils in England and Wales had not even reached the first level of the CRE's (1999) 'Standard on Race Equality', and only half had a comprehensive equal opportunities policy (for an overview of law and regulation see the next chapter). The record of putting policy into practice is also highly variable. There has in fact been no shortage of guidance on good practice since the 1970s, yet we still seem to have to revisit the same territory again and again. The *Race and Housing Inquiry* (2001) was set up partly because of evidence that the housing association sector seemed to be performing badly in terms of race equality.

Recent research involving the present author (Phillips and Unsworth, 2002) found that 'race equality' obligations were still generally very narrowly conceptualised and operationalised for both RSLs and local authorities. Too many organisations viewed their responsibilities in terms of narrowly defined ethnic targets and quotas, and employed very few minority ethnic staff. The commitment to meeting targets was itself variable and sometimes poorly thought out. One large association set its targets for black and minority ethnic representation at local authority level because the computer system used to record lettings could only cope with this level of geographical detail. In general, it was assumed that as long as an organisation could demonstrate that their annual lettings were in line with the ethnic make-up of the locality, then this was sufficient to discharge their 'race equality' obligations. More radical changes demand a transformation of the institutional culture, which would see fuller integration of black and minority ethnic issues into mainstream strategic thinking and practice. Meanwhile, as we see in the next chapter, the framework of expectations developed in recent years by central government really requires proactive and strategic thinking as well as cultural change, and the pressures for these seem likely to continue.

The private rented sector

The private rented sector, although small, still has roles to play. Back in the 1970s, minority ethnic groups were very heavily dependent on private rented housing; 30 per cent of Black-Caribbean and 35 per cent of Indian households rented privately in 1971. By 2001, both of these groups had largely moved out of private renting, only 7 per cent of Black-Caribbeans and 10 per cent of Indians living in this sector (compared with 8 per cent of white British). However, private renting still plays a relatively important role for Black-Africans (18 per cent), who are concentrated in the London housing market, and for the Chinese (18 per cent). In particular localities, such as London and Dover, the private rented sector houses large numbers of refugees and asylum seekers.

The quality of private rented accommodation which is affordable for people on moderate incomes, or covered by housing benefit limits, is still often very poor. The *English House Condition Survey* (2001) shows that nearly half (49 per cent) of private tenants live in 'non-decent' accommodation. The position has improved somewhat over the last decade, but this group of tenants is still significantly worse off than those in better parts of the social rented sector (for example, 27 per cent of RSL tenants live in non-decent housing, although it is worse for council tenants at 42 per cent).

Despite the poor quality of much private rental housing, rents are high because of the shortage of rented housing in most markets, not just in London or even metropolitan areas, and it has become common for deposits to be required. Many landlords are unwilling to accept prospective tenants dependent on income support. There is also little security of tenure; assured short-hold tenancies for six months have become the norm for new private lettings. However, this means that there are difficulties in obtaining shorter lettings to tide over emergencies. A number of local authorities and voluntary organisations have set up schemes to help vulnerable tenants access private rental accommodation through rent deposit and bond schemes, with the aim of moderating the worst effects of competing for a place to rent in the private market (see the *National Rent Deposit Forum* for examples of good practice; see internet sources at the end of this book). The initiatives include working with and providing support for landlords, many of whom are suspicious of certain types of tenants (e.g. ex-offenders, refugees, homeless people), bond and rent-in-advance schemes, housing benefit advice, and home grants schemes to help with improvements to the property and furnishings. The organisers of schemes include churches, councils and housing associations, and many draw on Supporting People funds. For example, Croydon Churches Housing Association pays the landlord the deposit and one month's rent in advance. In this case, the landlord banks this advance for a year and keeps it as a gift for the tenants if they renew the tenancy for a further twelve months, thus encouraging stability of tenure. The greatest limitation to these schemes relates to the restricted funds of voluntary sector organisations, which can usually only provide support in the early years of accommodation. The aim is to get tenants to a stage where they can secure a lettings contract.

The National Asylum Support Service (NASS) uses the private rental sector for the housing of asylum seekers. The accommodation may be poor and there have been incidents of exploitation and harassment by landlords. In 2003, for example, an independent inquiry for the Home Office found that the private property company Landmark Liverpool and NASS had not paid sufficient attention to the housing needs and rights of 2,000 asylum seekers, who had been housed in two tower blocks in Liverpool (the blocks having been sold to the private company by Liverpool Council, who had deemed them unfit for their tenants). We say more on such matters in Chapters 6 and 7. Problems have also arisen when NASS has paid above market rates for accommodation within the private rental sector. This has led to rent inflation in local private rental markets, fuelling public misunderstanding of the level of government financial support for this vulnerable group and placing pressure on affordable accommodation in this sector. Problems can be particularly acute in London, where affordability is a major issue, because many refugees tend to gravitate there, despite government programmes of dispersal.

Conclusion

The achievements and constraints for black and minority ethnic people in the housing market may be understood in terms of a number of inter-linked processes:

1. Growing minority ethnic empowerment, through socio-economic advancement and greater skills in negotiating the housing market.

Minority ethnic progress within the housing market of the twenty-first century reflects the different housing demands and strategies of a more settled population and its subsequent generations, the improved financial capacity of many to meet those demands, broad societal changes which have removed some of the housing market barriers to minority ethnic progress, and the capabilities of minority ethnic groups themselves to resist discrimination and marginalisation and press for their housing entitlements. The emergence of the black minority ethnic voluntary housing movement is significant in this respect, but so too are the individual strategies employed by households in resisting, for example, the discrimination and harassment that has confined so many to the poorer inner city areas, or in organising to protect their interests in areas of urban renewal. Suburbanisation is not always easily achieved, even for those with the financial capacity to make the move. Some households go to extraordinary lengths to adapt their lifestyles to cope with the every-day risk of harassment. We can thus see that minority ethnic groups are far from passive victims of discrimination.

2. Growing diversity of black and minority ethnic backgrounds and experiences, giving rise to a wide range of demands, needs and aspirations.

An appreciation of the diversity of experience, both within and between groups, is fundamental to our understanding of the current position and future prospects for black and minority ethnic groups in the housing market. Chapter 1 highlighted this when referring to the *diversity agenda*. For some purposes, for instance, we can no longer talk meaningfully about 'South Asians' as an undifferentiated group. Length of settlement, levels of education and employment status, housing outcomes and cultural factors serve to distinguish between Indians, Pakistanis and Bangladeshis. Given some of the recent events noted in Chapter 5, we should also acknowledge the particular pattern of hostility and exclusion faced by many Muslim families in their search for decent housing. The inclusion of information on religious groups in the 2001 Census, for the first time, helps enable us to monitor Muslim housing achievements and constraints. At time of writing, a report on Muslim housing experiences has just been published, dealing with housing profiles and conditions, and with case studies indicating child poverty and housing deprivation amongst this group (Housing Corporation, 2004: see also Chapter 1).

The recognition of growing diversity has clear policy implications; housing strategies and equality targets need to take account of ethnic differentiation in housing need, tenure preferences, locational requirements and housing market behaviour. For instance, the diversity of experience amongst homeless youth, in terms of gender, age, location and minority ethnic group, has important implications for statutory and voluntary service provision for this group. Equally, new housing demands will emerge with the demographic maturity of the minority ethnic groups, with a growing need for more varied housing options for minority ethnic elders.

3. The continuing impact that institutional racism and harassment may have on housing choices.

Despite growing minority empowerment, white institutions retain overwhelming power in the allocation of housing and employment resources. The development of avoidance strategies based on fear and experience of discrimination and/or racist harassment has, in the past, promoted what some have referred to as market segmentation or a 'dual housing market'. This was most clearly evident in the 1970s and 1980s as a result of black and minority ethnic groups often restricting their search for accommodation to particular neighbourhoods and to poorer sections of the housing market. Whilst market segmentation has found its clearest expression in the private rental sector, where there has been a tradition of renting from a landlord of a similar ethnic origin, comparable processes have long been at work in the owner-occupied sector as well. Although there is now widespread use of mainstream housing institutions by black and minority ethnic groups, we have seen that institutional discrimination, including racialised steering, can still restrict housing and neighbourhood choices. For some, continuing suspicion of mainstream institutions perpetuates the tradition of word-of-mouth exchanges of information and private funding arrangements. This inevitably limits the range and price of properties considered for purchase to the poorer, cheaper end of the market. The network of black-led housing associations, whilst providing black and minority ethnic people with access to better quality housing than in the past, offers a limited range of neighbourhoods through the city, since most of their properties are in inner areas.

4. The continuing desire for ethnic clustering.

It is clear that many black and minority ethnic people still prefer to live in areas with some families of a similar background. Cultural and religious ties can therefore influence a family's decision about where to look for housing in both the inner city areas and the suburbs. Some, according to a national survey of black and minority ethnic neighbourhood preferences (Lakey, 1997), would prefer to live in an area where people from their own ethnic group are in the majority. This is particularly true for people of Pakistani and Bangladeshi origin and reflects both cultural reasons and the value gained from being able to access local community networks.

The process of clustering has given rise to emotive discussions about so-called 'self-segregation' by minority ethnic groups, with assumptions being made about supposedly negative effects from people living 'parallel lives'. As Chapter 5 shows, this has been fuelled by the reports and ensuing debates surrounding the racialised disturbances in northern cities in 2001. We believe, however, that it is important to challenge the idea that an expressed preference for living close to people from a similar ethnic group is the same as *voluntary segregation*, as has so often been implied. Recent research with the Asian communities of Leeds and Bradford also indicates that a degree of residential separation is not indicative of an unwillingness to mix with people from other ethnic groups (Phillips *et al.*, 2003). Spatially segregated living very often arises through *bounded choices*, which reflect both cultural values and practicalities in terms of support (especially for those with limited English), as well as perceived constraints on where black and minority ethnic people can live. These constraints may be a result of financial limitations, anxieties about harassment, unequal opportunities in the housing market and/or fears about not being accepted in areas away from established neighbourhoods. As Chapter 10 shows, some black and minority ethnic households are very worried about the idea of living in an 'all white' neighbourhood because of fears about racism, harassment and cultural isolation. The presence of a 'familiar' face can be reassuring and help to overcome a sense of isolation, especially for women and older members of the household.

Recognition of the importance of bounded choices has specific implications for housing policy-makers and service providers. As discussed earlier, there is a need to widen minority ethnic area choices by supporting moves to new areas when desired. There is also a need to recognise the value of ethnic clustering and focus efforts on the regeneration of declining neighbourhoods that have become the basis for vibrant, supportive communities.

5. New household formation and affordability issues.

The formation of new black and minority ethnic households is likely to increase significantly. Recent projections suggest that, by 2011, the number of households headed by someone of minority ethnic origin will increase by 39 per cent compared with 18 per cent for white British heads of households. This reflects the age structure of the minority ethnic population, family size and over-crowding levels. Over-crowding is likely to increase as younger family members marry. Research into the views of five minority ethnic groups in Leeds (Law *et al.*, 1996) and, more recently, Asian families in Leeds and Bradford (Phillips *et al.*, 2003) has pointed to the complexity of processes influencing household formation and re-formation. Decisions on whether or not to move out of the parental home reflect financial pressures, changing views of family life and perceived housing options. The desire for extended family living under one roof, and thus large accommodation, persists amongst many Asian families, perhaps especially Muslims. This restricts housing choices across the social classes. The search by middle class families for suburban housing, for example, is often governed by the desire for property with sufficient room to build an extension. Nevertheless, the potential for the formation of smaller households is also evident for all black and minority ethnic groups. The greatest pressure for new household formation lies with Pakistani and Bangladeshi families, because of their youthful age structure and the high incidence of over-crowding within the traditional inner areas of terraced housing. However, as was previously noted, these groups also currently occupy the weakest position in the housing and employment markets, and may thus encounter difficulties in securing decent, affordable, and large enough accommodation in their preferred locations.

There is no doubt that families of South Asian origin in particular retain a strong preference for home ownership. There are nevertheless very real economic constraints on these households achieving this goal. Exploring ways in which a mix of affordable home ownership and social renting could be achieved in preferred areas of settlement could be a valuable way forward. The greater emphasis since 1998 on 'Mixed and Flexible Tenure' (MFT) options in the Low Cost Home Ownership programme has been widely acclaimed by housing policy analysts and by the Joseph Rowntree Foundation as a positive step towards greater choice and flexibility for low-income households (Terry and Joseph 1998; Martin and Watkinson, 2003). MFT schemes contain tenants, shared owners and full owners. All have the opportunity to alter their tenure if their circumstances change. Shared owners can either increase or reduce the share of the property they own. This type of reform has the potential to integrate tenures within designated neighbourhoods, thus helping to combat the stigma of social housing areas, and to give greater financial choice to low-income households. However, according to a Housing Corporation report (1998), minority ethnic groups often have a poor level of knowledge about the low cost housing options available to them through such schemes. Empowering black and minority ethnic groups through improved dissemination of information would seem to be a high priority for widening potential housing choices. At the same time it is important that adopting any goal for 'mixed' areas should fit with expressed preferences amongst relatively disadvantaged households, so that mixing does not become a route to gentrification or social engineering (see also Chapter 5).

Chapter 3:
The growth of law and regulation

Malcolm Harrison

Our task on legal and regulatory issues is to sketch the trends affecting people from minority ethnic groups already settled in the UK, commenting on implications for housing. While aware of ongoing problems, we also draw attention to the positive side of the history, noting how understanding moved beyond assimilation or conciliation, anti-racist strategies and the restricting of direct discriminatory actions, and into the domains of institutional racisms, diversity and cultural sensitivity.

This chapter is necessarily selective, offering an overview and interpretation rather than a detailed guide. Asylum and immigration practices will only be touched upon briefly, because these matters are covered later by Lisa Hunt and John Perry. Furthermore, although there has been a tendency for some years for government to align provisions across gender, 'race', and disability as far as rights and expectations are concerned, discussion below concentrates on trends in policies and practices revolving around 'race relations' legislation, and linked to issues concerning ethnicity. Here there is a growing array of advisory documents, good practice 'toolkits', and other resources available for practitioners, from a range of sources, and readers can pursue many of these via websites. The CIH has published a succinct good practice briefing entitled *Equality and Diversity* (Blackaby and Larner, 2003), giving a clear summary on the legislative framework, legal and policy context, development of diversity strategies, communications issues, and performance management. It includes good practice examples, and relates to a range of diversity issues (including disability, ethnicity, and gender). The CIH has also helped sponsor a substantial good practice guide on BME housing strategies for local authorities and their partners (Blackaby and Chahal, 2000). In May 2005, the CRE published a lengthy consultation draft of its new statutory code of practice on racial equality in housing, and this code will provide extensive guidance in due course.

Box 10: Note for readers

Our usual convention of placing 'race' or 'racial' in quotation marks (noted in Chapter 1) has been set aside in many instances in this chapter, because these words are used so frequently without qualification within legal and official documents. The same applies to the word 'colour' for this chapter.

A long and important journey for the law

A crucial element in the journey to better ethnic relations has been the development of a structure of robust legal provisions. A strong legal framework is an essential foundation for securing equality of treatment for job applicants, in promotion processes, and for lettings and allocations of tenancies. It is also important when countering harassment, and in dealing with such matters as fair practice in the awarding of contracts. There has been a cumulative development in legal provisions over time, with increasing recognition that firmer rules are required, and acknowledgement that discrimination may be both direct and indirect. Central building blocks in previous decades have been the Race Relations Act of 1965, the Race Relations Act of 1968, and the Race Relations Act of 1976.

While not enough in itself, the law can offer remedies for those treated unfairly, and some protection against the abuse of power and administrative discretion. The merits of a firm legal framework were made particularly clear in a white paper produced by the government in 1975, which paved the way for the important 1976 Act (Home Office, *Racial Discrimination*, Cmnd. 6234). Amongst the points referred to in that white paper were those shown in the box below.

Box 11: The benefits of firm laws

1. Legislation is the essential pre-condition for an effective policy to combat the problems experienced by minority groups and to promote equality of opportunity and treatment.

2. Legislation is a necessary pre-condition for dealing with explicit discriminatory actions or accumulated disadvantages. To fail to provide a remedy against an injustice strikes at the rule of law, and to abandon a whole group of people in society without legal redress against unfair discrimination is to leave them with no option but to find their own redress.

3. The law has an important declaratory effect, and can give support to those who do not wish to discriminate but who would otherwise feel compelled to do so by social pressure.

4. Law can make crude, overt forms of discrimination less common. We could argue that this then has ongoing effects on public perceptions of what is normal and acceptable.

5. Legislation is capable of dealing not only with discriminatory acts but with patterns of discrimination, particularly with patterns which, because of the effects of past discrimination, may not any longer involve explicit acts of discrimination.

(See Home Office, *Racial Discrimination*, Cmnd. 6234, 1975.)

The persistence of the patterns referred to under 5 has remained a key issue, and one with which policy-makers, analysts and researchers continue to grapple.

The 1965-1976 legislation and other developments

In summary, the Race Relations Act of 1965 made it unlawful to discriminate on racial grounds in specified places of public resort, and contained provisions dealing with racial restrictions on the transfer of tenancies and penalising incitement to racial hatred. It created a Race Relations Board and local conciliation committees to investigate complaints and attempt to settle differences. The Race Relations Act of 1968 went further, extending the scope of the law so that it applied to a wide range of situations in employment, housing, the provision of goods, facilities and services to the public, and publication or display of discriminatory advertisements or notices. The 1968 Act reconstituted the Race Relations Board, and (together with regional conciliation committees) it had a duty to investigate complaints of unlawful discrimination (although some were dealt with through other channels). The 1968 Act also created a Community Relations Commission (CRC) to complement the Board, and provision was made for salaries of local community relations officers to be paid by the Commission. There was a network of local voluntary Community Relations Councils to which these officers were responsible. A key aim at the time was to promote harmonious community relations.

It was felt by the mid-1970s, however, that the legislation had proved unable to deal with widespread patterns of discrimination, perhaps especially in employment and housing. One important weakness was the narrowness of the definition of unlawful discrimination upon which it was based (the less favourable treatment of one person than of another on the ground of colour, race or ethnic or national origins). Action could be taken where a discriminatory motive had led to adverse treatment of an identifiable victim, but the law as it stood did not cover less intentionally discriminatory practices which might be having unjustifiable discriminatory effects on members of minority groups. It was felt that law should go further, to cater also for instances where practices might appear fair in a formal sense when dealing with an individual, but be discriminatory in their operation and effect.

The 1976 Race Relations Act outlaws racial discrimination in (amongst other areas) employment, the provision of goods, facilities and services, and the disposal and management of premises in England, Scotland and Wales, and there is parallel coverage in the Race Relations (Northern Ireland) Order 1997. The legal framework allows employers to make an exception by discriminating in an appointment, when a person's race, ethnicity or origins is a genuine occupational qualification for a job. For example, a housing provider might need staff with specific cultural knowledge and language skills in order to support Chinese elders in a sheltered scheme.

Importantly, the 1976 Act sought to deal with some of the earlier limitations in legislation, and introduced the concepts of direct and indirect discrimination. Thus the way was opened for dealing more effectively with instances where a general practice or rule of an organisation might seem unrelated to any purpose to discriminate, but nonetheless would have that effect. We might consider as an example the practice of allocating tenancies to 'sons and daughters' of existing residents of a neighbourhood. A requirement reflecting this aim might have no explicit connection whatsoever with ethnicity or the 'white/non-white' divide, yet in practical terms could mean that only white people would be able to be offered tenancies, if the existing population of the area was predominantly white. This could be interpreted as indirect discrimination. The act also indicated how far and when it would be lawful for positive action to be taken to provide services or access to education, training, etc. Furthermore, under Section 71 of the act, local authorities and certain other public bodies were required to make appropriate arrangements with a view to securing that their various functions would be carried out with due regard to the need to eliminate unlawful discrimination and to promote equality of opportunity and good relations between persons of different racial groups.

On the organisational front, the Commission for Racial Equality (CRE) was established, replacing the two earlier bodies, and with three central duties. It would work towards the elimination of discrimination, promote equality of opportunity and good relations between persons of different groups, and keep under review the working of the new act. The Commission has issued codes of practice for the promotion of equality and prevention of discrimination in the areas of employment, rented housing, and non-rented (owner-occupied) housing. Although codes of this type do not have direct legal force, they can serve as evidence in court proceedings. The CRE Code of Practice in Rented Housing recommended implementation of an equal opportunities policy, and keeping ethnic records and monitoring systems. The records could serve as a source of information on the needs of various communities, and could be analysed to ensure that services were being provided equitably.

Various dissatisfactions continued following the 1976 Act. It was argued that the extension of the law to cover indirect discrimination did not work (as the majority of cases heard still concerned direct discrimination), while codes of practice in fields such as housing and employment were poorly implemented (see Law, 1996, pp. 11-12; cf CRE, 1985b). On the other hand, there seems to have been gradual adoption of equal opportunity policies, and legal provisions proved valuable for those seeking improvements in housing practices, as well as a stimulus to important research and investigative work in this field. CRE powers to issue non-discrimination notices were important; as for instance when one was issued against Tower Hamlets in 1988, for discrimination in homelessness and allocations practice. Nonetheless, it has long been understood that other steps need to occur in parallel with legal development, strategies for investment being especially important. Furthermore, issues of religious discrimination were not covered directly in the legislation referred to above (although certain religious groups received some protection), and the situation in Northern Ireland highlighted the case for action more generally across the UK. The Northern

Ireland Act 1998 included the requirement for public bodies carrying out their functions to have regard to the need to promote equality of opportunity between people of different religious belief, political opinion, racial group, age, marital status or sexual orientation, and to have regard to the desirability of promoting good relations between persons of different groups. Equality Schemes have to be prepared and submitted to the Equality Commission for Northern Ireland.

Under a European Community Directive, the UK has been required to implement legislation in relation to discrimination on grounds of religion or belief, and this has now been followed through by government (parallel regulations also being introduced on sexual orientation). Thus the Employment Equality (Religion or Belief) Regulations came into force in late 2003. They covered England, Wales and Scotland, with separate legislation to follow for Northern Ireland. The rules, focused on the employment sphere, are aimed at inhibiting direct and indirect discrimination, harassment and victimisation, and religion here is cast broadly (properly allowing for protection for people with varied philosophical and ethical positions). This is part of the consequences of the European Union establishing a common framework to tackle unfair discrimination on the grounds of sex, race, disability, sexual orientation, religion and age. The Race Directive (2000) prohibits race discrimination in employment and training, provision of goods and services (including housing), education and social protection (and strengthens UK law on specific matters such as the way indirect discrimination is defined). Along with the influence of EU Directives, general human rights legislation affects housing. The Human Rights Act of 1998 is relevant to the way that some housing organisations (or 'public authorities') are expected to handle diversity and equality issues, including the avoidance of discrimination and the upholding of rights regarding respect for the home (private and family life) and peaceful enjoyment of possessions. The European Convention on Human Rights states that the enjoyment of rights and freedoms set forth in the Convention (such as the right to respect for the home) is to be secured without discrimination on grounds of sex, race, colour, language, religion, association with a national minority, and so forth.

An additional issue is the impact of devolution legislation within the UK, which placed varying equality duties on government organisations. Chaney (2004, p. 66) points out that the Welsh Assembly's duty is distinctive in its all-embracing scope, paying regard to the principle that there should be '... *equality of opportunity for all people*'. Each national devolved administration may develop different strategies to some degree.

Strengthening the Race Relations Act

There was only limited proactive effort at central government level to improve ethnic relations and equal opportunities performance during the Conservative period of office that began in 1979. In the late 1990s, however, Labour's arrival in government changed the environment. Furthermore, the Lawrence Inquiry report (published in 1999, and arising from the official inquiry following the death of

Stephen Lawrence) soon provided a further and specific stimulus to changing strategies, since it pointed to the adverse part potentially played by institutional racism in public services (see Macpherson, 1999). This phenomenon (touched on earlier in the book) was seen as the collective failure of an organisation to provide an appropriate and professional service to people because of their colour, culture or ethnic origin. Institutional racism might be seen or detected in processes, attitudes and behaviour, amounting to discrimination through unwitting prejudice, ignorance, or thoughtless and racist stereotyping which disadvantage minority ethnic people.

Box 12: 'Institutional racism'

This is usually taken to mean the collective failure of an organisation to provide an appropriate and professional service to people because of their colour, culture or ethnic origin.

Going beyond the concept of indirect discrimination, the idea of institutional racism raises questions about the internal culture of organisations, their level of understanding of diverse communities and needs, and the sensitivity of their services.

Taking the Lawrence Report seriously implies a strategic response within housing organisations, helping to ensure that policies are fully translated into practice, and underpinned by an appropriate office culture, staff training, monitoring, and evaluation of outcomes.

The Labour government moved to respond to the limitations of the 1976 framework. The main provisions of the Race Relations (Amendment) Act 2000 came into force in 2001. It strengthened and extended the scope or application of the 1976 Race Relations Act rather than replacing it. Although the law is targeted directly at the public sector – hospitals, schools, police services, local councils and central government actors – the expectations of the new legislation should influence practice in the private and voluntary sectors too. The 2000 measure strengthened the 1976 Act in two key ways (see Box 13).

Box 13: The Race Relations (Amendment) Act 2000

This act extended protection against racial discrimination by public authorities.

It also strengthened the duties of public authorities. They have a new and enforceable positive duty concerning the promotion of equal opportunities and good race relations. In carrying out their functions they should also have due regard to the need to eliminate unlawful racial discrimination. The CRE has power to issue a compliance notice.

A recent Home Office consultation document indicates that over 43,000 public bodies are now under a positive duty to promote racial equality and good race relations. All should develop a Race Equality Scheme and make race impact assessments (*Strength in Diversity*, 2004, pp. 12-14).

Before the act came into force it seemed likely that it would imply somewhat revised ways of thinking and working for officials both in the public service and within voluntary and non-profit organisations involved with implementing public policies. In general terms, discrimination would be prohibited in all functions of public authorities, and the act was defining a 'public authority' widely. Anyone whose work involves functions seen as being of a public nature must not discriminate while carrying out those functions, and this potentially may embrace private or voluntary agencies carrying out public functions (such as providing residential care). Exceptions to the requirements relate to those areas that central government has long been reluctant to open up to scrutiny or make subject to challenge (such as the functions of the security services, judicial proceedings, and certain immigration and nationality functions, where in some circumstances it remains lawful to discriminate on grounds of nationality or ethnic or national origin, although not in terms of colour or race).

At first sight it might be thought that the changes were not really all that significant, because the UK already had law which outlawed many types of negative discrimination, while the aim of supporting good ethnic relations had been a very long-established one. This, however, might be to under-estimate the potential of the shift that has occurred. One key change was that it became unlawful for any public authority to discriminate on racial grounds – directly, indirectly or by victimisation – in carrying out any of its functions, and this might also affect some private organisations responsible for carrying out such functions.

The other big change lies in the positive duty noted above. The Commission for Racial Equality has commented that, in the long term, this duty may be the most significant aspect of the amended Race Relations Act, '... *because it gives statutory force to the imperative of tackling institutional racism*' (CRE, 2000). The idea is for public authorities to have a strengthened obligation, leading them to pay due regard to the need to eliminate unlawful discrimination, and to promote equality of opportunity and good race relations in carrying out their functions. They need to consider the implications right across the range of their activities. In the housing case this might include thinking about tenancy allocations and management, investment strategies, 'Housing Plus' services, and so forth. Powers were taken for government ministers (including Scottish ministers) to impose specific duties on particular types of organisations: the list of agencies covered included local authorities, regional development agencies and enterprise networks, health authorities and NHS trusts, the Housing Corporation, Scottish Homes (now Communities Scotland) and housing action trusts.

Many public bodies, covered by the specific duties, were to produce a *Race Equality Scheme*, showing clear plans for delivery in external and internal work. Local authorities and the Housing Corporation were included. Expectations of such bodies included setting out arrangements for ensuring access to information and services, monitoring existing policies, assessing and consulting on proposed policies and their impact on equality and in employment, and carrying out ethnic monitoring of all staff, at all career stages, from application to exit interview. An important element was to be the inclusion of 'race equality impact assessments' of new policies and projects, as part of a strategic approach. As noted elsewhere, the CRE has published online guidance for this. If such evaluations become a routine part of policy processes, effects could potentially be very great. It was also anticipated that codes of practice related to the legal duties would become available to provide practical guidance (following the well-established UK tradition that we have already touched upon). Very importantly, the new duty was made legally enforceable (with the potential for compliance notices and court actions), and, alongside the CRE's enforcement powers, roles were opened up for more inspection or audit from central government. Although the public authorities to which the new duty was to apply would constitute a narrower list than those required not to discriminate, further bodies would be affected indirectly. English RSLs would be in this category, via the regulatory powers of the Housing Corporation.

It should be added that despite the heightened emphasis on being proactive, UK law in most contexts stops short of supporting direct positive discrimination or affirmative action (the US term). Where groups are under-represented in an area of work, or amongst those seeking a service, it has been seen as acceptable to pursue training or outreach strategies to create a more level playing field under the banner of 'positive action'. A good example noted in Chapter 1 has been PATH (Positive Action Training in Housing) that has brought people through into particular career tracks or helped give them skills needed to compete. Nonetheless, posts cannot normally be offered to people from minorities to the exclusion of other groups unless there is a job-specific justification (such as the need for particular community language skills).

Codes, guidance, performance expectations and strategies

Extensive official advice and information has been available in recent years to guide or direct housing providers and allied organisations. Given the large amount of documentary material produced, we comment selectively now, the main aim being to illustrate trends and general features.

We have already noted the role of the CRE in providing codes. The present Code of Practice in Rented Housing applies to all rented housing, but is apparently rarely tested outside the public sector. It refers to the elimination of racial discrimination and promotion of equal opportunities. Most substantial landlords are targeted, although some smaller ones have not been expected to meet all detailed provisions. The recommendations refer to forms of discrimination, victimisation, pressure or instructions to discriminate, and the positive duties of public bodies. Specific matters dealt with include licences and consents for disposals, liability of employers, advertisements, exemptions, access to housing, its quality, and unlawful barriers, records and monitoring systems, service delivery, harassment, and equal opportunity policies and their implementation through action programmes. The latter is usefully taken to include identifying unmet needs (such as those of minority ethnic elders). Local authorities, however, by no means all meet CRE Code expectations (London Boroughs apparently having been most likely to do so, and Unitary Authorities, Welsh Authorities and District Councils outside the Metropolitans least likely).

The parallel code on owner-occupied housing also deals with a wide range of inter-linked concerns. They include direct and indirect unlawful discrimination, victimisation, instructions or pressure to discriminate, acting on instructions or pressure, refusals to provide premises of like quality, provision on different terms, disposal of premises, advertisements, liability of employers, records, communications, harassment, estate agency, consumer credit, access to housing, quality, positive action, segregation, and finance and lending criteria. Organisations covered by the code are expected to adopt a simple written equal opportunity policy setting out their commitment and summarising actions to be taken, and advice is offered on policy implementation, ongoing reviews, dissemination and training.

A new code currently in preparation will replace the previous ones, taking account of legal developments and current concerns such as community cohesion. There will be separate versions for England, Wales and Scotland (but Northern Ireland is covered by distinctive legislation). There is likely to be extensive guidance on good practice, and the code will apply to all providers of housing and related services, across the tenures.

The duty to work to eliminate unlawful racial discrimination and promote equal opportunities and good race relations is not optional for bodies such as local authorities (and a CRE Code of Practice was produced in 2001 on the duty to promote racial equality; see 2002). Authorities must meet their obligations even if BME populations in their areas are small. The CRE indicates various outcomes that can be expected if the duty is being met properly by authorities. These are grouped in terms of 'community satisfaction and equal opportunities', 'staff satisfaction and equal opportunities', and 'confidence and respect'. Evidence of meeting the duty may be found in a committed leadership (with minority ethnic personnel not marginalised or expected only to concern themselves with work on diversity and equality). Race equality is to be central to the way local authorities work. Procedures should be in place for assessing policy proposals for their possible impact on race equality (see above), and steps be taken to identify needs in communities and ensure people know about consultation. Authorities may use both formal and community-based approaches to consultation. There is to be monitoring of effects of policies, publishing of assessments, consultations, publication of a race equality scheme, race equality objectives for partnership and contracted-out work, and other actions.

Box 14: The CRE and its proposed replacement, the CEHR

The CRE has been an important source of information, guidance and regulation. For detail of current approaches and expectations, readers are recommended to consult the CRE's website (see further information at the end of this book). The CRE has published useful guides on ethnic monitoring, and on the duty to promote race equality.

Central government may replace the CRE and the other equality rights commissions with a single all-purpose body, a 'Commission for Equality and Human Rights'. This would cater for more dimensions of equality than are covered by the existing bodies. It can be argued that, if this change goes ahead, it may prove damaging for minority ethnic groups (and for disabled people), if their concerns rank lower than before, their voices are diluted or subordinated, or scarce resources are spread more thinly.

There may be links between this plan and some of the discussion noted in Chapter 5 in relation to the community cohesion agenda. The white paper (below) itself makes explicit reference to promoting citizenship and a cohesive society, and to community cohesion work. Press reporting has indicated that a *'lighter touch'* is to be applied to the private sector (*The Guardian*, 13th May 2004), while the white paper refers to *'listening to business needs'*, *'flexible dialogue'*, etc. The tone is bland, and the document holds out little hope of significant forward movement in anti-racist work. Government can be criticised for its inaction on issues of private sector monitoring, reporting and duties.

There is likely to be some continuity in frameworks of practice expectations if the change goes ahead, although resources may be limited. Apparently there was what was called in one press report a *'last minute revolt'* by the CRE against the plans (see M. Dean in *The Guardian*, 1st September 2004).

(See Secretaries of State for Trade and Industry and Constitutional Affairs, *Fairness For All: A New Commission for Equality and Human Rights*, Cm. 6185, 2004.)

Departments and agencies

Specific central and devolved government departments and agencies play crucial roles alongside the CRE. In 2001, in England, the then DTLR Housing Directorate produced an important Action Plan (see Box 15). This highlighted the department's own obligations, demonstrating commitment to improvements in line with the Race Relations (Amendment) Act. More recent statements available on the ODPM website have shown continued positive development: see ODPM (Housing Directorate) *Action Plan Update No. 2, 2002.*

Box 15: The DTLR Action Plan of 2001 – an important landmark

The department acknowledged the diversity of needs and aspirations amongst black and minority ethnic groups, and showed a very sound grasp of many key issues for housing and minorities.

The statement indicated the strategic role of local authorities in the context created by the new act, not only as housing providers in their own right, but also in identifying need, planning and co-ordinating action at local level. Their performance would be assessed by the Housing Directorate through Best Value inspections, and Best Value housing reviews which must involve BME communities and reflect their views on performance (while this would be paralleled by Housing Corporation requirements for RSLs).

There was specific reference to the department's guidance on involving BME groups in regeneration proposals.

Links were also made in the statement to other areas of policy concern, such as allocations and homelessness, young people, stock transfers and older people.

Gypsies and Travellers were covered in references to delivering on the Gypsy Site Refurbishment Programme (2001-2004) aimed at helping local authorities maintain the existing network of sites, and to research in this field (including issues of provision and need, site closures and pitch losses).

(See DTLR, *Addressing the housing needs of black and minority ethnic people,* a DTLR [Housing Directorate] Action Plan, 2001: and *Update.*)

In many ways the sophisticated *Action Plan* statement was an impressive reflection of the very long way that central government practice had come since the 1960s. It seems reasonable to see the 2001 document as having been something of a landmark (even though there might be disagreement here and there with details, and ongoing difficulties in carrying through some of the good intentions). Similar progress may be noted in other parts of the UK at formal levels. For instance, in 2001 the Welsh Assembly consulted on its Black and Minority Ethnic Housing Strategy, and the Black Minority Ethnic Housing Action Plan for Wales was launched in 2002. It was anticipated that by April 2004 all local authorities and RSLs here would have an individual BME housing strategy, or be a partner to a regional and/or multi-agency one. RSLs were also to have Race Equality Plans in place by then (for more information on Wales, see Tomlins, 2003; and BME Housing Project, 2003).

In recent years, extensive guidance has come from governmental bodies in a variety of specific contexts. For example, for local authorities in England, Housing Investment Programme Guidance issued in 2000 stressed (and we simplify to summarise):

- that housing authorities should ensure that the needs and aspirations of black and minority ethnic people and communities form an integral part of local housing strategy;

- the importance of measuring housing need by ethnicity;
- the importance of working with partners and stakeholders to meet black and minority ethnic housing needs;
- the need for housing authorities to demonstrate evidence of strategies to tackle discrimination and harassment; and
- that authorities should adopt the Home Office Code of Practice on the Reporting and Recording of Racist Incidents.

ODPM guidance on allocation of accommodation has indicated that local authorities are to ensure that allocation policies and procedures do not discriminate, directly or indirectly, on grounds of race, ethnicity, sex or disability (for fuller comment on lettings practice, see Blackaby and Larner, 2003, p. 11; also Chapter 8).

Local authorities are subject to performance expectations under Best Value requirements, which have related to matters such as whether they had adopted the CRE's equality standard for local government, and, if so, which of five levels they had reached. Blackaby and Larner's briefing highlights three relevant Best Value performance indicators for 2003-2004 for English local authorities, focused on satisfaction of tenants with overall services, their satisfaction with opportunities for participation in management and decision-making, and whether the authority follows the CRE's code on rented housing and standards in tackling harassment. Equality and diversity performance indicators have apparently been becoming key potential drivers for efforts to secure improvement. The 'duty to promote race equality' under the 2000 Act requires production of a Race Equality Scheme (as already noted above) every three years with annual review of progress, a timetabled action plan, and active communication to the public and to staff. Service delivery indicators have included:

- the widening of the ethnic profile of service users;
- improving service outcomes for ethnic groups and reducing differences;
- improving satisfaction rates among users of all ethnic groups and reducing any differences;
- improving confidence in reporting of racial incidents;
- satisfaction of tenants.

There are further indicators for employment and training.

Considering particular governmental regulatory mechanisms, we can highlight inspection. The national Housing Inspection process (developed as part of the Audit Commission Inspection Service) appears to offer a significant means of examining local authority performance and encouraging change. The Inspectorate's primary role has been to support improvements in the performance of local housing authorities through inspection, as well as by promoting good practice through publications and seminars, and through engagement in relevant policy debate. For instance, the Commission has examined Best Value

Performance Indicators for the information they offer on how well local authorities in England and Wales are doing in providing equality of services.

In Scotland, Communities Scotland has responsibility for regulating all social landlords, homelessness functions and factoring services provided by local councils and RSLs ('factoring' generally refers to property management). Communities Scotland, the Scottish Federation of Housing Associations and the Confederation of Scottish Local Authorities have published performance standards for social landlords and homelessness functions, one guiding standard being about embracing diversity, promoting equal opportunities and eliminating unlawful discrimination (see Blackaby and Larner, 2003, pp. 5 and 18, which also summarises briefly for Wales and Northern Ireland). In Scotland, RSLs are encouraged to undertake equality and diversity audits, but it seems that performance may be patchy. Some individual RSLs, however, have pushed things forward (encouraged by commitments relating to geographical areas of operation, or to meeting specialised needs such as those of BME elders). Communities Scotland itself is involved in a range of proactive initiatives, as well as carrying forward its general functions relating to housing regeneration and social justice (for its Race Equality Scheme see Communities Scotland website).

Guidelines and expectations for RSLs/housing associations

For England, which is home for the majority of the UK's black minority ethnic households, the Housing Corporation (as principal funder and regulator of RSLs) launched a *Black and Minority Ethnic Housing Policy* in 1998, seeking to develop in RSLs a culture empowering black and minority ethnic communities, and integrating their needs and aspirations into every-day business (this built on earlier Corporation initiatives). In summary, RSL governing bodies were expected to confirm that they operated effective equal opportunities policies and procedures and reviewed them regularly, that they reviewed performance against the CRE codes of practice, that they had a strategy supporting recruitment, retention and progress of people from minority communities, and that there was a strategy to ensure that management and development services responded to black and minority ethnic housing needs. Standards for RSLs in Scotland were produced by Scottish Homes and the Scottish Federation of Housing Associations, and there were similar developments in Wales.

Regulation and guidance continued to develop in the era of Race Equality Schemes (the Corporation's Scheme appearing in 2002). The Housing Corporation produced a Regulatory Code for RSLs, requiring them to act on all aspects of equality and diversity, and with BME-related targets. RSLs were expected to be working towards these obligations from April 2002, their performance scrutinised by the Corporation's Inspection Team (see Blackaby and Larner, 2003, p. 5 for summary). The Code meant a wider range of information being accessible to the Corporation, including business plans, risk management strategies and BME/equality and diversity strategies and action plans. Tenant involvement was a key element, both as part of the inspection process and in providing feedback on landlord performance. The Regulatory Code and Guidance from 2002 indicates that associations are to demonstrate when carrying out their functions their commitment to equal opportunities. They must work towards the elimination of discrimination and demonstrate an equitable approach to the rights and responsibilities of all individuals. They should promote good relations between people of different racial groups, and must also have an equalities and diversity policy that incorporates specific targets in relation to BME people on lettings, tenant satisfaction, racist harassment, membership of governing body, staffing, tenants' representation, suppliers and contractors (see para 2.7 of the Code). RSLs may conduct their own equality and diversity audits. Evidently, in today's environment, RSLs need to have effective race equality plans, with priorities, targets, timetables, and procedures for monitoring and consultation made clear. RSLs are also expected to operate under Best Value principles.

The Housing Corporation has had commitments to research and monitoring via projects, and coherent strategies for progress review as far as the Corporation's *Black and Minority Ethnic Housing Policy* is concerned. Alongside its Regulatory Code imposing the duty of the Race Relations (Amendment) Act 2000 on RSLs, the Corporation has been involved with innovations such as the *'RaceActionNet'* website developed by Lemos & Crane (see Chapter 9 in our book), and further codes of practice. A management tool has been produced (*the 'race equality toolkit'*) for RSLs and regulators to undertake 'race' equality audits and benchmark performance within the Best Value framework. This was launched in spring 2002. Summarising the situation, we can say that for practitioners in RSLs and councils there is now some first-rate detailed guidance available, sometimes building on research findings or specific survey exercises. There is also some ongoing development of supportive and advisory networks.

The breadth and nature of formal commitment by the Corporation today can be seen (for instance) in policy statements such as *Equality and Diversity: Policy and Strategies* (2003b), which (amongst a large array of goals) aims to provide a *'... framework for continuous improvement'* (see 1.4). The Corporation's Race Equality Scheme includes the aim of promoting good relations between people from different 'racial' groups, as well as tackling unlawful discrimination and promoting equality of opportunity. The importance of regulatory bodies and their published guidelines has been enhanced by the link with availability of funding. Although Corporation requirements have not had the status of law, guidelines nonetheless have force, and regulators have means of encouraging better practice. An interesting feature of developments is that tenants acquired a voice in inspection processes, with 30 appointed 'tenant inspectors' apparently providing an important part of this. It seems that a high proportion have probably come from BME communities (see *Black Housing*, 2003). The Corporation has produced Good Practice Notes linked to obligations in the Regulatory Code, to help clarify expectations of how associations achieve compliance (for example *Note 8, Equality and Diversity*, February 2004). It is worth adding that performance expectations may extend 'downwards' in certain circumstances to organisations like residents' associations, with recognition criteria and rules offering mechanisms for regulating practices and reducing discrimination (again see Blackaby and Larner, p. 16).

Responsibility for inspection of housing associations has now passed to the Audit Commission Housing Inspectorate. The Housing Corporation, however, has provided guidelines, and will work closely with the Inspectorate and follow up any recommendations as appropriate. The inspection remit consists of inspecting the quality of services and the arrangements housing associations have in place for improvement, and there is a responsibility to report to the Corporation matters considered to be of regulatory concern.

Independent housing organisations including the National Housing Federation and the Federation of Black Housing Organisations have produced their own publications, exhortation, codes, research or advice over the years, and have worked with or pressed official bodies to develop positive approaches. One high profile report published in 2001 was the Race and Housing Inquiry *Challenge Report*, resulting from collaboration between the National Housing Federation, CRE, FBHO and Housing Corporation. An important recommended Code of Practice followed, for action on race equality by housing associations, covering expected outcomes and standards. Progress in reviews and action on race equality by associations has been researched recently, with evidence of positive work but some limitations.

An additional point concerns the community cohesion agenda, which will be discussed more fully in Chapter 5. It seems that this has begun to affect performance measures, inspection, and ideas about Best Value indicators (see Community Cohesion Panel, 2004, p. 19). This needs to be approached with caution, both in terms of the principles involved in applying such a vague concept to performance measures, and as regards selection of specific indicators.

(See websites at the end of this book for Audit Commission and Housing Corporation information, including the online housing *'race equality toolkit'*.)

Harassment and hate crimes

The issue of harassment has been a difficult one over many years, and there have been frequent attempts to encourage better practice. Given coverage elsewhere in this book, comments now can be brief. Criticisms have been voiced about the lack of support infrastructure and sensitive access points to help those who have experienced victimisation, and the under-development of independent community-based monitoring and support agencies (for an overview see Chapter 9). In recent years there has been evidence of a degree of valuable co-operation between key players in pursuit of better practice, nationally as well as locally. For instance, the then DETR produced *Tackling Racial Harassment: Code of Practice for Social Landlords*, in co-operation with the Housing Corporation and the National

Assembly for Wales (see DETR *et al.*, 2001). Anti-harassment policies related to racism may tie up with action on other 'hate crimes', and benefit from multi-agency working. The range of possible responses is wide. Blackaby and Larner's CIH *Briefing* notes that the remedies against perpetrators embrace both civil and criminal ones, including possession orders, injunctions or interdictions, anti-social behaviour orders, parenting orders, and child curfew orders, as well as action by the police in cases of assault, criminal damage, threatening words or behaviour, sending or making grossly offensive or threatening letters or phone calls, and racial hatred offences. If a landlord fails to take action to protect a tenant suffering harassment it may in effect be reinforcing a breach of the tenant's human rights (such as the rights to respect for home and family life) (see Blackaby and Larner, 2003, p. 14). Effective actions of other kinds may include more provision of information, offers of alternative properties to those who cannot remain in their present homes, good facilities for reporting of incidents, support for victims and witnesses, identification of perpetrators, prevention measures such as alarms, and taking full account of harassment in assessments of housing priority needs.

Box 16 : Links with other aspects of local practice

It should not be forgotten that anti-harassment strategies are potentially multi-agency in character, and that the legal basis for action has been primarily in public order provisions. Thus, one of the essential elements within policies on anti-social behaviour in neighbourhoods will often be a set of good practices for dealing with harassment and any wider inter-group tensions or conflicts. It will also be important to monitor implementation of measures taken against anti-social behaviour to ensure that their impact is not disproportionately affecting people identified as perpetrators who are non-white. In addition, harassment may be a crucial issue for action under the community cohesion agenda (see Chapter Five).

Cautious optimism?

Governments cannot always solve problems of behaviour and attitudes, but they can help create appropriate environments within which things can progress more satisfactorily. The UK has seen a gradual intensification of central government's formal commitments to improving those environments. Consequently, the policy scene differs markedly from that of 15 to 20 years ago. Reform preoccupations in earlier decades cast anti-racism strategies primarily in terms of monitoring and resisting direct discrimination, exposing and seeking change in systematic and frequently overt bad practice around a 'black/white' divide, starting to tackle broad 'racial inequalities', bringing resources into specific inner urban localities to counter economic decline, and (as time passed) promotional and exploratory work on equal opportunities through codes of practice and investigations (for an account of change, see Law, 1996, chapter 1). There have been several forces leading to this agenda gradually becoming more complex in the fields that most concern us. The development and growth of the black voluntary housing movement helped influence debates, highlighting issues of community empowerment and cultural sensitivity. Meanwhile, on a broader front, the governmental agenda gradually changed with recognition of increasing diversity and 'difference' across households and localities, and growth in numbers of minority ethnic people. A heightened interest in autonomy and involvement for groups gradually developed in the policy arena, or at least in official discourse which touched upon such matters positively. As we have indicated above, monitoring, regulation, advice and audit developed considerably in scope and complication. Sophisticated advice and guidance has become available for provider organisations, while official bodies like the Housing Corporation have engaged in important promotional or research work (see Harrison with Phillips, 2003, pp. 87-88, 90-91).

Quite apart from reviewing their own direct activities, social landlords and local authorities may be expected increasingly to embed diversity and equality agenda principles in their dealings with a range of bodies, partners and outside individuals (see Blackaby and Larner, 2003, on commissioning and partnering). The use of consultants, external contractors, tradespeople, or suppliers requires scrutiny and monitoring to ensure good practice in investment. Achieving equality through contracts has long been acknowledged as an important issue, and has been the subject of advice from the CRE and others. Apart from ensuring that contractors' employment practices are satisfactory, organisations with substantial spending budgets have sometimes wanted to encourage involvement of local labour, or of appropriate minority ethnic firms, in bidding for or obtaining of contracts. Despite the interest in the topic, the first 'freestanding' substantial systematic study on the issue – *Constructing equality* (by Harrison and Davies) – did not appear until 1995. This research involved case study work demonstrating clearly that surprisingly little of the expenditure flowing through housing associations was finding its way to black-run firms or contractors.

More recently, Sodhi and Steele carried out a study focused on London which included interviewing and a postal survey of RSLs. Although able to refer to a few other reports, Sodhi and Steele state nonetheless that '... *only scant attention has been given to RSLs' investment powers in terms of construction and maintenance work*' (2000, p. 11). We might add that expenditure via services, suppliers and consultants had received even less research attention. A positive tactic used over the years has been to develop local registers of potential firms, so as to reflect diversity locally or counter previous patterns of exclusion in commissioning of work. Contracting remains difficult territory, however, because of the nature of private markets in this field, the longstanding tight limits placed on any moves towards affirmative action in the UK, and even (it has been suggested) because of other aspects of central government policy. For RSLs, however, a good start may be to ensure that the businesses they regularly spend money with have diversity and equality policies that are sufficiently comprehensive and adequately resourced or followed through.

At the level of general principles and leadership, government has in recent years adopted an increasingly positive position in relation both to securing racial equality or equal opportunities and in terms of encouraging sensitivity to diversity. The law has been strengthened, and there is commitment to race equality performance indicators aimed at monitoring the contribution public services are making, and ensuring that they are more adaptable and responsive to the communities they serve. At the detailed level, encouragement has been given for firmer action against racist harassment, and for fuller BME participation and inclusion in a variety of settings (for example in neighbourhood warden schemes). It has been made clear that housing strategies should be based on a proper assessment of the needs of local minority ethnic populations, and that 'mainstream' bodies should work with minority ethnic RSLs and community groups. Unfortunately, government can be criticised justifiably for its input into debates and actions on asylum seekers and refugees, with negative effects on ethnic relations more generally. Adding to this, very recently (as we shall see in Chapter 5) some unfortunate steps backward in thinking seem to have occurred following urban disturbances in northern England early in the new decade.

Benefits and costs of regulation

One feature of the present era is that service providers and planners face an increasing complexity of exhortations, official demands and legal requirements. Britain is becoming what is sometimes referred to as an 'audit society', and there genuinely are heavy burdens for many kinds of practitioners in terms of bureaucracy, record-keeping and daily interactions with a range of other participants. While this general tendency is often mentioned amongst those who challenge managerial trends in public services, such discussion rarely picks out equal opportunities work as potentially problematic, perhaps because this field at least is one where regulation has proved very productive. Nonetheless, some issues need noting.

Much of the machinery of regulation, audit and monitoring is very necessary, since without it equality of opportunities and fair practices would slip down the agenda. Without regulation (and regular and transparent monitoring) there is very limited scope for revealing, challenging or correcting bad practice that may occur. On the other hand, commitment does not come cheaply for housing and community development organisations. Professional practitioners (and some volunteers) may carry increased workloads and have more sources of authority or advice to respond to. Monitoring, formal strategic planning, internal auditing, consultation processes, and so forth, may all require staffing, management and reporting systems. Parts of this chapter indicate how complex regulation is becoming, even though we have only skimmed the stream of advisory materials, and there are sharp contrasts between what is expected of public, voluntary or socially-orientated bodies on the one hand, and many private organisations and small-scale businesses on the other.

A genuine danger is that regulatory demands may end up generating a primarily paper response, or one that means going through the motions in order to satisfy some external observer, rather than producing significant changes. Central government agencies need to consider the environments in which local practice takes place, when reviewing regulatory mechanisms and their impact. An understanding is needed of constraints on internal organisational cultural change posed by pressures which may conflict with equality or diversity goals. Possible barriers to consider might include lack of resources, competition and pressure from other priorities, managerial and financial needs, and (perhaps) the implications of other trends in government's policies and expectations. Explanations of poor performance on equality or diversity that fall back on generalised claims about institutionalised racism in housing are not likely to prove sufficient. Furthermore, regulation cannot usually compensate for problems such as a lack of investment in services, dwellings, training, or preventative anti-racist work. It remains crucial to have enough resources to enable policies to take hold, whether for RSLs or local authorities.

Box 17: Adapting to the demands of an 'audit society'

Machinery for regulation, audit and monitoring is essential, since without it equality of opportunities and fair practices would slip down the housing, community development, or regeneration agenda, but there are costs involved, and real commitment cannot come cheaply for organisations.

It is important for central government and its agencies not only to develop machinery that can facilitate measurement and regulation, but also to understand the environments in which local practice takes place, and to keep under review the regulatory mechanisms and their impact. An understanding is needed of the constraints on positive internal organisational cultural change posed by pressures of finance, 'consultation fatigue', staffing, other governmental demands, or commercialisation.

Concerns continue about how far housing providers and services organisations are actually fulfilling expectations on good practice, on monitoring, or on partnerships and participation. Research findings at the start of the present decade cast doubt on the extent to which effective action by RSLs had followed external exhortation and criticism, and it is unclear how far good practices have been sufficiently built into daily proceedings on a permanent and regularised basis. Some work sponsored by the Housing Corporation suggested that performance of RSLs in England in delivering and monitoring services had been less satisfactory than might have been hoped (Somerville *et al.*, 2000; Tomlins *et al.*, 2001; Robinson *et al.*, 2002). Their equality policies may still sometimes lack depth and breadth (although they have become more comprehensive), and there are ongoing doubts about the adequacy of record-keeping and monitoring, consultation with communities, outcomes on contractors and consultants, employment of staff, lettings, and investment. Specific areas requiring further effort include responses to harassment, and barriers or limitations that may persist with language, communications or utilisation of advice services (see for instance Gidley *et al.*, 1999).

One key issue at a general level concerns the actual processes of guidance, supervision and monitoring of providers, and the impact of guidelines in specific environments. More research is needed of the type that the Housing Corporation commissioned to analyse the outcomes of 'ethnic coding' in investment decision-making, and the monitoring potential of investment code data (Robinson *et al.*, 2002). Housing guidance and regulation itself needs to be monitored and regulated, to see what works best. For instance, there are concerns about the burdens that inspection for local government imposes on service providers, and perhaps there may be limits on how far relatively non-specialist inspectors can be expected to generate tangible improvements (see JRF, 2004b for relevant analysis). At central government level, and for devolved government, there should also be further development of 'foresight' evaluation practices, whereby ongoing social audit processes provide sensitive analyses about likely effects of changing policies and law. The merits of 'equality testing' or impact assessment are now acknowledged officially, and it will be important to monitor how far and with what effects such practices become genuine and standard features of public policy development, at regional, local and national levels.

Chapter 4:
Urban policy responses

Malcolm Harrison

To complement our summary of trends in law and regulation, we now consider developments elsewhere on the UK policy agenda, by reviewing the history of urban policies. This is a very selective rather than comprehensive account, designed mainly to provide background on key policy issues affecting minority ethnic groups. To some degree, our commentary also reflects the fact that a large majority of the UK's black and minority ethnic households live in urban England, where their presence has been a longstanding driver for governmental action. Although there are distinctive policy histories in other parts of the UK, engagement with black minority ethnic groups in England has been more extensive, and is inevitably the central focus for a discussion of policies.

The context: neighbourhoods and deprivation

Chapter 2 indicated that some BME communities face considerable socio-economic disadvantage and occupy poor housing. In overall terms they live in disproportionate numbers within districts where there are multiple problems of environmental quality, socio-economic deprivation, poor job opportunities, and over-burdened or under-resourced services. Processes influencing socio-economic conditions in inner areas have included selective out-migration of better-off households, and uneven patterns of employment change and job loss within and between regions. Opportunities for residents in many places have been restricted by adverse labour market conditions, deindustrialisation, and lack of personal capital, as well as by infrastructure problems, poor services, and inadequate inward investment. Some peripheral urban areas, freestanding industrial towns or outer estates of social rented housing have been affected by rather similar processes.

Relative poverty remains crucial for neighbourhood conditions and life chances, and has been influenced by central government strategies on pay, taxation, pensions, child support, transport, and benefits. Striking examples of the gulf between low-income lifestyles and those of the better-off have been found through investigations of specific localities. In a study of certain Liverpool neighbourhoods, for instance, Andersen *et al.* (1999) indicate that even facilities available in or close by an area may be out of reach for locals. One of their informants mentions a public sports centre too expensive (despite modest prices) for local people, so that *'... unless you are working you can't afford to go ...'*.

The speaker adds that this is '... *so sad when it's our area*' (p. 40). Contrasting with such experiences, there are now numerous expensive private sports and healthy lifestyle centres established for those middle class people for whom cost represents a small consideration. Deprivations affect predominantly white populations in some localities as well as BME households in others. Perhaps in some places white people in run-down areas are even worse off than minority ethnic counterparts, if there are strong kinship or cultural resources available to the latter. On the other hand, distinctive penalties are experienced across minority groups as a consequence of the combination of problems they may face, including discrimination, disproportionately low incomes, and lack of access into particular job circuits, networks and locations.

Inner area policies before 1997

UK central government has concerned itself frequently since the 1960s with inner city and old industrial urban areas where minority ethnic groups live. Governments have sought to combat problems by focusing resources through area-based strategies of varying kinds. Urban policy has tended to comprise different sets of initiatives rather unevenly linked together. There has long been something of a distinction between the 'bending' or re-orientating of mainstream spending programmes to take account of inner urban disadvantage, and creating explicit urban policies as separate additions to the policy agenda. Policy development can be summarised in terms of a series of stages. The initiatives of the 1960s were characterised as in part concerned with an ameliorative social pathology approach built on an account of deprivation and social and economic isolation, and concerned with (amongst other goals) a community development philosophy. In that period policies were influenced by reactions to political turmoil over racism and potential urban conflicts. A shift in direction came in the 1970s, with increasing acceptance of economic and structural explanations of urban decline, although social welfare concerns remained on the agenda during the Labour period that ended in 1979. Conservative governments subsequently confirmed ongoing public commitment to the inner cities, but strategies were affected by desires to bring in private capital and contain or cut direct public expenditures. Stewart refers to a phase of policy:

> '... *predicted ... on a strategy of physical regeneration which drew in major financial resources from the private sector, used public expenditure as the leverage for property led urban regeneration, and featured new institutions and instruments of policy such as Urban Development Corporations and Urban Development Grant*' (Stewart, 1994, p. 134).

There then followed some movement in the direction of collaborative partnerships between levels of government and public and private sectors, with incorporation of a wider range of interests into policy implementation, and explicit competition over resource allocation. In the last stages of Conservative strategy there seemed to be efforts to address problems of compartmentalism, with the setting up of a new Single Regeneration Budget (SRB) system to be run through integrated regional offices. From 1994, 20 targeted programmes, including specific urban and housing programmes, were to be brought together in this system, supporting regeneration and economic development.

Numerous criticisms were made about the programmes that operated from the 1960s onwards. Organisational frameworks did too little for local democracy and empowerment, sometimes relying on ad hoc agencies and appointed teams with inadequate accountability to local people. There was not enough change in mainstream strategies to help the poor, despite some bending of investment patterns in the direction of prioritised localities (such as housing stress areas). Gains for disadvantaged communities from area programmes could be undermined by cuts in general governmental investment levels. As far as outcomes for BME groups over the 1960s-1997 period were concerned, clear evidence of direct improvements was limited. Brownill and Darke (1998) argued that while 'race' had often been on the policy agenda, this had usually been implicit rather than explicit. They also noted some patchy performance in specifying strategies to benefit and involve minority ethnic communities, and some reduction in 'ring fenced' resources directed to minority groups' needs with the advent of the SRB.

There was a tradition over the decades that targets and planning were set in largely 'neutral' terms, not tied specifically to minorities but to inner cities in general. Surprisingly few elements of expenditure were harnessed overtly to needs defined specifically in terms of minority ethnic groups, although for some years Section 11 monies under the 1966 Local Government Act had the potential to be an exception, as did the Housing Corporation's investments through black-run housing associations (see below), while there was support also for community centres and specific groups. Valued projects were created, but were often vulnerable to cuts in funding, leading to the criticism that there was 'funding for failure' in a context where black and minority ethnic community organisations or representatives were drawn into governmental programmes (Harrison, 1995, p. 77, etc.). Established white-run bodies frequently seemed to shape the agenda and pre-empt funds. Dependency of black-run enterprises could develop, as they became clients of larger white-run partners, or sought short-term discretionary public funding. With dependency came dangers of patronage.

A comprehensive account of urban policy would review public investment not simply in terms of its immediate declared aims, but also through taking account of its 'ripple effects'. Investments could be examined for their indirect impact on the opportunities of different groups. Although there was some encouragement for BME businesses over the periods we are reviewing, minority ethnic tradespeople and firms seemed to obtain only a very limited share of the indirect benefits of capital investment in social housing (Harrison and Davies, 1995; Sodhi and Steele,

2000), and this was most likely replicated in other fields. There was little to suggest that large volume expenditures on property development, purchasing, maintenance and infrastructure were systematically feeding the growth of local black-run businesses, or even giving them a reasonable share of opportunities. This issue remains important today, being relevant to developing a community cohesion or inclusion strategy in the employment domain.

Urban policies since 1997

It is difficult to characterise fairly the Labour strategies that have operated since 1997, given the wide range of channels through which relevant actions have occurred, and the shortage of immediately-accessible data on outcomes, although Chapter 3 indicated growing commitment to equality in services provision. It should also be noted that there is a European dimension, a regional development dimension within Britain, and ongoing changes from devolution, all of which affect urban BME communities. Given that shifts in general services, regulation and taxation also continue to affect the inner cities, the impact of public policies is extremely complex. The huge variety of policy fields ranges from care and support (Supporting People) to law and order, or from benefits policy to choice-based lettings. Imrie and Raco (2003, pp. 14-16) list over 150 policy programmes that have '... *some relevance to urban policy'*. Sometimes policy seems to point in contradictory directions. For example, on the one hand government improves the economic position for poorer households by cutting the burden of stamp duty in disadvantaged areas (see *Black Housing*, 121, 2002, p. 22), yet on the other it slides towards imposing damaging burdens upon them: notably an expectation for production of a seller's 'home information pack' that might hit low-income inner city owner-occupiers disproportionately hard financially, and that has been inadequately tested and justified (see Housing Act 2004, SS. 155, 163).

The collection edited by Imrie and Raco emphasises the importance of 'community' both as an object of policy and a policy instrument for New Labour, and points to connections between ideas about urban revitalisation and political goals of stimulating 'active citizenship' (shaped by the duty to contribute with others for the public good) (see 2003, pp. 4-6, 22-23). Amongst its goals, government apparently intends to build capacities for communities to help themselves (p. 21), but critics may perceive this as shifting responsibilities for problems further onto households that experience them. Labour's language of urban renaissance includes vague terms like 'social capital' as well as 'social cohesion' (see Kearns, 2003, pp. 37-60), with the potential to label residents in terms of supposed characteristics held heavily responsible for their lack of material success. Indeed, the terminology may underpin designs for 'mixing' which come close to 'gentrification' plans. Lees (2003) offers insights into the negative implications (in terms of gentrification) of the government's Urban Task Force report and Urban white paper. Loss of funding may function as a punishment when local residents resist such changes, revealing limits in government's commitment to real participation (see Imrie and Raco, 2003, pp. 28-29).

Meanwhile, New Labour at UK level shows scant interest in intervening in private market processes or modifying trends in service restructuring which disadvantage low-income residents. Although Labour may have lost some faith in the capacity of stand-alone special initiatives to address urban disadvantage, and supposedly favours bending 'mainstream' welfare spending and general service provision to help deprived localities, area-based initiatives have not been supplanted (see Imrie and Raco, p. 19; Hastings, 2003, p. 85). Nonetheless, a 'multi-level' approach has been advocated. Local Strategic Partnerships in England and Community Planning Partnerships in Scotland are vehicles here, with neighbourhood-level programmes and projects placed within a broader context (Hastings, 2003, p. 86). There is also an ongoing drive to develop contributions from 'active' community organisations, perhaps fuelled partly by the intention to substitute dutiful volunteers and slimly-funded local bodies for the reduced capacities of direct public sector providers (cf Imrie and Raco, pp. 21-22). In developing 'Community Strategies', local authorities are expected to construct relationships not only with area-based communities but also other communities of interest (see ibid., p. 239).

Thinking on urban policies since 1997 has included a strong emphasis on regeneration, and this is sometimes linked up with the aim of reducing social exclusion, as well as with strategies for neighbourhood renewal. The Social Exclusion Unit (established to improve co-ordination of government action to tackle social exclusion) identified a need for a national strategy to revitalise deprived neighbourhoods, and 'Policy Action Teams' began to produce material contributing to developing this. The work has been a potential source of analyses and recommendations for organisations such as social landlords (see especially Cabinet Office, 2000). The Single Regeneration Budget, referred to above, initially continued with modifications under Labour (although it was subsequently wound down). In 1998 the New Deal for Communities programme began, with investment aiming £2 billion at 39 severely deprived neighbourhoods over ten years, and in 2001 a £ 1.8 billion Neighbourhood Renewal Fund was launched, to enable deprived districts to improve housing, employment, safety, economic performance, education and health. Government has also encouraged schemes under the Private Finance Initiative and Public/Private Partnerships, although these are expensive and their inclusiveness for minority ethnic firms, investors and potential employees is uncertain.

Today there are many possible official funding sources for regeneration, ranging from the New Deal to European Community programmes. A variety of initiatives have operated for particular sectors (such as Health Action Zones and education strategies) or in parallel with larger funding streams. In 2000, for instance, the Home Office announced a new 'race equality' grant. The underlying theme was about 'connecting communities', and areas were identified where the £5 million funding might help (community networks, opportunity schemes, working towards more representative services, and positive images) (see Home Office, 2000). 'Faith communities' were referred to here alongside ethnicity, and government also noted the intention to give the most disadvantaged minority ethnic communities and individuals greater access to, and influence over, policy-makers and service providers. The reviving theme of social integration was evident in the statement that work needed to be done to bring all communities closer together, '... *because communities connecting with each other can help bring about genuine understanding and appreciation of the value of diversity'* (p. 6). Recent governmental preoccupations with people seeking asylum have raised the profile of integration policies. For instance, there have been Home Office integration strategy statements (see Home Office, 2000a and 2004a), and acknowledgement of the roles of housing and community development in this context.

Critics sometimes doubt the depth of governmental commitment to minority ethnic groups, and some reports indicate a continuity of problems from earlier periods. Beazley and Loftman (2001) comment on urban policy failure in providing benefits to minority ethnic communities, and a 'fairly bleak' picture for minority ethnic groups in relation to regeneration. They argue that, in terms of success in securing funding '... *the results for BME groups are not good'*, and barriers remain for voluntary and community organisations in accessing and managing funds (pp. 38-40). Nonetheless, they indicate the significance of the development of 'Race Equality Guidance' in area-based regeneration (particularly in the New Deal for Communities programme). Certainly we should not overlook positive gains that may have been made from specific types of renewal and neighbourhood regeneration programmes. There is considerable ongoing uncertainty about 'what works' or does not work (and for whom), while multi-agency activities and holistic concerns make comprehensive appraisal in some regeneration settings a potentially complex task. Yet central government has shown increasing concern to draw in minority groups and ensure that they benefit from area regeneration. An important trend within practice has been the giving of fuller recognition to concerns about community engagement, although this may not be easy to achieve or sustain outside ad hoc short-term projects. There are of course questions to ask about the costs of participation and partnership for people drawn in as knowledgeable participants or as representatives of interests or organisations. Someone might feel that he or she has responsibilities but no power, and black minority-run organisations need proper financial or other recompense if key personnel are involved in providing large amounts of advice and expertise.

Before saying more on housing, we summarise general lessons in two boxes, one highlighting conclusions from the policy record, and the other suggesting positive steps.

Box 18: Key conclusions from the history of urban policies from the 1960s to the present

The limitations of an area focus
1. Policies focused on particular localities are unlikely to be enough to solve some of the more persistent problems, especially those associated with low incomes. A focus on neighbourhoods, and the capacities of people within them to 'self-manage' problems, cannot be adequate on its own.

2. Positive local strategies can be offset or undermined by governmental policies in other spheres, or by trends in living costs or private markets. For example, it is likely that large numbers of poor people have suffered increasingly from severe debt problems whose escalation has been allowed by government's failure to protect consumers with tighter regulation and interest charge capping. Or, to take another example, in some ways it has been middle class groups that have been the 'winners' in more general processes of urban change (including expenditure on infrastructure). In some periods their ability to choose housing on the edges of the city or beyond was facilitated by tax concessions on the company car and associated benefits, and mortgage interest tax relief and freedom from capital gains tax for owner-occupiers.

Lack of evidence of positive gains for BME households
3. Little systematic national research evidence is readily available to show whether black minority ethnic groups have substantially benefited from regeneration exercises, although that does not mean that this has not occurred in specific places. Urban policies have aimed at tackling problems on a locality basis, but assisting minority groups has sometimes been more of an implicit than explicit element in regeneration programmes and spending. Some policies likely to have been beneficial have been receiving reduced government support in recent years, notably those aiding renewal for owner-occupiers. Policies and investment patterns were rarely subjected, until recently, to any type of developed 'equality testing'.

The limitations of a physical emphasis
4. Achieving higher physical standards for dwellings and local environments may not on its own produce sustainable neighbourhoods in social and economic terms (especially if rents and other costs rise).

5. If physical renewal or regeneration involves dislocation, reduced choice, or loss of ownership for a household, this may negatively offset improvements to the housing environment.

Problems arising from the diversity of local interests and needs
6. Localities may contain complex groupings and interests, with tensions over possible options, processes of partnering or co-operation, and interactions between officials, leaders and grass roots actors. Even with effective consultation, the path ahead may not be straightforward. For instance, collaborative progress could be affected by inter-generational differences in experiences or aspirations as well as divergence related to gender, ethnic grouping, etc.

Getting the right organisational frameworks can be crucial
7. Organisational arrangements are important, particularly where they bring black minority ethnic people into positions of responsibility, leadership, and control (individually or collectively) over assets and decisions. A similar point may be made for white people within disadvantaged neighbourhoods. Whatever the ethnic composition of an area, 'top-down' externally-led policies may be viewed with suspicion locally. →

There have been important political dimensions in the development of urban policies with regards to BME communities

8. Urban programmes have been significant politically. Black and minority ethnic-led social, business and community organisations and activists developed or mobilised through a long series of interactions with official organisations and potential white-run partners, and sometimes gained assurance, cohesion and standing through engagements around specific programmes. At the same time, white-run organisations learned something of the implications of racism and cultural diversity.

9. One important stimulus to policy development has been the series of urban disturbances that have taken place at various moments since the late 1950s. Although there have been several drivers for such incidents, the outbreaks of the 1980s were seen to some degree as challenges to policing practices and other aspects of institutional power through mobilisations on the streets. The establishing of the Housing Corporation's programme for developing black and minority ethnic housing associations in the mid-1980s owed something to specific disturbances that had preceded it, and without such challenges the pace of policy change more generally would have been slower. Riots, disturbances or uprisings (a term sometimes used) are hazardous, exhausting, and costly ways of resisting oppressive practices or securing positive change, but have sometimes helped stimulate a reformist agenda (cf Ben-Tovim *et al.*, 1986, pp. 115-117).

Box 19: Approaches that might help towards progress

Working 'with the grain' of people's preferences, and empowering people through control of assets

1. Regeneration policy-makers could more regularly aim strategies at 'working with the grain' of people's own ideas about their preferences, and facilitating households' desired 'housing pathways' where feasible. This would require knowledge and collaboration from local people through which to build scenarios about future community trajectories. There should be thinking in advance about how to locate and work with small, less known, or more geographically dispersed communities, bearing in mind their relative 'invisibility' in some policy environments (for Somali experiences see Cole and Robinson, 2003).

2. Evaluation of area programmes should relate more closely to local perceptions at grass roots of what those programmes should have achieved, and research and community development work should allow for proper funding of local participants, advisors and volunteers.

3. 'Empowerment' for individuals or groups could be part of the explicit agenda, meaning that minority ethnic communities would have more access to control and ownership of assets. A similar point applies with low-income white communities. The BME housing associations have shown what can be achieved, but a range of options need to be kept in view (including co-ops and self-build).

Developing and testing policies effectively and sensitively

4. 'Equality testing' or impact assessment should be developed further and attempted more frequently, along with audits of performance and outcomes.

5. Mainstream services should be made more relevant to the circumstances of people from minority ethnic communities, with adequate monitoring of outcomes and involvement of people from the communities in design and delivery. 'Strategic mainstreaming' remains important, relating to the long sought-after prospect that mainstream budgets and operations might be more seriously diverted in the direction of greater sensitivity and particular minority ethnic needs.

6. Policies should link effectively with diversity, taking account of cultural resources that may exist, and if appropriate using this as one of the routes to capacity building in community development.

Housing policy effects from the 1960s to today

The relative significance of housing within urban policies since the 1960s has varied across places and programmes, but mainstream housing policies and practices have had numerous effects on inner city residents, even when not presented as parts of government urban strategy. Developments affecting BME households have ranged from changes in social rented housing allocation policies to the provision of hostels for women or assistance for the homeless, and from regeneration investment trends to council mortgages. We sketch selectively a few of the issues now, to highlight some key current housing concerns within the urban policy agenda (complementing comments in Chapter 2). It should be kept in mind that government has shown strong interest in the neighbourhood level in recent years, with a variety of initiatives or implements (such as Housing Regeneration Companies recently).

Renewal and regeneration

The impact on households from physical neighbourhood renewal has been a longstanding issue, and it is often thought that demolition strategies in early decades worked against minorities (although Werbner suggested benefits in Manchester: see 1990, pp. 28-31). Some of our material in Chapter 10 highlights the sense of personal or collective loss that could occur through renewal programmes, and there is certainly no systematic national evidence that clearance benefited black people. After the 1970s, although clearance never regained the prominence it had once had within national housing policy, demolition remained an option in specific settings, sometimes as part of a broader package of measures. Today it has relevance particularly in the context of regeneration, including that envisaged under government's housing market renewal strategy in England, but remains potentially contentious. Interestingly, it appears that a reprieve has recently been won in one Lancashire area where the versatility of older housing makes it useful for minority ethnic households. Here, a press report indicates interest in adapting dwellings for extended families by the process of combining two dwellings into one (see Hetherington and Weaver, 2004). Another report (in *Black Housing*, 121, 2002) arising from a different context, by a community activist from a London district, refers to a local view that residents should have a 'right to return' after demolition, conflicting with the local authority's plans (Oshodi, 2002, p. 20). As we suggest in our chapter on needs, there can be something of a gap between local perceptions on the one hand, and available policy levers and solutions on the other (and this may remain problematic in an era when demolition has moved up the policy agenda). A key issue for clearance has long been the potential loss of individual ownership. Thus, the viability of creating new pathways which satisfactorily reconstruct this (or something with comparable collective benefits) could be crucial, alongside issues of location, safety from harassment, and local facilities.

Another longstanding issue for renewal programmes has concerned investment patterns. Despite notions about targeting deprived priority areas, focusing resources on council estates in recent periods probably 'side-stepped' some problems of deprivation, *'... because the most disadvantaged areas for minority ethnic groups'* were *'... of mixed tenure'* (JRF, 2000, p. 1). Negative impressions of outcomes here, however, rest on insights only from specific places and moments, and it remains impossible to weigh up the present regeneration scene accurately without further data. One accessible study on renewal outcomes is an interesting 'before and after' analysis of a London locality scheme that certainly did include minority ethnic households (see Ambrose, 2000; Ambrose and MacDonald, 2001). This research covered a population including a high percentage of Bangladeshis. The authors noted health and other improvements after regeneration, although perhaps offset by negative trends in some aspects of mainstream services spending, and with potential local implications in terms of raised household costs (rents, costs of moving, etc.). Unfortunately there is little comparable material from elsewhere.

It is perhaps too early properly to evaluate the Housing Market Renewal Pathfinder projects (referred to above) aimed at tackling low demand, housing market failure and abandonment (although funds for improvement and demolition seem relatively modest, given the scale of problems; see Baker, 2004). A preliminary appraisal by Cameron, however, suggests that BME communities might provide key contributions to market renewal and neighbourhood restructuring, and notes that there is some recognition of the specific renewal potential arising from minority ethnic housing demand. In South Yorkshire, new homes aimed at BME communities apparently have been identified as a specific output target. On the other hand, drawing on Audit Commission material for three other market renewal areas, Cameron suggests that there has been some neglect of BME housing needs and aspirations. He also identifies the danger of BME communities being discussed primarily in terms of problems rather than opportunities in market renewal contexts, and the negative nature of a focus on supposed ghetto-isation and the issue of dispersal. (I am grateful to Stuart Cameron for observations here.) One line of more general criticism about the pathfinders concerns lack of social inclusivity and the likelihood of creating what Atkinson refers to as *'... secondary social costs'*, through *'... state-sponsored gentrification'*. He notes fears that these enterprises are largely undemocratic, *'... and will destroy existing communities in ways reminiscent of earlier waves of demolition and clearance activity'* (2004, p. 124).

Turning to private sector dwellings, a lesson from the past seems to be that improvement grant spending had considerable merits. Information from John Perry suggests that some Midlands and North of England councils achieved significant levels of take-up with improvement support for owner-occupiers amongst minority ethnic households in the late 1970s and 1980s (the renewal efforts being enhanced by an emphasis on local advice centres, BME staff, and translation and interpreter arrangements). Work by Bowes *et al.* (1998, pp. 101-

102) points to continuing likely benefits for minority ethnic households in the first half of the1990s in two other English towns. Systematic data from independent investigations seem scarce, but findings from Leeds (an exception where information was reviewed) support the argument that this type of funding has been important for minority ethnic households (Law, 1996, p. 107), although not reaching every potential target group. The positive potential of grants and allied support may have been applicable also for agency services (such as Care and Repair) and Disabled Facilities Grant (DFG) (although again see Law, 1996). When general funds were available, however, questions sometimes arose about sensitivity in terms of advice in appropriate community languages and staffing. There might be problems too with delays, affordability, quality of workmanship or relationships with white builders, while ethnic monitoring data were limited (Ratcliffe, 1992). In the present period, the lack of comprehensive and well-resourced policies for improving older private housing probably works against minority ethnic households from specific groups. Although there is much talk about a sustainability agenda, implications of this for expanding the programmes of older housing expenditure and support have not been seriously addressed.

Allen has recently summarised problems over improvement programmes while discussing health issues, and notes the problem of waiting time and the policy shift away from grants (apart from the DFG) towards loan and equity release schemes. Current official discourse apparently includes reference to a 'grant dependency culture', an interpretation that seems to under-rate the importance of chronic illness and poverty, and perhaps seeks to justify pushing poor people towards burdensome debts (for observations see Allen, forthcoming). As an additional point, it has been suggested that funding for inner city improvement work may have had localised political side-effects, insofar as there may have been resentment within adjacent white populations on council estates about the support being given to minority ethnic owner-occupiers.

Other local investment policies assisted minority ethnic owner-occupiers in the past, but have more or less vanished from today's agenda. It seems likely that local authority mortgage loans frequently brought benefits over a long period. Indeed, as early as 1967 Burney wrote that, '... *barring perhaps the National Health Service, the mortgage finance available from the majority of local authorities has probably been the public service from which immigrants have gained most benefit*' (Burney, 1967, p. 34). Perhaps the closest parallels today might lie in the policy growth areas of assisted purchase and shared equity, but it is not clear how far BME households benefit from these. A lack of developed systems for acceptable financing for Muslims may be a potential barrier to ownership in some cases. Certainly the issue of Islamic financing (with funding arrangements offering alternatives to standard mortgage interest-based systems) is important. It is notable that Islamic mortgages are now being taken seriously by funders (see *Black Housing*, June/Oct 2003, pp. 6-7), and further developments seem likely (see Rahman, 2004; also Housing Corporation, 2004a, footnote 9).

Box 20: Housing renewal policies

There is little solid evidence of BME households having gained from clearance and redevelopment in earlier years, and we have too few independent studies of more recent regeneration exercises.

Improvement grants have had considerable potential to help low-income BME households living in owner-occupied dwellings. As we noted in Box 18, this type of expenditure has had lower priority with central government in recent years.

A sustainability programme for pre-1919 housing neighbourhoods could usefully build on past examples of success with improvement programmes, and perhaps link this where viable and appropriate with other policies such as assistance with purchase.

Social rented housing

When it comes to allocation practices, much has changed since the 'classic' studies of discrimination mentioned in Chapter 1. We lack up-to-date material on local councils, but what is known for RSLs suggests that considerable effort has gone into responding to minority ethnic households' needs, albeit with limitations in benefits achieved. Well informed practitioners and 'champions' for equal opportunities have, over the last two decades, frequently involved themselves in developing improved practices, despite constraints. Case study and survey work by the present writer with housing associations in the early 1990s indicated some excellent innovation and good practice (although somewhat patchy), alongside many ongoing limitations and difficulties. Unfortunately there has been a rather intermittent record of independent research and monitoring, so it is hard to weigh up progress. Nonetheless, although relating to England rather than the UK generally, there is recent informative material about performance from four substantial reports (Ratcliffe *et al.*, 2001; Tomlins *et al.*, 2001; Somerville *et al.*, 2000; Robinson *et al.*, 2002), as well as material about associations from narrower official monitoring exercises (for instance in Housing Corporation, 2002). The reports point to ongoing problems in delivery and targeting of accommodation, and indicate that issues such as employment by housing providers need continuing attention.

Perhaps most important, there is a continuing shortage of good quality social rented lettings in reasonably desirable areas, and this seems likely to affect increased numbers of BME and white households if house prices outstrip capacity to pay for mortgages. How this is carried through into localised effects on access and choice for specific categories of households from minority ethnic communities is unknown. On indirect benefits from investment and contracts in housing, one of the studies cited above indicates that '... *the use of BME contractors and consultants is a major area of work requiring the attention of RSLs*', and that recruitment of contractors and consultants '... *was a reactive process, benefiting those already familiar with RSLs' networks and ways of working*' (Tomlins *et al.*, 2001, pp. 52-53).

BME housing associations

Over the period from the mid-1980s, black-run housing associations established themselves as significant players on the housing policy scene, at least in England. It was 'top-slicing' of mainstream Housing Corporation budgets for social rented housing investment that facilitated their development. One view is that they became the 'jewel in the crown' in the urban policy repertoire, through providing role models, access into policy for previously excluded groups, and culturally-sensitive services (long seen as a facet of practice where white-run associations had remained deficient). Although growth and consolidation has been by no means easy, the development of the black and minority ethnic voluntary housing movement stands out as an impressive achievement with lasting impact on the policy scene. By the mid-1990s, however, the Housing Corporation's black and minority ethnic housing associations strategy had become unacceptable to Conservative ministers, fitting poorly with the goal of prioritising provider competition rather than encouraging particular community-based organisations.

The associations recovered their position within policy somewhat after 1997. Labour's arrival in office led to restored political support from the centre, and to a new policy statement from the Housing Corporation confirming the significance of minority ethnic housing needs and issues. Nonetheless, the Corporation today prioritises the meeting of BME housing needs by all housing associations, and is perhaps less concerned than in early phases to promote the BME associations as such. Extensive appraisals are available elsewhere of the development and roles of BME RSLs (for history see Harrison, 1995, 1998, 2002; Harrison et al., 1996). The BME associations have faced challenges because of a changing investment environment and issues such as national rent restructuring, as well as because of the need to adapt services to meet potentially changing demands (such as those from smaller or emergent groups of BME households). They house white tenants as well as those from minorities (for whom they are well placed to cater). One view is that unfortunately the funding and policy environment today may be less responsive to new or emergent groups (and their needs and participation) than in the 1980s, and that there is inadequate flexibility and innovative potential in the availability of support (I am grateful to David Mullins for observations here).

A recent CIH report (Lupton and Perry, 2004) points up a number of issues for future development amongst BME RSLs. On the one hand, a small number have a successful development role, and cater effectively for mixed client groups while providing culturally-sensitive services to a range of BME communities. On the other hand, many smaller associations remain community-based, and face an environment in which development funding may be concentrated with larger players. One way forward might be further diversification, with smaller associations offering specific skills in neighbourhood regeneration, or services for new client groups, refugees and asylum seekers, while providing contracted services to assist larger associations to operate properly in terms of cultural sensitivity, consultation, referrals, advocacy, and so forth. Key questions concern the extent to which government is prepared to provide adequate resources, the terms on which this might be done, and the kinds of collaborative and partnership relationships that can sustain autonomy and BME client empowerment while facilitating co-operation. Some steps have been taken by government to help on rent restructuring, but doubts remain about the financial environment (see *Black Housing*, October 2004, p. 7). The potential role of BME associations in the context of local authority stock transfers was under-valued as an issue until fairly recently, but is now receiving more attention from government. (See the ODPM's website for a summary of work on stock transfers by Hann and Bowes, *Black and Minority Ethnic Housing Associations and their involvement in Local Authority Stock Transfers*; this is also helpful on the positive contributions of the associations. See also *Black Housing*, September 2004, p. 17.).

Box 21: The BME-run housing associations

Despite obstacles, the black and minority ethnic housing associations have established themselves as highly significant players on the housing policy scene in England. They may be seen as having been the 'jewel in the crown' in the urban policy repertoire of the 1980s-2000 period, with a majority of members of their governing bodies (80 per cent or more) drawn from BME backgrounds. Their growth was internationally an almost unique example of successful separate organisational development through dedication of substantial funds from a mainstream national budget to minority ethnic self-management of needs over several years (see Harrison, 1995), although parallels exist for indigenous minorities in some other Western countries.

BME associations have provided successful role models, access for voices from previously excluded groups, and culturally-sensitive services. It is important for them to consolidate their position and expertise, and move forward through new activities, both individually and in partnership and collaboration with other bodies. Taken together, the 23 largest manage over 20,000 housing units, with a gross turnover of £82 million. BME associations may manage their own stock or homes provided by other RSLs, provide specific services and a bridge to communities for white-run partners or client associations, and act as catalysts to improved understanding and meeting of needs. They may provide 'gateways' into housing and allied services for specific client groups who might not otherwise come forward.

It has often been argued that BME associations have been especially good at adding value to housing services through 'Housing Plus' activities, thereby connecting with allied concerns and needs in the communities they seek to serve. Sometimes the term 'community investment' is preferred instead here, to reflect the hope that such activities need not be simply 'add-on' optional extras in local housing strategies. Today the associations have important potential roles through stock transfer, low cost and shared ownership, regeneration and market renewal, and community cohesion work. Federal or group working arrangements with other associations sometimes may be a way forward for growth and diversification, provided enough autonomy can be retained.

→

Critics have suggested that separate organisational development led by people from minorities may fragment consumers (thereby encouraging the development of 'dual' housing markets), while BME organisations might foster an inward-looking approach that undermines multi-culturalism and inclusiveness. On the first point an answer is to improve joint working amongst social landlords so as to build on the capacity of BME associations to attract potential minority tenants and provide culturally-sensitive services. The second charge is not supported by the overall record. Of course it remains important for all landlords to work within regimes that ensure they remain inclusive, and have channels for co-operation with a variety of potential partners when appropriate.

For contemporary challenges see Lupton and Perry, *The Future of BME Housing Associations*, CIH (2004). For factors contributing to success and failure, and issues of management, structure and supervision, see the Housing Corporation Source Research Report 69, *Black and minority ethnic housing associations: the challenge of growth and viability* (2003a).

Alongside the BME RSLs registered with the Housing Corporation, there are numerous non-registered bodies, voluntary service providers, and allied community organisations. For example, a refuge may cater particularly for women from minority communities, or a homelessness facility may offer resources for specific minority ethnic clients. Urban policy-makers and larger voluntary sector 'players' may connect in some instances with such organisations through funding or other support.

Housing trends under Labour

The 1997 shift from Conservative to Labour had several effects. Labour's aim of improving the quality of social rented housing in the direction of 'decent standards' is significant, although rent levels and benefit arrangements remain crucial for households' welfare and options. Strategies on homelessness under Labour are more comprehensive and proactive than under the Conservatives, and this may be helping some minority ethnic households. Stock transfer policies appear more uncertain in their merits. Although positive statements have been made about involving minority ethnic groups, it is not clear how far this has actually happened, or how far organisational arrangements catering for a measure of community control or collective representation have developed or will do so in England, where most black minority ethnic households live.

Chapter 5:
From community cohesion to an inclusion and co-operation agenda

Malcolm Harrison

Notions about community have long played a part in urban strategies. The arrival of New Labour in power, however, brought a renewed emphasis on '... *active involvement and development of communities as core to the successful regeneration of British cities'* (Imrie and Raco, 2003, preface). This chapter appraises one specific idea in government's repertoire, the concept of community cohesion. We note the questionable nature of some underlying assumptions, but also explore constructive possibilities for local practice. In particular, the chapter sets out a summary of ways forward in Box 23.

Background

During 2001 there were disturbances involving substantial numbers of people in disadvantaged areas of several towns and cities in northern England, against a backcloth of tensions over policing, white/South Asian conflicts, and right wing political activity. Although the causes of tension were complex, and particular to times and places, the political dimension and police/community relationships appear to have been important factors. The overt right wing agenda apparently included Belfast-style 'peace walls' to divide Asian and white communities in Oldham, a boycott of South Asian businesses, and 'repatriation' for non-whites, while the presence or threat of right wing combatants or activists locally proved highly provocative. People from minority ethnic communities took action on the streets. In Bradford certainly (and perhaps elsewhere), some of the younger generation amongst South Asians felt that their community was being threatened (for a rare detailed study see Bagguley and Hussain, 2003). It may be that ethnic solidarities played an enhanced defensive role when disturbances developed, given the strengths of local South Asian communities and the recently heightened hostile targeting of Asian youth, religion and culture within popular debates.

When considering the underlying causes of the disturbances, we should not overlook what Burnett refers to as, '... *the wealth of research documenting the discriminatory imposition of formal police powers upon certain Asian communities'* (2004, p. 10). Important roles have also been played by the national and local press (see Community Cohesion Independent Review Team, 2001, p. 45). Nationally, there had been a process of labelling and criminalisation in public debate relating to Asian male youth, which – taken alongside ongoing racist influences within some policing – made it perhaps unsurprising that the police force '*... rounded on Asian youth more vehemently than on White racism*' (Amin, 2002, p. 961). Meanwhile, for some white residents, right wing political activity apparently capitalised on ill feeling about the allocation of local regeneration funding, and the notion that neighbourhoods occupied by white people were 'missing out on funds' in favour of Asian areas. This was alongside the political impact of more general controversies over asylum seekers, and hostility to Islam, supplementing 'traditional' racist claims being voiced that '*... people of African origin have a predisposition towards criminality*', or that those from the Indian subcontinent '*... make slums out of good areas and also bring bad attitudes and disease*' (see Loney, 2003). The events in 2001 mirrored a series of earlier disturbances, but had distinctive features and generated very specific governmental reactions.

The Cantle Report and its orientations

Responding to the disturbances, central government established a ministerial group on public order and community cohesion, to consider how national policies might be used to promote this latter goal, based '*... upon shared values and a celebration of diversity*', and appointed a review team led by Ted Cantle, which consulted and reported (see Denham's foreword in Community Cohesion Independent Review Team, 2001). Of the official reports published following the disturbances, the *Cantle Report* (Community Cohesion Independent Review Team, 2001) became the most well known and influential.

The *Cantle Report* summarised its proposals into 67 statements, ranging from the grand to the very specific. Recommendations included a call for each local area to prepare a plan (as part of the Community Strategy) to improve community cohesion (6.6), with a parallel communication strategy. Longstanding concerns such as issues of recruitment and career progression in agencies should be tackled (6.9, 6.56), and programmes '*... must be devised ... to promote contact and understanding between and within, the black and ethnic minorities, and the white community and faiths*' (6.27). It was stated that schools should consider ways in which they might ensure that their intake would be representative of the range of cultures and ethnicity locally, with admissions policies ideally avoiding more than 75 per cent of pupils from one culture or ethnic background in multi-cultural areas (6.38). Thus, '*Church and faith leaders should ... voluntarily limit the faith intake in both new and existing independent and state sector schools*' (6.39).

It was also felt that funding bodies should:

> '*... presume against separate funding for distinct communities, and require collaborative working, save for those circumstances where the need for funding is genuinely only evident in one section of the community and can*

only be provided separately' (6.45). Funding bids should be *'... based on evidenced need, on a thematic basis, rather than particular communities and should not generally relate to areas that reinforce cultural boundaries'* (6.47).

Recommendations specific to housing included the assessment of allocation systems and development programmes with a view to ensuring more contact between different communities and reducing tension, together with *'... more ambitious and creative strategies'* to *'... provide more mixed housing areas, with supportive mechanisms for minorities facing intimidation and harassment'* (6.57). The report's overall agenda mixed valuable proposals built sensibly on practical knowledge of previous experiences, with suggestions implying a shift towards 'social engineering', or to an emphasis on greater citizenship responsibilities and assimilation for minorities.

With the *Cantle Report* setting the tone, numerous other related official documents and statements have appeared (and the flow was continuing as we completed this chapter). In 2002 came *Guidance on Community Cohesion* for local authorities and their partners, published by the Local Government Association (LGA), with the Office of the Deputy Prime Minister (ODPM), Home Office, CRE and Inter Faith Network. The working definition of community cohesion at this point embraced a common vision and sense of belonging *'... for all communities'*, with appreciation and positive valuing of the diversity of people's different backgrounds and circumstances. There was an emphasis on people from differing backgrounds having similar life opportunities, and the development of strong and positive relationships between people from different backgrounds in the workplace, schools and neighbourhoods (LGA *et al.*, 2002, p. 6). The LGA document's notion of everyone having a 'common vision' may seem unrealistically optimistic, although people with diverse views often share perspectives on specific practical issues and ways forward.

Central government sought to generate measures to bring community cohesion into the mainstream agenda, and established a Community Cohesion Unit within the Home Office, as well as an expert advisory panel and supporting practitioner groups. In 2003 a pathfinder programme was launched, with development and dissemination of good practice as the goals (see Robinson *et al.*, 2004). Altogether, 14 pathfinder and 14 'shadow' pathfinder areas were approved. Further steps included a consultation exercise to aid development of a new Community Cohesion and Race Equality Strategy (see Home Office, *Strength in Diversity*, 2004). *Strength in Diversity* refers to structural inequalities and the legacy of discrimination, along with commenting on building active citizenship, a sense of pride in being British, and a sense of belonging (pp. 5, 6). Echoing other reports, it refers to the *'... risk that people exercise their choices in a way that leads to them living separate or parallel lives, where they do not interact with people from different backgrounds, beliefs or traditions'*, and then focuses on the aim of fostering mutual understanding and respect between people from different backgrounds and cultures (p. 16).

In discourses about the disturbances, issues of separateness and segregation were given some emphasis (see for instance Ministerial Group on Public Order and Community Cohesion, 2001, 2.13-2.19). This echoed elements in the earlier Ouseley Report on Bradford (Ouseley, 2001). Amongst other things, Ouseley highlighted '... *community fragmentation along social, cultural, ethnic and religious lines*', identifying an apparently '... *very worrying drift towards self-segregation*' and the '... *necessity of arresting and reversing this process*' (see his foreword). He referred to people retreating into '... *comfort zones*' made up of other residents like themselves (p. 16). In the community cohesion debate, the issue of separateness became important for housing and for education.

Critics sensed in the debate a possibility of deprived communities being blamed for their own deprivation, with cultural separatism (supposedly fuelling a process of self-segregation) being implicitly assumed to play a significant role in generating tensions, consolidating divisions, and even perhaps the condoning of criminality. With emphasis placed on perceptions that people lead 'parallel lives' (with differing low-income communities living, working and socialising separately), the spotlight was being taken away from issues such as deficient policing, racist political activity, uneven economic development, or ongoing practices amongst white-run institutions and households that contributed to segregation. Thinking seemed to be skewed by contemporary political alarms and 'moral panics' about Islam, 'Asian youth', and alien cultures, reinforced by concerns about the impact of asylum seekers and other migrants (for discussion related to crime see Kalra, 2003). To some degree Asian young men had moved in popularised perceptions from being categorised '... *as primarily law-abiding and/or victims of crime ... to being associated with criminality, drugs, violence and disorder*' (see Webster, 1997, p. 65). Multi-culturalism itself was implicitly in the firing line, and challenges to it became more overt (for discussion see Back *et al.*, 2002; Ouseley, 2004).

The second Cantle Report

In July 2004 a second Cantle Report was published (the final report of the Community Cohesion Panel, *The End of Parallel Lives?*), underpinned by contributions from practitioner groups covering specific fields. The tone and central preoccupations were much as before, but the text provides further insights into assumptions and developing priorities. The Panel believed that a most important part of the agenda is the development of shared values to support a new sense of belonging for all groups, in what is firmly recognised as a multi-cultural Britain (pp. 11, 7). The latter point was emphasised again when (writing in the press in the same month) the Panel Chair argued that *'More integration has to be a good thing, but it should maintain the multiculturalism model that allows differences to be respected'* (Cantle, 2004). Amongst specific suggestions in the report is one that more should be done to '... *manage settlement'*, to complement the management of migration. In this context the '... *social and psychological needs of communities must be managed'* (p. 7), with additional resources being made available earlier. This management of settlement clearly concerns newcomers such as people seeking asylum, but there is also a feeling here that white communities need to be engaged and their needs (social and psychological) should be addressed (p. 12). Constructively, the authors stress the need to link community cohesion with the '... *racial equality agenda'*, that is '... *still essential to tackle disadvantage'* (p. 8).

Less sure-footedly, the Panel suggested that the Office for National Statistics should monitor the concentration and segregation of communities and use the information to inform policy (an issue on which we comment below), although elsewhere reference is made to a vague but potentially more promising idea of having better data on '... *community dynamics'* (p. 17). The Panel expressed its hope that the statutory duty to promote 'good race relations' will be effectively discharged through the community cohesion agenda, and will be regarded effectively as being synonymous with it (p. 57).

Detailed material is presented in the report arising from the practitioner groups, referring to numerous practical points, developments or needs (such as the accessibility of services for BME, refugee and marginalised communities, the appropriateness of health and social care services, ways of improving employment rates for BME and white groups in deprived communities, and others). For policing, mention is included of the integration of:

> '... *mapping tension, criminality and offender densities with the National Intelligence Model to inform appropriate levels of police responses and effort and to prioritise targets'*, and '... *identification, on a geographic basis, of significant or disproportionate criminality, fear, and disorder in order to prevent or pre-empt community fragmentation or breakdown'* (p. 40).

Three early priorities identified for the housing group are the housing needs of asylum seekers and refugees, the lettings process and its impact on segregation (where concerns include enhancing choice in lettings), and the contribution of the private sector to cohesion. Interestingly, there is reference to the potential impact of lettings patterns on school pupil population profiles, and to the need for the private sectors to adopt good practice guidelines (p. 39). Under the Regeneration heading concern is expressed about area-based initiatives, where resentments apparently arise from perceptions of favoured treatment, and some suggestions are made about how to improve matters. In effect, on many issues the second *Cantle Report* mirrors the assumptions of the first. It points to some positive ideas and developments, but hangs onto some worrying specific baggage, such as a suspiciously crude assimilationist perspective on the funding of groups (see pp. 50-51).

A backward political adventure?

There was something of a double standard in the way that the new 'moral panic' about separatism surfaced. It is nearly 30 years since the present writer first heard the claim that some Christian denominational schools were serving as a means to preferred self-segregation by white families, it being difficult for minority ethnic children to gain entry to them. Today, many white-run schools strive for inclusiveness, yet barriers have not all disappeared. Indeed, just a couple of years ago I was told by a parent from a West Yorkshire Muslim background that her child had been rejected by a much preferred Roman Catholic school, because neither the mother nor child would 'fit in' (even though the mother was studying successfully at postgraduate level and a very well-acclimatised member of 'mainstream' UK society). Yet over the years since challenges were first heard about indirect racist effects from religious schools in England, government has rarely seemed much concerned about any exclusive consequences that Christian denominational admissions practices and academic management might have had. With the arrival of a number of recognised Muslim schools, and increasing proportions of South Asian children in existing state schools, national politicians suddenly discovered that religious or cultural separatism could be threatening to community cohesion. It seems that there are over 6,800 maintained Christian schools, by contrast with 33 Jewish, 4 Muslim and 2 Sikh ones (Community Cohesion Panel, 2004, p. 31); although presumably these figures do not include institutions with less support or formal recognition (and a report in *The Guardian* on 25th January 2005, refers to 107 independent Muslim schools).

A parallel case is the housing one. No national outcry has ever occurred about the persistence of particular white 'strongholds' within working class or lower middle class housing areas, although researchers have often challenged processes by which black people were kept out. No-one would suggest that many privately-owned rural and suburban areas are a threat to community cohesion because so few non-white people live there, or because some villages have become preserves for the immensely rich. More likely a village would be held up as a shining example not only of the persistence of localised community but of a contribution to a wider positive civic environment (although even in rural life tensions might be noted about 'outsiders', or over English language speakers settling in parts of Wales). Yet we are being led to believe that streets or areas where black minority ethnic people form a majority may be a threat to civic order and community, however benignly this message is explained or connected with proposals (see Ministerial Group on Public Order and Community Cohesion, 2001, 3.23). There is also the message that minorities 'keep themselves apart' rather than joining in wider participation, although evidence suggests that racist barriers to such engagement are frequent. Meanwhile, when it comes to residential segregation, the pattern of white households' choices remains dominant in shaping outcomes. It is worth noting that anecdotal information from US scholars points to some white people eagerly seeking out 'segregation indices' data, so as to refine their choices of housing areas well away from black people.

As this book has already intimated, one ought to be sceptical about the notion that separation based on clustering is *in itself* necessarily problematic, and it is clear that some well informed housing practitioners are cautious about that idea (see below, Robinson *et al.*, 2004). Going further, we should be wary of inclinations towards social engineering to create mixing or to 'correct' patterns of separation in a top-down manner, supposedly for the sake of integration. The past research record shows not only that black people were disadvantaged by being concentrated through allocation practices into areas of inferior housing, but also that there were failed (and illegal) attempts to disperse non-white people locationally when social rented housing was being allocated, in response to fears about the 'threat' posed by numbers of non-whites living together. In providing a summary, Smith reminds us of the Birmingham instance where (between 1969 and 1975), in response to pressure from white tenants, a dispersal policy was implemented, to ensure that in future allocations each black household would be separated by at least five white tenancies (see Smith, 1989, pp. 99-101). She observes that to have succeeded as a mechanism to promote 'racial equality', dispersal would have had to offer black tenants privileged access to the better parts of the housing stock, a strategy that local politicians would not have entertained.

No serious analyst today would suggest a crude quota approach of the type described. Instead, emphasis should be on facilitating equality of access in terms of quality of properties and areas, and responding to the preferences of individual needy households (of all kinds). Any broader considerations of creating a 'social mix' have to be justified by demonstrable benefits for households who are in the weakest positions or potentially vulnerable, while a key target might well be the widening of real choices for those households. None of this denies that there are places where diverse households live together successfully, while within the owner-occupier market there is undoubtedly a measure of minority ethnic suburbanisation into areas of previously predominantly white residence, a process which is likely to be primarily about getting better dwellings and environments. While spatial mixing may be sought by some households, however, it should neither be prioritised for its own sake, nor imposed from above.

One implication of the new climate of thinking might be that separate organisational development or separate specialist provision could be seen as problematic by funders or politicians, with minority ethnic organisations perceived as potentially less appropriate channels for support. Such organisations have often started up to provide more sensitive services or create new voices within policy contexts, but many have had to struggle to overcome disadvantages of resources. Information from a Rowntree study suggests that they may often have been expected to demonstrate standards of equality of representation and inclusiveness beyond what they perceived to be the case for their funders, or for many white-led organisations (JRF, 2004, p. 3). The JRF report that notes this also observes that without the black and minority ethnic voluntary and community sector, many involved individuals would not have made the move into other areas of civic engagement, while the sector provides innovative and inclusive projects and schemes, and reaches people who would otherwise remain on society's margins.

Seeing separate minority ethnic organisations as a danger to civic development would usually be misleading. Yet, in a 'post-multi-cultural' political environment, the roles of BME-focused services (whether run by BME groups or by white-led organisations) seem more likely to be challenged. A 2004 housing press report refers to an East London development aimed at Asian elders, on which 'tabloid papers' had 'declared war'. Apparently the scheme was commissioned after research had uncovered a need for extra care services among a borough's Bangladeshi community, and would be able to provide the specialised facilities and food needed (Beveridge, 2004). In evaluating combinations of specialised, separated and integrated schemes, what matters primarily is 'what works' and how far the most urgent targets are being tackled. In this respect BME organisations and BME-focused schemes have proved their worth. In fact – so far – the reaction against multi-culturalism may not have become very problematic for housing provision. To some extent the role of BME housing associations in community cohesion has been 'flagged up' positively. It would be important, though, not to impose unreasonable targets (such as prioritising 'mixing' in schemes) on such bodies if these targets conflicted with the needs they served, and when similar targets were not being required of the full range of white-run associations in a region.

Looking at the community cohesion debate more generally, one has a sense of the resurgence of some problems identified earlier in this book (for critical comments on recent thinking see Mason, 2003, pp. 2-3; Burnett, 2004). Particularly important is the danger of revitalised processes of stereotyping, now linked with a fear of enclaves of supposed 'alien cultures', at a time when we had become accustomed to recognition of diversities within as well as between groups, and to acknowledgements of the importance of good information about what is happening 'on the ground'. In other words, the clock may have been turned back at national level. This might have parallels in events elsewhere in Europe. For example, Musterd comments informatively on changes in the Dutch political climate, where policies for rapid assimilation have apparently superseded the idea that each culture should have opportunities to develop its own norms, values and interests (albeit within limits) (see Musterd, 2003, p. 627). In Britain, one influence has been a 'backlash' against the growing visibility and strength of culturally distinct communities located in specific neighbourhoods, and the impact of Islam in particular. Rather paradoxically, this backlash immediately followed a period when praise had been directed towards 'faith communities' and their potential contributions to welfare and community development, although implications of their positive engagement in fields like urban renewal had not really been adequately explored (for a useful report see JRF, 2003b).

One possibility is that the 'diversity agenda' may have been moving in the direction of a stronger top-down management of ethnic divisions, that (while acknowledging the strengths of communities) seeks more fully to measure and identify groups with a view to containing and modifying their distinctiveness, and handling where appropriate any supposedly 'deviant' tendencies (see Harrison and Law, 1997, for Law's concept of 'ethnic managerialism'). Local partnerships for managing crime and anti-social behaviour might seek to enlist community leaderships in handling such tendencies under the banner of community cohesion (although anti-social behaviour is something about which genuine concern runs across differing communities; see Chapter 10). At a more general level, both young male Asians and the areas they live in may have become labelled as problematic.

In reality, people living in particular deprived areas sometimes fill socio-economic positions previously occupied by other disadvantaged working class inner city residents. Some take on similar economic activities and hazardous lifestyles, and are exposed to pressures and temptations from today's national trends in crime, youth cultures, substance abuse, violence and poverty, as well as facing poor quality services and housing. At the same time, relations with the criminal justice system and the host community (and matters of 'turf' or territory) are complicated by the daily experience of racist hostilities. In effect, causation is complex, whether we are considering issues of crime or tensions on the streets. Negative stereotyping of male Asian youth (and perhaps particularly Muslims) might encourage over-dependence on containment or punitive measures, at the expense of more constructive, holistic or supportive approaches. The degree of geographical separation neither offers a satisfactory explanation for behaviours and attitudes, nor explains why community relations seem better in one town than another. Reflecting on the terrorist bombings of July 2005 to which we refer in our Preface, we can add that neither spatial separation nor overt cultural separatism seems to offer much of a guide to potential threats.

Contested concepts and the research agenda

The concept of community cohesion is novel both for UK institutions and in public debate here (although we gather that a great deal has apparently been written about community cohesion in North America: see Appendix C in the *Cantle Report*). The idea is capable of multiple interpretations, and has resonances with other broad concepts such as 'social capital', 'social cohesion', or 'the social glue' (see Forrest and Kearns, 1999). Central, however, is a conception of community which is laden with normative intent, implying that perceived 'micro-communities' at very local level should 'mesh into' or have counterparts at or across some higher level of community, not least because otherwise they may come into tension with each other. Scholars know, however, that the concept of community is itself open to dispute at any level, being perceived in a variety of ways by differing observers depending on contexts of time, perspective and setting. What are actually important are usually people's particular interactions, interdependencies and collaborations in diverse and very specific institutional, economic, cultural or geographical contexts (such as the workplace, college, voluntary bodies, or politics), and actors are unlikely to be static occupiers of one particular social space alone. When it comes to interactions outside the small locality, questions arise about the agenda being envisaged for community cohesion, since its implication may be an assimilationist model in which the entrenched barriers and values of white communities pass relatively unchallenged, while the cultural domain of minority ethnic households is pushed back into a private realm (see Robinson, 2004, p. 8). Certainly there are dubious connotations in the thinking. Writers have begun exploring its wider implications in the context of New Labour thought, and the connections with ideas about social capital, social cohesion and social mix in general (see Robinson, 2004; also Imrie and Raco, 2003).

Ideas about researching community cohesion should not depend heavily on statistical exercises measuring degrees of residential segregation, daily interaction or participation which rely on categorising people tightly under predetermined 'ethnic' headings (as if this was necessarily a reliable or central guide to their identities or relations with wider society). Policy analysts should be very cautious when developing 'indicators', and avoid placing weight on 'top-down' exercises that produce 'indices of segregation' or other measures of supposed separateness. There have been doubts about earlier governmental endorsements of a social exclusion agenda, and measurement of exclusion, given potential difficulties in defining and agreeing exactly what that term means, but at least it has the potential to be interpreted in the light of grass roots perceptions of relative disadvantage. The position on community cohesion is different. There is nothing wrong with gathering information about where people live and why, and what they feel about their future housing trajectories. It is also reasonable to examine residential segregation, or any systematic patterns and practices of exclusion from avenues for participation. One must be careful, however, about what data are assumed to mean, how they are interpreted, and the extent to which information succeeds or fails in capturing people's own conceptions of identity, belonging or exclusion.

At an apparently technical level, care is needed with statistics. In an important account referring to Bradford, Simpson shows that understanding migration effects and population change over time is essential when considering concentration or dispersal. The paper shows that increasing residential segregation of South Asian communities is a myth (2004, p. 668), and reveals that there has been considerable dispersal of the South Asian population. (See Simpson, 2004, p. 671; for related analysis see Phillips, forthcoming). The suburbanisation process has been under-rated politically, as has the fragmentation within, as well as between, minority groups, not least in respect of socio-economic variations affecting viable locality choice. Simpson's critique also reminds us that – internationally – studies of segregation emerged from the 'Chicago School' in the USA, and '... *have seen concentrations of any non-White group as negative*' (p. 664). I believe that in recent years such pejorative social science traditions have carried little intellectual weight in the UK by comparison with North America and parts of continental Europe. Battle must be joined to resist their incursion into mainstream UK thinking, especially where they imply that concentration of non-whites in itself is a problem or a threat to be measured and then 'treated' as if it were a pathological issue. It should not be forgotten that it is population concentrations of white people that are the most geographically isolated from other groups.

In case the reader is in any doubt on the implications of a focus on indicators of segregation, consider the case of UK Jewish communities (for studies here see work by the Institute for Jewish Policy Research, including Waterman, 2003). It would be hard to conceive of benefits for public policy from officials attempting precisely to identify distinctly Jewish households and measure their degree of spatial separation, in order to appraise their successful integration into UK society. Their inclusion and integration has been a long socio-economic process, with barriers overcome and cultural accommodations made. It is interesting to know where Jewish people are most likely to decide to live, but this is a product of a mixture of motivations and circumstances, and their settlement patterns as such (which may involve some clustering) tell us little about integration. Furthermore, it would be bizarre if official bodies attempted to 'plot' or measure '... *the extent and nature of cross-cultural contact*' for Jewish people, or to monitor that over time (which is one thing suggested for differing groups in official advice in LGA *et al.*, 2002; see p. 17). Current official interest in measurement derives from a wish to appraise Muslim assimilation in particular, and is potentially racist.

One marker of successful integration might be the extent to which people are able to enjoy rights and every-day opportunities that others take for granted, while another indicator might be the degree of incorporation and inclusion by UK institutions (such as colleges, trades unions, businesses, housing providers and political organisations). Changes in these things are certainly worth monitoring, and have long been on the agenda, as have measures of intolerance and racisms (or lack of these). One must nevertheless be cautious about the underpinnings of any statistical work, and about future attempts to model the supposed 'integrated individual' or community. For minority ethnic groups generally, UK traditions of concentrating research and monitoring on institutional performance, and relating this to social inclusion, fairer access and participation, should remain central for policy-related work. Box 22 summarises dangers to be avoided in the general community cohesion debate.

Box 22: Misleading assumptions and approaches that should be avoided in the community cohesion agenda

1. The labelling of specific minority ethnic communities or religious groups as 'problematic', with stereotypes developing about their supposed tendencies to 'self-segregate' and 'unwillingness' to acclimatise to Western values. (See Chapter 10 for life at grass roots; also Simpson, 2004, and Phillips, forthcoming, on the myth of increased residential self-segregation.)

2. Adopting stereotypes of South Asian young men in inner urban areas which present them as potentially threatening in ways that echo the images that developed of African/Caribbean youth of the recent past (with supposedly disproportionate group 'tendencies' to criminality, disorder, or a drugs culture). Similarly, adopting parallel crude stereotypes about disaffected white youth. Such stereotypes (whether of white or black) might lead to over-dependence on punitive measures against anti-social behaviour at the expense of more constructive or holistic approaches, and divert resources away from an attack on causative factors.

   (Causative factors worth considering may include: unemployment; educational and income issues; racisms; punitive rather than preventative drug control regimes, with consequential growth in drug dealing as a hidden economic activity and generator of violence; policing failures; poor services and housing; or loss of local facilities.)

3. Under-valuing the development and potential contributions of organisations begun or led by a majority of minority ethnic people as separate channels for funding or managing services. Assuming that they will undermine civic development through their separatism, despite the fact they are normally subject to at least the same standards and requirements as other participating bodies.

4. Assuming that minority ethnic groups and their organisations as a general category have generally been over-privileged through the investments and policies of government and voluntary bodies, and that this is a major issue that policy-makers should highlight.

5. Assuming that sustainable 'mixed' communities can readily be brought about within areas of settlement in a 'top-down' way, through housing allocation and management, without closely considering people's experiences and preferences. Under-estimating and failing to tackle the barriers and difficulties that have to be overcome for more 'mixing' to occur.

6. Assuming that identifying degrees of physical separation of non-white people in statistical terms will provide key indicators of a lack of community cohesion or of other problems. This would build on assumptions that geographical separation of culturally distinctive groups into different areas of residence is in itself necessarily harmful (which is unproven), and might involve fruitless research investigations of supposed divisions and groupings which may have less meaning or permanence than is imagined. Local or regional authorities should not be drawn into any substantial expenditure on work of this type unless its benefits are absolutely clear. There are dangers of classifying individual people in much too simplistic a way, and even perhaps of implicitly assuming that some pre-determined notion of 'deviance' may apply to them. None of this is to deny the benefits of knowing more about people's residence and trajectories.

→

7. Moving the 'diversity agenda' in the direction of a stronger top-down management of ethnic divisions, which seeks more fully to measure and identify groups with a view to containing and modifying their distinctiveness, or to help handle their supposed 'deviant elements' (a revitalised 'ethnic managerialism'). (Our criticism of this trend does not mean that multi-culturalism should have no limits; see Chapter 11.)

8. Assuming that tackling inter-community or ethnic relations problems is something needed urgently in certain northern towns where South Asian groups live in substantial numbers in old housing areas, but is less pressing or significant elsewhere (cf Robinson *et al.*, 2004, p. 59).

The applicability of community cohesion in housing

Although Robinson argues that housing policy and practice remain largely disengaged from the community cohesion agenda (Robinson, 2004, p. 14), this may change as national policies roll forward. In an important forthcoming paper for the journal *Urban Studies*, he points up the way in which housing policy and provision have been seen as major determinants of the shape of communities in official reports, and singled out for having contributed to segregation. Housing interventions are considered capable of promoting residential integration.

The *Guidance on Community Cohesion* document made particular comments about housing (LGA *et al.*, 2002, pp. 36-40; as updated 2/4/2004), and provides useful illustration (although reflecting thinking at particular moments within an ongoing stream of official statements). The relevant section in the *Guidance* boldly asserts that concentrations of people from one ethnic background in certain areas of housing, and their separation from other groups living in adjacent areas, have '... *contributed significantly to inter-community tensions and conflict*' (p. 36). More modestly, reference is made to barriers in terms of access and the apparent potential of choice-based lettings to help break them down, as well as the merits there might be of an ambitious target for improving the quality of run-down private sector homes. Housing agencies are urged to review provision, considering its impact upon cross-cultural contact and community cohesion, and to consult communities about preferences and barriers. Housing's impact on access to other services is also to be reviewed, the needs of under-represented groups and young people are to be considered, and there should be work with private landlords, developers and estate agents, challenging potentially discriminatory practices. Housing authorities should improve awareness of (and access to) social housing for groups which are currently under-represented, and 'race equality' and community cohesion issues should be built into consideration of stock and management transfer. Other matters to be reviewed might include allocations policies, involvement of residents, implementation of 'race' and diversity action plans, and establishing of support for households such as asylum seekers or Travellers. Furthermore, land use planning should be reformed to enable more intervention in specifying mix of properties and tenures on sites, with community cohesion recognised as a legitimate objective in planning guidance.

What is evident overall in the LGA document is the mixed character of the package. Well-established practical goals are combined with more doubtful expectations about what should and can be achieved. Robinson observes that the *Guidance*, and reports for Burnley and Oldham, all emphasise the importance of local authorities and housing associations working to ensure that relevant and appropriate provision is made available in order to increase the attractiveness of properties to minority ethnic households, and he also notes the need for larger houses and for adequate grant allocations for new social housing development even in low demand areas (Robinson, D., 2003, p. 2).

A Sheffield Hallam University team has researched the contribution of housing management to community cohesion, sponsored by the CIH and the Housing Corporation (Robinson *et al.*, 2004). Their study is complemented by other CIH reports, including a good practice guide (see below). The research report tackles how community cohesion is perceived and understood, as well as the roles and management of social rented housing. There were variations in local understandings, and the team's informants reflected on a variety of issues, priorities and concerns when asked what they understood by the term (including equality, understanding and acceptance, participation, increasing choice and fostering social mix, and quality of life; see p. 10). The general consensus, however, was that community cohesion should be concerned with tackling inequality in access to resources and services and promoting greater understanding and harmony between ethnic groups. The authors note a tendency to interpret the new agenda in terms of familiar territory concerning equality concerns and allied legal obligations. The programme is expected also to embrace other dimensions of social division, and locally this might extend to the inclusion of youth issues and shared challenges across groups (p. 13). For example, one informant touched on efforts to bring disaffected young white males '... *back on board*' (p. 14).

Although segregation was an important concern for many of the study's respondents, opinions differed about whether it was actually a problem, whether it was an issue that should be tackled, what interventions might be appropriate, and how tackling segregation might promote or undermine community cohesion (see section 2.3.3). One association director even observed that '... *my most sustainable schemes are mono-cultural*' (p. 15). Residential integration was not necessarily seen as essential for interaction to take place, and reservations about promoting residential integration appeared to recognise that people often live in segregated communities for good reason. Indeed, the tenor, realism and sensitivity of several of the comments cited were impressive. A key theme was the importance of choice.

Although it seemed that housing's role was not being explicitly emphasised very much in most pathfinder areas, there was a view that housing management had key roles to play: in provision of relevant and appropriate housing opportunities, in allocations and lettings, through community participation, involvement and development, via equality of opportunity, and through tenancy support and management. Current housing activities are probably already addressing some of the more positive aspects of a community cohesion agenda. Robinson *et al.* provide examples of practical efforts in hand or completed. These include a development extending the locational choice of the local minority ethnic population, stock conversion as a means of responding to inadequacies in the local stock profile, bringing residents together in a regeneration planning process, improving the staff profile (or training routes) to make the workforce more representative, changing or enhancing allocations and lettings practices, tenancy support improvements, and training local people to report hate crime incidents. Amongst other points the authors highlight collaborative working between landlords and across policy sectors, and the importance of a staff base representative of the local population, skilled in community languages, and alert to situations of different groups.

Blackaby's Good Practice Guide for CIH, *Community Cohension and Housing* (2004), examines related concerns. Although the author interprets matters in the light of official guidelines, there is often a properly cautious touch. In relation to the circumstances of individuals and households, understanding the spatial dimension of preferences and constraints is seen as *'... of central importance'* (p. 22). A good practice example reflecting a practical interpretation of how to develop community cohesion is taken from Oldham Housing Investment Partnership and Aksa Housing Association (pp. 30-31). Here the aims are to:

- develop and maintain contact with hard-to-reach groups;
- provide tenancy support complementing the work of other service providers;
- co-ordinate and promote community development activity (and develop new projects and activities to encourage social and residential integration and cultural awareness);
- support communities in moving to non-traditional areas;
- forge multi-agency partnerships to tailor services to deliver more effectively to meet specific needs in deprived areas; and
- promote 'racial equality' and cultural awareness within tenants' and residents' associations.

Unsurprisingly, Blackaby pays attention to the creating of 'mixed neighbourhoods', although indicating that this should not be about compulsion but extending choices and creating new opportunities (p. 36). Along with discussing the potential of new development and filling vacant dwellings, the study mentions redevelopment, conversion and refurbishment programmes to re-model currently unpopular areas (see p. 41). Important issues for the planning of schemes include measures to support what has been created, and selecting the right location (such as sites in 'intermediate' areas outside but within reasonable reach of traditional areas of settlement (p. 44)). Strategies to open up new opportunities are held unlikely to succeed if they simply provide housing and ignore wider issues, such as housing management, support and local amenities (p. 50); the guide lists components of an effective support strategy. Citing one of the few earlier evaluations in this field (Hawtin *et al.*, 1999), Blackaby highlights the need to work with all newly selected tenants, integration of the needs and aspirations of existing communities with implementation of the project, promotional work among existing residents, agreement over nominations systems, and full commitment of all relevant agencies. Approaches to grouped or co-ordinated lettings for black and minority ethnic households are also dealt with (p. 58).

More generally, the study also explores the role that housing associations can play in bringing about strong and positive relationships between people of differing ethnic groups (including tackling and reducing harassment, becoming positive role models as organisations, building bridges with new minority ethnic communities, and involving young people). A chapter dealing with investment decisions argues for the continuing significance of area-targeted strategies, emphasising such matters as the importance of robust data on needs, an open bidding process, and criteria developed in consultation with community representatives. Perhaps a key underlying goal may be to secure defensible systems in political and administrative terms, with clear rules for allocation and prioritising of funding (see p. 83). On monitoring, the guide recommends attempting to collect information about the ethnicity and age of alleged perpetrators of harassment and anti-social behaviour and of the parties involved in neighbourhood disputes (p. 25). We suggest that it is important to monitor the impact and character of actions against perpetrators to see if there is any indication of indirect or institutional racism. Near the end of the report it is suggested that priority should be given to examining the role that black and minority ethnic housing associations should play in delivering the community cohesion agenda.

What is striking about this guide is its combination of practical strategies and innovations with the language of goals and assumptions that government imposes via the official community cohesion discourse. This is a hopeful sign, suggesting that good practice will continue to develop locally despite flaws in thinking at national level. Positive elements of the agenda show a substantial advance in sophistication from earlier decades. Although the picture is patchy across organisations, useful developments are being delivered (or re-labelled) under the banner of community cohesion, while local practitioners can probably be selective about which strategies to adopt (something in any case made easier by government's emphasis on local responsibility). Readers may note that the CIH has sponsored additional work, including a briefing paper on lettings that is available electronically (Fotheringham and Perry, 2003). This indicates the merits of identifying 'bridging' neighbourhoods to enable BME households to move away from their existing settlement areas.

Charting a positive path: an inclusion and co-operation agenda

If we want cities and towns to have less potent divisions, there are barriers to overcome, collective capacities to develop, communications and knowledge to improve, and participatory and co-operative enterprises and frameworks to sustain or create. There is also the pressing issue of assisting voluntary integration of asylum seekers. None of this requires us to embrace the more misleading assumptions noted in this chapter, but in constructing a way forward in Box 23 we can draw on some useful insights from community cohesion debates.

It has become clearer, for instance, that investment strategies should be transparent and their outcomes carefully monitored, given the tendency for people to suspect they are receiving poorer shares than they should. In a recent Rowntree-supported study, researchers on religious groups and regeneration report that most of the groups they interviewed, including Christian, Hindu, Muslim and Sikh, had the perception that they were discriminated against in the allocation of funding (JRF, 2003b). More general research on religious discrimination in England and Wales has also confirmed that some minority religious groups (including Muslims) perceive and report unfair treatment in housing. This is a reminder of the need for good communication. Practices for access to services and tenancies should also be clear and well founded, and there should be mechanisms in place for proactively enlarging choice and pathways, reducing barriers posed by harassment or fear, and developing inter-organisational and cross-community collaborations. One of the most important results from the community cohesion debate should be a confirmation that these issues need revisiting, and that more concern should be given than in the past to the dynamics of inter-group relationships, and the fit between group needs, investment prioritisation, and overall urban planning. Furthermore, the strengths of established communities should be acknowledged. It is interesting to read, in the press report about Lancashire renewal noted in Chapter 4, that community cohesion has apparently been cited as a justification for not proceeding with a demolition scheme (Hetherington and Weaver, 2004).

In Chapter 2, Deborah Phillips has already touched on some ways forward in housing, and pointed out that understanding underlying causes of social division and tensions has significance for the pathfinder and shadow pathfinder areas identified as recipients of government support for its community cohesion programme. What is needed is concrete local knowledge alongside more co-operation and collaboration. The range of available measures must be tested against what succeeds in particular circumstances, and a pragmatic approach will build on local experiences. Chapter 8 comments on the significance of control of assets in housing and allied fields, and it might be that more federal arrangements for representing the grass roots in developing, managing and allocating resources would have merits in social housing contexts. Perhaps people in cities might be brought together in shared enterprises that involve controlling or owning housing and other resources and environments collectively or collaboratively, and that might facilitate development of more interactions locally (although interactions may be difficult as well as harmonious, and learning processes slow).

Box 23: Towards an inclusion and co-operation agenda

Some key positive general principles for strategies (the targets overlap).

Establish and sustain a genuine multi-directional and open learning environment
This would involve:
- Better monitoring and consultation, covering all disadvantaged groups (including those from white estates, and asylum seekers).
- Better communications by institutions, raising households' awareness of opportunities, methods of prioritising in resource allocation (in regeneration, etc.), and limitations on what can be done.
- Promoting better understanding across communities generally of constraints, fair methods, and rules, and implications of adhering to them.
- Ensuring that specific outreach work takes place where participation or contact is difficult; for example when a group is small or new to an area, or in a rural setting where minority ethnic households may be scattered, or when disabled people's needs have been under-valued.
- Encouraging mutual awareness by clarifying differences of perspectives and needs amongst groups and households.

Establish sustainable mechanisms for co-operation, capacity building and conflict resolution
This would include:
- Developing ways of bringing people together for practical and meaningful purposes, perhaps for neighbourhood management, or via federal relationships drawing organisations together in planning or implementation. Providing real leverage with public institutions.
- Focusing around control and management of assets and services, not just talk.
- Working towards more effective combinations of localised neighbourhood management or participation on the one hand, and cross-area interests and organisations on the other.
- Countering perceptions (such as those expressed to researchers looking into BME organisations' experience of local compacts) that voluntary and community organisations feel they are marginal to local policy debates, and used by mainstream and statutory agencies to deliver the latters' goals and targets rather than being fully involved in strategic policy discussion (JRF, 2002).
- Improving the stability of specialised and innovative services that are funded on a sponsorship and temporary basis and prove their worth.
- Properly funding the entry and contributions of BME experts into wider forums, so that involvement can be sustained. The *Guidance* document (see LGA *et al.*, 2002, pp. 19-20) recommends engaging with smaller community organisations as an aid to a 'bottom-up' approach to building community cohesion, but it will be important not to use funding too much as a lever or incentive to require meeting of imposed cross-cultural performance targets for minority ethnic organisations.
- Developing participation and capacity for co-operation and learning from each other at several levels, including the regional one.
- More inter-organisational activity, including housing bodies feeding into non-housing strategies and actions (ongoing CIH work is important here).
- Community investment and allied strategies integrated into business planning, regeneration planning, control of local assets, etc.
- Development of better services for youth.
- Monitoring and countering patterns of exclusion of groups from avenues of civic participation.
- Applying rules to ensure that participating bodies and community groups (such as residents' organisations) conform to good practice on inclusion, or (if not) are themselves trained, excluded or pressured.

→

Clarifying and keeping under review the mix and application of general rules, methodologies and standards

This would require:

- A transparent prioritisation process for investment undertaken on a reasonably fair and rational basis, with needs approached carefully and systematically across all communities. Provision and investment (e.g. conversions into larger units) should be accessible to all communities in relation to relative urgencies and problems being faced. Lettings practices should reflect carefully set rules which take into account urgency of needs and any significant issues of under-representation or exclusion experienced by minority ethnic people. As Blackaby and Larner (2003, p. 6) ask, bearing in mind the tensions that might be created when areas are prioritised for investment, *'... are there objective impartial systems for identifying priority areas for stock renovation?'*
- Thorough monitoring and reporting.
- Setting out of rules for direct employment and for performance expectations when public funds are provided to other bodies (including contractors).
- Setting any clear rules that might be needed about accommodating multi-cultural needs and the limits of this (see also Chapter 11).

Catering for diversity and acknowledging 'difference within difference'

Not everyone seen as 'white' is in a position of advantage, and the concept of 'difference within difference' can be applied here just as for minority groups (Mason, 2003, p. 3). Thus every grouping may have potential for differences and divisions within it. It is important not to lose sight of the broad range of households that face disadvantage, including many white people living in low-income estates. Organisations should:

- Continue to work towards making services more inclusive by developing cultural sensitivity, and making channels and criteria of provision better related to variations in need.
- Acknowledge that all ethnic communities contain variations in terms of households, opportunities and assets, and that there are smaller minority groups and disadvantaged white groups that deserve attention.
- Engage specific categories within minority and white communities: including elders; disabled people and those with chronic illness; women as well as men; asylum seekers; people with differing sexual orientations; youth; people who are especially vulnerable through isolation or other reasons.
- Offer incentives and support to make consultations more inclusive, and cross-cut or avoid ethnic managerialism focused through hierarchies and cultural sets which down-play other needs.
- Keep inequalities in opportunities and conditions under review.

Widening choice and assisting positive pathways

Policy-makers should:

- Be familiar with the kinds of barriers households face, and review prospects for overcoming these in particular districts. The Bradford report on *Breaking Down the Barriers* (Ratcliffe *et al.*, 2001) may be useful here. In areas with strong demands on social renting, access should be monitored to see what is happening for specific household categories.
- Audit for equality of opportunities on a regular basis.
- Seek to reduce harassment and fear so as to widen locational choice; and develop support mechanisms and capacity building.
- Ease the paths of asylum seekers to establishing themselves (see Chapter 7). For instance, the Home Office is apparently committed to an integration strategy for refugees emphasising the need for personalised programmes of support during the crucial weeks after a person is granted refugee status (see Home Office, 2004, p. 18).
- Consider strategies which incorporate diverse lettings and tenure options (including group or linked lettings) with appropriate housing management support and with marketing aimed at minority ethnic communities. (See also Chapter 2.) →

Tackling racisms and the social climates in which they are sustained
- Key foci within community cohesion strategies may be white-run organisations and disadvantaged white communities.
- Hate crimes and intimidation need to be understood and countered. The promulgation of racist beliefs and programmes by any sources should be challenged.
- Support and proactive intervention may be especially useful when important changes are taking place, such as the arrival of substantial numbers of new households in an area.

Conclusions

In many ways British cities are fragmented as well as very unequal places, and there is a strong case for trying to increase solidarities as well as tackling economic disadvantage. Yet this chapter has expressed reservations about some ingredients in community cohesion thinking. The present writer is particularly sceptical about the goal of mixed and balanced communities, as encapsulated in recent official discussions, at least insofar as this is to be reached by top-down strategies. The hope of thereby achieving behavioural modifications is highly doubtful. 'Mixing' in housing areas will not of itself necessarily increase positive social interactions between types of households, or secure stability. Of course there may sometimes be benefits when there are a variety of socio-economic groups or household types in a neighbourhood. Mixed tenures or dwelling sizes may be useful in some contexts, while mixing of age groups may be valued for practical reasons by some minority communities. Strategies to create such situations, however, need to be carefully weighed, in the light of their benefits and costs for specific categories of households. It has long been recognised that encouraging the better-off into an area may squeeze out poorer households, while 'integrating' low-income vulnerable disabled people into 'the community' has placed some in poor housing in exposed situations with relatively little support. This latter type of 'mixing' cannot be satisfactory (despite the dangers of segregating disabled people).

If given an ethnic or religious dimension, 'mixing strategies' would need to be driven 'grass roots-up' rather than 'top-down', reflecting genuine needs and preferences and spontaneous processes of change. They might also need resourcing. The responses of white households over time to areas of mixed ethnicity may prove crucial, and no area of mixed residence is likely to remain static, especially since some white people with choices may leave. More generally, certain types of mixed areas may actually be less sustainable than mono-cultural ones in the long term, and black minority ethnic households may derive benefits from living near to others like themselves (even though some may also be attracted by the idea of living in a mixed community with a percentage of white people). In Northern Ireland, certainly, the prospects seem limited for improving integration and positive interactions across the religious divide through housing developments (O'Hara, 2004).

As well as challenging aspects of currently influential thinking, this chapter has touched on constructive ways forward. The ideas brought together in Box 23 represent an initial sketch rather than a fully-developed plan, but the aim is not to provide a comprehensive solution to a complex set of problems. Rather, we offer an outline for an alternative approach. It sets aside some of the more damaging assumptions that have appeared in the community cohesion debates as far as minority ethnic people are concerned, and we hope it fits better with positive processes of social change, adaptation and interaction within UK cities.

Chapter 6:
Refugees and people seeking asylum: history and context

Lisa Hunt

In recent years, the issue of asylum has become a major concern, not just in the UK, but across the whole of Western Europe. Every day, newspapers seem to carry stories about asylum seekers and refugees, and as the number of applicants has increased, countries have responded by restricting entry or access to social and economic rights. The UK is no exception, and despite an increase in civil wars, political oppression, and ethnic and religious conflict around the globe, the motives of recent arrivals have been questioned and the official view can often be forceful, as the claim in Box 24 illustrates.

Box 24

'There is no doubt that the asylum system is being abused by those seeking to migrate for purely economic reasons. Many claims are simply a tissue of lies' (Home Office, 1998).

There has been a succession of legal and policy developments in recent years, which have built on the idea that the UK needs to support 'genuine' refugees, while at the same time should be deterring 'bogus' claims. Indeed there seems to be fear and suspicion of asylum seekers running through many contemporary debates. Although hostile reactions sometimes suggest that the UK is targeted by a disproportionately large number of asylum seekers, the real figures do not appear to justify such claims (for data and comment see Chapter 7, Figures 7.1 and 7.2, etc.). To help readers come to grips with some of the issues, the sections below provide coverage of definitions and general historical background, and offer a brief interpretation of trends. Chapter 7 then takes up the more recent story, focusing in particular on issues that need to be understood by people involved with housing practice.

Definitions

Before looking at the immigration and asylum legislation, it is worth noting what some of the terms mean. The term *asylum seeker* can be used to denote someone who has put in an application for asylum and is now awaiting a decision from the Home Office. They are not permitted to work until they have obtained refugee

---

status, and rather than entering the mainstream benefit system they are supported by the National Asylum Support Service (NASS), which was established under the Immigration and Asylum Act (1999). Some get no support at all; for instance, 'failed' asylum seekers whose claims have been refused, but who have not yet been removed for whatever reason. A *refugee* is someone who has been recognised within the terms set out in the United Nations Convention Relating to the Status of Refugees (1951). See Box 25.

Box 25: UN definition of a refugee:

'... any person who, owing to a well-founded fear of being persecuted for reasons of race, religion, nationality, membership of a particular social group or political opinion, is outside the country of [his/her] nationality and is unable or, owing to such fear, is unwilling to avail [him/herself] of the protection of that country'.

Refugees are granted indefinite leave to remain/enter, and are given the same rights as other UK residents such as permission to work and entry to the mainstream benefits system. They also have the right to family reunification. In some cases, an asylum seeker can be granted *'humanitarian protection'* status or *'discretionary leave'*, both of which replaced what was previously known as *Exceptional Leave to Remain (ELR)*. When an asylum seeker is granted 'humanitarian protection' status, it means that although their application has been unsuccessful, they are given leave to remain on humanitarian grounds, normally for a period of three years. At the end of this period, they can either be granted further protection or leave to remain, or arrangements will be made for them to return to their country of origin. 'Discretionary leave' is granted to applicants who do not qualify for refugee status or humanitarian protection, but cannot be removed due to legal obstacles, human rights issues, or a medical condition.

The history of controls and restrictions

The trend of restricting entry to the UK is not a new occurrence but began over a century ago. There appear to have been three phases of controls (see Cohen, 2001, and Hayter, 2000). The first phase was the restriction of Jewish immigration at the beginning of the twentieth century; the second phase was the restriction of African/Caribbean and Asian immigration during the 1960s; and the third phase of restrictions relates to the present time. This began towards the end of the 1980s, gathering momentum during the 1990s and continuing into this century. In this third phase, it is believed that population movements have taken on new characteristics. Thus they are apparently characterised by having their origins increasingly in the 'developing world', involving migrants with less in common culturally with Europeans than previous arrivals, and involving people arriving illegally, apparently often through use of false documentation and trafficking networks (Hansen and King, 2000).

Phase one

For most of the nineteenth century, due to the development of the British economy and empire and the subsequent need for labour, the UK had little use for immigration controls. This changed at the beginning of the twentieth century with the arrival of increasing numbers of Jewish refugees, mainly from Eastern Europe. In the large cities, their arrival was blamed for problems such as over-crowding, ill-health and criminality. No real evidence was found to support these claims, but the government nonetheless chose to curtail immigration by passing the 1905 Aliens Act. The basic premise of this act was that vessels carrying 20 or more steerage passengers would stop at designated ports, and immigration officers would be given the power to refuse entry to those who were unable to support themselves. In some ways the thrust of this legislation is strikingly familiar for anyone looking at welfare and employment debates today. This act signified the first time that a link was being made between immigration and welfare, with the idea of 'no recourse to public funds' a central feature. There were also contradictory arguments, with Jewish refugees being accused of taking British jobs, but at the same time of living off welfare. The First World War saw the passing of further legislation. During the time of national emergency, it seemed justifiable to remove or detain non-British nationals. The government's 1914 Aliens Restriction Act, which prohibited the entry of 'aliens', was intended to last for the duration of the war, but was extended in 1919.

Economic considerations dominated the interwar years and as unemployment increased it was felt that the UK could not find any more openings for refugees. Britain was also slow to respond to the persecution of Jews in mainland Europe, and when those fleeing Nazism began to arrive, it was left to the discretion of the Home Office to decide who was allowed entry. The official position on the granting of asylum is illustrated by the extract in Box 26 from a Home Office memorandum.

Box 26

'The so called right of asylum...is not the right of a foreigner to admission. But the right of the State, if it thinks fit, to receive a foreigner fleeing persecution' (1934, cited in Shah, 2000, p. 46).

In the aftermath of the Second World War, economic considerations dominated once again, but it was recruitment of labour that was required rather than the restriction of entry. As was indicated briefly in Chapter 1, the UK began recruiting those who could in some way benefit British society, and the government granted acceptance to thousands of displaced persons (DPs), particularly able-bodied men from Poland and other Eastern European countries. Once the UK had exhausted this supply of labour it turned to the Caribbean and Indian sub-continent for workers.

Phase two

This phase began in the 1960s with the restriction of black and Asian immigration. There was fear among trade unions and the white working class that they would now have to compete with immigrants for jobs, housing and welfare. After an outbreak of racist violence towards the end of the 1950s, policy-makers began to believe that action needed to be taken. This is often seen as a period when the issue of immigration became 'racialised' (the views of Enoch Powell, for example, are associated with this era), and cutting down on non-white immigrants was presented as being essential to maintaining good 'race relations'. Consequently there was a succession of measures beginning with the Commonwealth Immigration Act (1962), and culminating in the Immigration Act (1988). The result of the legislation was the erosion of the rights of entry for people from Africa and the Indian sub-continent, and a reduction of their citizenship rights in the UK (Bloch, 2000). Entry to the UK would become limited to family reunion, or the entry of refugees and people seeking asylum. As the next phase illustrates, however, the entry of this latter group would eventually be called into question as well.

Phase three

We now focus on the most recent pieces of legislation aimed directly at asylum seekers and refugees, starting with the Asylum and Immigration Appeals Act (1993), and continuing to the more recent Asylum and Immigration (Treatment of Claimants, etc.) Act (2004). The measures are summarised, and the implications indicated for asylum seekers in terms of access to social and economic rights. The chapter also touches briefly on what we know about the experiences of asylum seekers and refugees in recent years.

The chapter ends with a chronology that outlines the main pieces of legislation passed from the 1980s to the present day. This also notes European developments as it is important to look at UK policy within the context of Europe as a whole, particularly given the call in recent years for 'harmonisation' of European policy. The aim of this is to stop so-called 'asylum shopping', whereby it is argued that asylum seekers are 'choosing' countries with more liberal immigration regimes. Some argue, however, that this move towards a 'harmonisation' of policy is simply an attempt uniformly to increase restriction (see Joly, 1997). The chronology also includes reference to some of the events that have led to refugee movements around the world. It is in no way an exhaustive list of all wars and conflicts that have occurred, but helps to highlight some of the incidents that have caused people to leave their countries of origin.

The Conservative response

When elected in 1979, the Conservative government aimed to reduce expectations of the state's role. There were a number of debates and media inspired 'moral panics' around what was regarded as a 'dependency culture', and the welfare system was portrayed as something that could be easily abused. There was also a supposed new threat in the form of asylum seekers, whom the government believed were being pulled to Britain by the overgenerous welfare system. As a result, a succession of measures were introduced, including Carriers Liability (see chronology for explanation) and visa requirements for certain countries. In 1993, the government introduced the first piece of legislation that dealt specifically with the issue of asylum. The Asylum and Immigration Appeals Act included measures such as curtailing rights to social housing; introducing fingerprinting of asylum seekers; extension of Carriers Liability; and a declaration that those whose claims had been turned down would have only 48 hours in which to lodge an appeal.

As asylum applications continued to grow, however, just three years later the government introduced the Asylum and Immigration Act (1996). This had two main strands, one aimed at restricting entry to the UK, and the other at reducing the social and economic rights of those who had managed to enter. The first strand included the introduction of the 'White List', a list of countries that were considered 'safe'. Any applicants from these countries could therefore automatically be excluded, and their claim deemed unfounded or 'bogus'. It also introduced criminal sanctions for those found helping asylum seekers into the UK, and increased police powers in immigration offences. The second strand of this act related specifically to social security provision and employment opportunities. In relation to welfare provision, the government attempted to create two categories of asylum seeker; those who applied at 'port of entry', who were regarded as genuine and were therefore entitled to support, and those who applied 'in country' or those appealing against a negative decision on their request for asylum. 'In country' applicants were seen as potentially 'bogus' and would have to rely on support from local authorities under the National Assistance Act (1948). (Section 21 of this act provided for residential accommodation for persons aged 18 or over who by reason of age, infirmity or any other circumstances were in need of care and attention not otherwise available to them.)

The media response towards 'in country' applicants is illustrated by the quotation in Box 27 from the *Daily Mail* of 1995.

Box 27: Press comment

'The easiest way to clamber on board the Great British Gravy Train is to enter the country on a visitor's visa or slip in illegally. Then if you're caught just claim political asylum' (cited in Bloch and Levy, 1999).

(For further recent examples of press style see Chapter 7.)

There are reasons, however, why someone may not apply immediately at 'port of entry'; for example, a fear of people in official positions, particularly those in uniform, as persecution may have occurred at the hands of such people in their own country. This measure was therefore challenged in court. In relation to employment, asylum seekers were refused a work permit until they had been in the UK for six months. A clause was also added stating that employers found hiring people without appropriate documentation would be subject to fines of up to £5,000. This had racist implications in that employers may be deterred from hiring anyone of minority ethnic background, and it was found that some employers were carrying out checks on employees on their appearance and accent. The extra burden of checking documentation was also seen to deter employers from taking on those asylum seekers and refugees who were legally allowed to work. The provisions in this act were aimed primarily at reducing the economic incentives that were supposedly attracting people to come to the UK in the first place.

The approach of New Labour

Although the 1996 Act faced a great deal of opposition, not least from the Labour party, the issue of asylum was gaining prominence with voters. When New Labour won the election they remained committed to the idea that people were entering the UK for economic reasons. Their 1998 white paper, *Fairer, Faster and Firmer – A Modern Approach to Immigration and Asylum*, made reference to the increasing cost to the tax payer and the view that 'bogus' claimants were 'clogging up the system' for those who were genuinely seeking asylum. Following this white paper, the government passed the Immigration and Asylum Act (1999), with the objective of discouraging and testing claims. Although this act abolished the 'White List', a list of 'designated safe countries of origin' replaced it, and Carriers Liability was extended to now include trucking companies and trains. The elements of the act most significant for this book, however, were those referring to social security provision and to the (re-)introduction of the dispersal of asylum seekers to regions away from London and the South East of England.

Social security provision

From April 2000, benefit agencies and local authorities were no longer responsible for supporting asylum seekers, and this job now fell onto NASS, which was set up to co-ordinate services for asylum seekers. The government believed that cash benefits provided too much of a pull factor for asylum seekers, and introduced a voucher system that would replace cash payments and be set at 70 per cent of income support (IS) level. This took asylum seekers out of the mainstream benefits system. The vouchers could only be spent at designated supermarkets where no change would be given, and so-called 'luxury' items could not be bought. Administratively this approach was more expensive for the government, but critics felt that the idea was to create a deliberately stigmatising system that would set asylum seekers apart from other UK residents.

Dispersal

The intention of this was to alleviate the burden of assistance in areas of high demand such as London and the South East, and arrangements for sending asylum seekers to one of 12 designated areas on a 'no choice' basis began in April 2000. When dispersing asylum seekers, the Home Office takes into account criteria such as whether there are existing multi-cultural communities, appropriate housing, and the scope to develop voluntary and community support. The decision is meant to be based on the location of agreed language clusters, although research suggests that this is not always adhered to. (Investigation by the present author confirms this point; see also Wilson, 2001.) There were criticisms of the use of dispersal, particularly the fear that asylum applicants were being placed in sub-standard accommodation, in areas that lacked the necessary support. There are several earlier examples of dispersal since 1945 that raise questions about its recent re-use. One was the dispersal of Ugandan Asians, who arrived in 1972 after their expulsion from Uganda by President Amin. The aim was to persuade those who had recently arrived to go elsewhere rather than settling in the so-called 'red areas' – the congested cities – which were regarded as having the most social and housing stress. There was also fear that providing homes in these areas would create racist reactions from local populations. What happened was that the local authorities that did respond to requests for housing were in areas from which the local population had moved due to the shortage of employment (Dines, 1973). As a result, refugees were settled inappropriately and a process of secondary migration occurred whereby families regrouped in areas of their choice; for example, where there were already established communities or more services available. The arrival of Vietnamese in 1978 provides further illustration. Again, the idea was to resettle refugee families throughout the UK, with an agreement that no more than ten and no less than four families should be housed in the same area. Research and analysis pointed again to a process of secondary migration (see Box 28 for conclusions from Robinson and Hale).

Box 28: Conclusions from earlier dispersal practices

'... any future policy for resettlement of refugees needs to be more carefully considered and more actively funded by central government. It is clear that many Vietnamese people have found dispersal in small groups unsatisfactory. Over half all households have responded by voluntarily moving into areas of nascent concentration ... If dispersal is to be considered beneficial to refugees ... then any future programme would have to address the issues of social isolation, absence of community facilities, and provision of services **in advance**, and it would have to be recognised that dispersal inherently requires greater financial resources and greater central government involvement'.

(Robinson and Hale, *The geography of Vietnamese secondary migration in the UK*, 1989, pp. 24-25, emphasis in original.)

Recent dispersal differs in some ways from earlier attempts. Previous strategies were more voluntaristic, and focused on 'quota' refugees (where the government had agreed upon numbers to be allowed entry). It has been suggested that reception and resettlement may have been refined over the years, and that today's context and outcomes in any case may be different. 'Spontaneous' refugees are seen politically as requiring more control than in the past, and local cost issues have been on the agenda (with a perceived need for 'burden sharing' across the country). It may be that secondary migration after dispersal is less likely now where local conditions and support make settlement more viable (for relevant discussion see Robinson, V., 2003 and 2003a). In any event, in the UK today, the areas that have been identified for cluster region status contain a high representation of the most deprived areas in the Social Exclusion Unit's catalogue (Pearl and Zetter, 2002). To disperse asylum seekers to these already deprived areas could therefore be serving to exacerbate the problems of an already disadvantaged group, often making them a target of racist abuse and violence. In some cases it is assumed that minority ethnic groups will automatically welcome other groups into their community, or that because someone is of the same religion they will be happy living in the same area regardless of cultural differences. With reference to housing, it is often the case that asylum seekers are placed in low demand areas.

As regards developing support, a report by Wilson (2001), looking at dispersal in West Yorkshire, highlights that although many organisations responded quickly to the arrival of asylum seekers, there was a general lack of resources and training of support staff, variations in quality of service provision, and (sometimes) reluctance from GPs, dentists and schools to take on asylum seekers. Research by the current author, also focused on West Yorkshire, has found that although the services have developed substantially since dispersal began (and indeed since the above report was published), providers still express concern about certain areas of provision. In particular, there is a lack of specialist services for victims of rape and torture, and a shortage of legal services that specialise in asylum and immigration. It is believed that these areas of expertise are still found mainly in and around London. Some service providers also make reference to housing shortages, particularly as increasing numbers of asylum seekers are choosing to remain in their dispersal area once they have been granted refugee status. This is especially problematic, as, under the terms of the 1999 Act, there is a requirement for people to move on from their NASS accommodation and to make alternative housing arrangements within 28 days of receiving a positive decision on their refugee status.

Bringing the debate up to date

With reference to employment, in July 2002 it was announced that the right to work after six months would be withdrawn, and that asylum seekers would have to wait until they had been granted refugee status. This, however, can take many years which poses two problems: it will increase the negative feelings of the indigenous population as people are forced to remain on support for longer periods of time, and it has implications for the mental health of asylum seekers. They are a heterogeneous group of people, and as such, many are doctors, nurses, accountants, teachers, and managers, with professional qualifications from their countries of origin. Service providers, again interviewed by the current author, point out that being unable to work can have a knock on effect on asylum seekers' mental health and can lead to depression. They observe that people no longer have that feeling of self worth that working provides, and this can exacerbate problems for those who have already suffered psychological and physical trauma. Some service providers also make reference to the fact that this country is missing opportunities, particularly in the health service (see Box 29).

Box 29: Excluding useful employees from work

'Certainly from a nursing point of view it seems farcical that the government pays thousands out for members of the Department of Health to go over to other Third World countries ... and take their nurses when we have nurses, people who can care, with training, right on our doorstep.'
(Community Health Nurse, West Yorkshire)

'The country's screaming out for nurses, and here we have a qualified, good, caring person who would be a great nurse, who speaks great English, and she can't do it, and she's wasted for want of a better word.'
(Support Worker, West Yorkshire)

Following the 2002 white paper, *Secure Borders, Safe Haven: Integration with Diversity in Modern Britain*, the government passed the Nationality, Immigration and Asylum Act, the fourth piece of legislation in a decade. The white paper included a commitment to phase out the voucher scheme and reintroduce the use of cash payments, although these would remain at 70 per cent of IS level, which still begs the question of why asylum seekers need less support than other destitute UK residents. It also included the government's commitment to maintaining the policy of dispersal. Another proposal was to build Accommodation Centres in rural areas, which would provide everything under one roof for asylum seekers, including education for their children. This idea was criticised for further segregating asylum seekers from mainstream services. The act also saw the return of the White List, which at the time of writing contained 24 countries. What probably received most criticism, however, was the decision to withdraw or deny NASS support for 'in country' applicants. Under Section 55, asylum applicants were only to receive NASS support if they could prove they had applied for asylum, met the criteria for destitution, and had applied for asylum 'as soon as reasonably practicable' after arrival in the UK. This measure echoes the earlier attempts in the Conservatives' 1996 Act. The implication of the new legislation has been an increase in homelessness and destitution amongst asylum seekers (see

Refugee Council, 2004a). Many people have been forced onto the streets, or are having to rely upon friends and relatives who themselves are already living below the poverty line. Also, when combined with restrictions on the right to work, it can force people into illegal work practices that leave them open to abuse and exploitation. Research by the current author, for example, has found that some women asylum seekers are being forced into prostitution. At the time of writing, Section 55 is under review following a ruling from the Court of Appeal which found that it was in breach of human rights requirements. The government has indicated that it intends to challenge the ruling in the House of Lords (Refugee Council, 2004, 'Asylum seekers win back their rights to basic food and shelter', http://www.refugeecouncil.org.uk/newsline04/relea171.htm). According to Dwyer and Brown (2004; see also Chapter 7), destitution still remains a serious issue for many asylum seekers, particularly those at the end of the process with no recourse to public funds.

Following the 2002 Act, further legislation was introduced into Parliament: the Asylum and Immigration (Treatment of Claimants, etc.) Act (2004). Provisions include: restricting asylum seekers' rights of appeal and access to higher courts; creating new penalties for people arriving without documentation; increasing removals to 'safe' third countries; and increasing the discretionary powers of immigration officers to arrest and detain. One of the other measures that has come under particular scrutiny is the removal of access to NASS support for families who are at the end of the asylum process. According to the Refugee Council (2004) this could lead to children being taken away from their families and into care. Aspects of current practices relating to housing in the present legal environment will be touched upon in Chapter 7.

In 2005, ahead of a General Election, the government announced a five year strategy, apparently aiming to 'agree' immigration that is in the public interest while preventing that which is not. The measures suggested included a new points system for immigrants based on qualifications, work experience and income, the ending of 'chain migration', and only permitting long-term settlement of skilled workers. The 'low skilled quota' would be phased out in favour of EU labour from new accession countries. There would also be fingerprinting of all visa applicants. With reference to asylum, the aim is to speed up the process via a single tier of appeal, and reduce delays before removal. Border controls would be strengthened, and successful asylum seekers would be granted temporary leave to remain rather than permanent status as refugees. If conditions in countries of origin had not improved after five years, then people would be allowed to stay.

Experiences of asylum seekers and refugees

While the aim of this chapter has been to outline key policy developments and the reasoning behind them, it is worth taking a brief insight into what is driving people from their countries of origin. With media attention focusing on 'bogus' refugees, and the government reducing the social and economic rights of asylum seekers, the reasons for people coming to the UK are often overlooked. As was mentioned in the introduction, civil wars, political oppression and ethnic and religious conflict have caused displacement of millions of people worldwide. In many cases, individuals have seen family and friends killed, and have themselves been victims of human rights abuses. Women asylum seekers and refugees may have experienced sexual abuse and exploitation, and in some cases men suffer this as well. Rape and sexual violence has often been a deliberate part of war. For example in Bosnia it was used as a tactic of 'ethnic cleansing', where women were raped in order to give birth to Serbian babies. Some female asylum seekers have faced forced sterilisation, female genital mutilation, or honour killings. They also have the same issues as men in terms of the need for protection against political oppression. Even when trauma is less severe, there may be a sense of loss and forced readjustment creating heavy demands on most refugees in their new environments. While refugees differ widely, they have had to flee their home country, often giving up a great deal to find a safe place for themselves and their families. As a reminder of this issue we close this chapter with two examples drawn from recent contact with asylum seekers in West Yorkshire.

Box 30: The loss and readjustment faced regularly by refugees

Pranvera* is an Albanian woman who came to the UK with her husband and two children. As a result of her involvement in the opposition Democratic Party, her life had been threatened by letters, phone calls and even in her home. Her children had also been threatened. Before she came to the UK, she and her husband both had good jobs. For 22 years Pranvera had worked at the same telecommunications company. As she points out, they were forced to leave everything behind:

'I came over here, left my job, my husband left [his] job, my sons left their school, their education and we left [our] family. Our parents they are old, who knows that we will see [them] again or not. We left our house, we left our friends, close friends, we left everything behind us just for one reason, to find the space, safe space'.

More severe trauma
Rose* is 19 and from Liberia. She came to the UK on her own with the help of a family friend. The rebels in her country came to her house one day and killed her father. She was then captured and held prisoner by the same group. Every day her life was threatened, and she was raped numerous times by her captors until her eventual release. As a result of this trauma she was left with a number of health problems both psychological and physical. After her arrival in the UK, and subsequent dispersal to West Yorkshire, she was rushed into hospital, and it was discovered that she was pregnant as a result of rape. She had a termination.

* Both informants' names have been changed here. The information is from research interviews by the author.

Table 6.1: Summary chronology

Important dates/ legislation	Measures introduced	World events
1979		Iran – Islamic Revolution Soviet Union invades Afghanistan. The conflict resulted in the death and displacement of millions of Afghanis
1980	Britain obliged Iranian citizens to obtain visas before their arrival in the UK Britain agreed to the idea of accepting a quota of Vietnamese refugees	Beginning of Iran – Iraq conflict 'Boat people' had been arriving in the UK from Vietnam for a year
1981 **British Nationality Act**	Citizenship through place of birth (*jus soli*) was replaced by citizenship through descent (*jus sanguinis*). This could exclude children born in Britain to Commonwealth immigrants	By this time over two million refugees had fled Vietnam, Laos and Cambodia following the Vietnam War
1982		War in the Falklands
1983		Conflict in Sri Lanka. There was a ceasefire in 1995 but it broke down only months later Sudan – start of civil war that has killed and displaced millions of Sudanese people
1985 **Agreement between the governments of the states of the Benelux Economic Union, the Federal Republic of Germany and the French Republic on the gradual abolition of the checks at their common borders (Schengen Agreement) (EU)**	This called for the abolition of checks at common borders and allows free movement of people from the signatory states. The emphasis was on external borders and the monitoring of non-EU citizens. The UK opted out of this agreement, as it wanted to maintain independent checks Britain obliged Sri Lankan citizens to obtain visas before their arrival in the UK	

Important dates/ legislation	Measures introduced	World events
1986 **Single European Act (EU)**	Aimed to establish the internal market with free movement of goods, capital, persons and services within member states. Raised the question of a need to co-ordinate rules on granting asylum	
1987 **Immigration (Carriers Liability) Act**	Penalised airlines and shipping companies for carrying passengers without appropriate documentation	
1988 **Immigration Act**	Ended the right to automatic entry of dependents of Commonwealth citizens who settled before 1973; introduced restrictions on right to appeal against deportation; increased powers of authorities to deal with 'overstayers' and illegal immigrants	Civil war breaks out in Somalia between the government and the opposition Somali National Movement (SNM). Over 600,000 people are forced to flee their homes
1989	Turkish citizens required to obtain visas before their arrival in the UK	
1990 **Convention determining the state responsible for examining applications for asylum lodged in one of the member states of the European Comm- unities (Dublin Convention) (EU)**	Introduced concept of 'first country of asylum', which aimed to stop multiple applications and also stop unsympathetic regimes passing asylum seekers to other member states without taking responsibility. Signed by the UK	Iraq invades Kuwait – Gulf War Liberia – civil war breaks out between army and rebel groups. Despite a number of ceasefires, conflict continued resulting in thousands being killed or displaced
1991	Asylum states including Britain begin to put emphasis on temporary protection rather than permanent asylum and citizenship	Conflict in Sierra Leone. There was a ceasefire in May 1996, however the conflict resulted in the displacement of more that half of the population Conflict in Yugoslavia

Important dates/ legislation	Measures introduced	World events
1992 **Treaty on European Union (Maastrict) (EU)**	Formal recognition of the need for co-ordination of asylum policy among member states UK orders that refugees get visas via consulates in Bosnia before entering this country	Conflict in Algeria – The military kill and detain thousands Conflict in Bosnia-Hercegovina. Tens of thousands of Bosnian women raped, and many people lost their homes due to 'ethnic cleansing' by Serbian authorities
1993 **Asylum and Immigration Appeals Act**	Extended Carriers Liability; introduced fingerprinting of asylum seekers; allowed only 48 hours in which to lodge an appeal against a negative decision; curtailed statutory duty of local authorities to provide social housing	
1994		Conflict in Rwanda – Genocidal killing Civil war in Yemen
1996 **Asylum and Immigration Act** **Housing Act**	Introduced the 'White List'; increased police powers in immigration offences; employment clause; proposed removal of support for 'in country' applicants; access to IS, housing benefit (HB), jobseeker's allowance (JSA), council tax benefit would only be granted to those whose country was deemed 'unsafe' Asylum seekers defined as non-qualifying for the purpose of the housing register	Amnesty International document human rights abuses experienced by Czech Roma Afghanistan – Taliban seize Kabul. Strict Sharia law is imposed which includes banning women from work and education
1997 **Amsterdam Treaty (EU)**	Continued the trend towards harmonisation of policy with reference to common list of non-member countries requiring visas before entry	

Important dates/ legislation	Measures introduced	World events
1997 – contd.	UK Home Office Minister reduces period of application for asylum seekers from 28 days to 5 days following the arrival of Czech Roma	
1998		Congo – conflict between ruling party and rebel forces
1999 **Immigration and Asylum Act**	Extended Carriers Liability to include trucking companies and trains, introduced new visa restrictions; introduced compulsory dispersal of asylum seekers; introduced the voucher system at 70 per cent IS level; requirement to move on from NASS accommodation within 28 days	Serbian authorities violate human rights of ethnic Albanians in the province of Kosovo
2001		Liberia – conflict between army and rebel groups War in Afghanistan following the September 11th attacks in the US
2002 **White paper: *Secure Borders, Safe Haven: Integration with Diversity in Modern Britain***	Proposed replacing vouchers with cash support; placed emphasis on control and removal of unsuccessful applicants; withdrawal of support for 'in country' applicants or those who do not apply as soon as is reasonably practicable (S. 55); applicants from 'safe countries' would have applications certified as unfounded and could be removed prior to appeal; proposed the use of induction centres near to ports to provide information about the process, and initial health screening; powers to detain and search widened; introduced idea of Accommodation Centres located away from the indigenous population; introduced the Application Registration Card (ARC)	Angola – ceasefire ends a 27 year conflict between ruling party and rebel forces that has killed hundreds of thousands of people

Important dates/ legislation	Measures introduced	World events
2002 – contd. **Nationality, Immigration and Asylum Act**	It was announced in July that asylum applicants would no longer be able to work or undertake vocational training until they received a positive decision It was announced in November that ELR was to be replaced by 'humanitarian protection' status or 'discretionary leave' Introduced measures outlined in the above white paper	
2003 **Asylum and Immigration (Treatment of Claimants, etc.) Bill proposals**	Implementation of Section 55. Removal of support from unsuccessful asylum seeking families; restricting rights to appeal and access to higher courts; greater scope given to the 'White List'; penalties for arriving in the UK without documentation; photocopying of passports on routes frequently used by asylum seekers	War in Iraq
2004 **Carriers Liability (Amendment) Regulations** **Asylum and Immigration (Treatment of Claimants, etc.) Act**	Proposed new 'control zones' outside the UK, plus new charging regulations Introduced measures outlined above	

Chapter 7:
Housing refugees and people seeking asylum

John Perry

How to deal with the numbers of asylum seekers and refugees has become a major political issue, especially since 2002 when the number of asylum seekers passed the 100,000 mark for the first time. Almost equally controversial has been the issue of where asylum seekers should live, and whether and how they should have access to local services. In terms of the debate on 'race' and community cohesion, the treatment of asylum seekers and refugees – most, of course, coming from minority ethnic groups – has become of paramount importance both in itself and in its wider implications for black and minority ethnic people.

This chapter looks principally at housing and related issues concerning asylum seekers and refugees, following the historical introduction in Chapter 6. To put the issues into the wider context of the book, we now approach them from the perspective of how we achieve greater social inclusion and improve community relations – or retain good relations where they already exist – in the places where refugees and asylum seekers have been placed or have found themselves. In 2002, the CIH worked with the Home Office Community Cohesion Unit that was set up following the publication of the *Cantle Report* (see Community Cohesion Independent Review Team, 2001, and Chapter 5) to establish a Housing Practitioner Group. One of its first acts was to examine the implications of the housing of asylum seekers and refugees for the communities in which they are being accommodated. The present chapter draws from the author's experience as part of this group, as well as in preparing a CIH policy paper on this issue and pursuing its recommendations with the Home Office and other bodies (see CIH, 2003).

The chapter first sets the context for discussion by looking at how we arrived at the present levels of demand for asylum, what the numbers mean and (in brief) how national policy has responded to them. We then look at how housing agencies have responded, and at the constraints and difficulties they face, both in terms of the deliberate limitations on the help that can be offered and through the problems caused by the treatment of the issues by politicians and the media. Finally, we consider proposals for change, being put forward by various organisations, that could improve social inclusion and community relations.

Asylum seekers and refugees in perspective

How did we get to the present position? Until recently, the number of asylum seekers coming to European countries had been growing considerably. Those coming to the UK numbered 20-40,000 per year in the early 1990s, then numbers began to exceed 60,000 per year from 1999 onwards and peaked in 2002 at over 80,000 (Figures in this paragraph exclude dependants. The figure in the introductory paragraph above included dependants). Numbers have now fallen substantially to a little under 34,000 (Figure 7.1). But even though the UK is one of the larger recipients of asylum seekers in Europe, in proportion to population size seven European countries receive more (Figure 7.2). Some developing countries adjacent to states that are in conflict – such as Iran, Burundi and Guinea – receive massively higher numbers of refugees than does the UK, yet are of course much poorer.

Figure 7.1: Applications for asylum in the UK 1993-2004

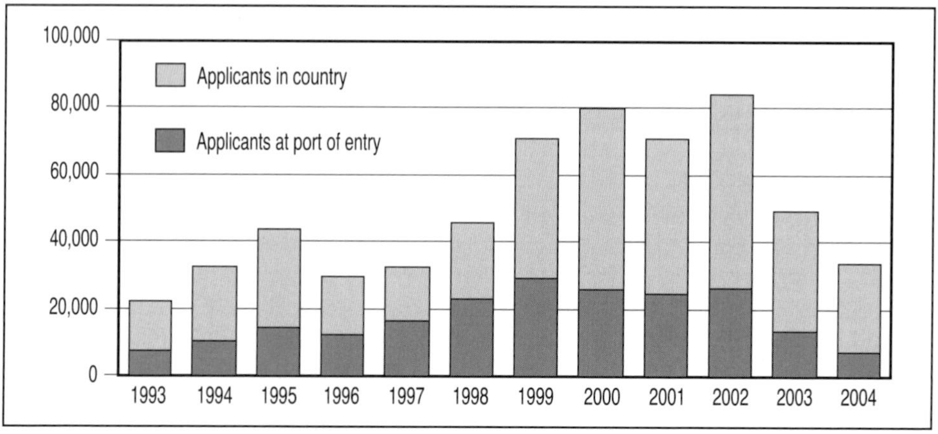

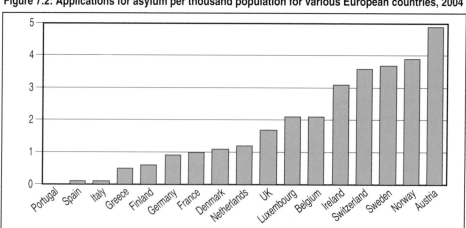

Source: Home Office, various statistics; figures exclude dependants.

Figure 7.2: Applications for asylum per thousand population for various European countries, 2004

Source: Home Office Asylum Statistics 1st Quarter 2005; data for Italy not available.

The main reason for applications appears to be conflict or human rights problems in different countries. The top four countries of origin of applicants in early 2005 were: Iran, Iraq, Somalia and China – all countries in the headlines for internal conflict and/or human rights problems. Countries where problems are decreasing – such as Afghanistan, Sri Lanka and Turkey – have seen big falls in numbers of asylum seekers in recent years (see Table 7.1).

Table 7.1: Top ten origin countries of asylum seekers, first quarter 2005

Iran	850
Iraq	525
Somalia	495
China	430
Dem. Rep. of Congo	335
Pakistan	320
India	310
Afghanistan	285
Sudan	275
Eritrea	265
Other nationalities	2,930
Total	**7,020**

Source: Home Office Asylum Statistics 1st Quarter 2005.

The growth in numbers coming here has led to tighter controls on entry, sometimes effectively forcing people to arrive either illegally or on a false pretext (e.g. as visitors). It has also led to restrictions on the help available (e.g. the short-lived voucher system). As Chapter 6 indicates, there has been a long history of developing controls, but recent periods have had some distinctive features. In 2002, the government introduced rules (the notorious Section 55 of the Nationality, Immigration and Asylum Act) preventing asylum seekers who fail to make their claims immediately when they arrive from receiving even basic assistance, despite the fact that, proportionally, such 'late' claims come from people whose cases are more likely to be accepted (see Crawley, 2003).

The growth in numbers overwhelmed both the processing system (leading to long delays whilst applicants' status was resolved) and the systems for housing and caring for the people themselves. This led to drastic revision of procedures and to the setting up of NASS, and the scheme for dispersing asylum seekers to various parts of the country (see also Chapter 6, which notes some earlier dispersal attempts). After widely-reported initial problems, the dispersal scheme achieved its main aim of shifting significant numbers away from either ports of entry or main conurbations like London to which asylum seekers have often gravitated (see Figure 7.3).

Figure 7.3: Regional dispersal of asylum seekers, 2005

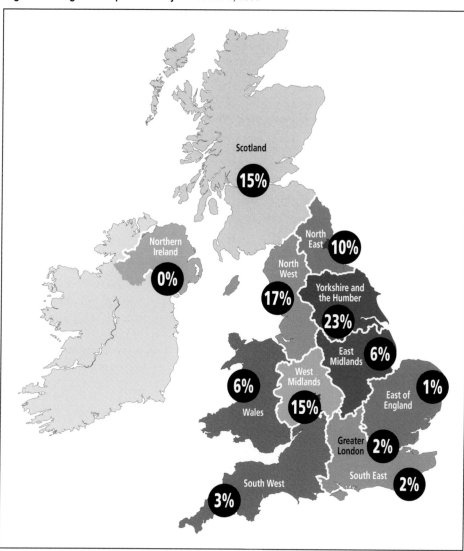

Source: Home Office Asylum Statistics 1st Quarter 2005.

The other main policy response was to reduce and strictly limit the help available to asylum applicants from public authorities. Asylum seekers now receive only certain limited kinds of help and are prevented from working (see Chapter 6). Refugees (successful asylum seekers) have more permanent status and greater freedoms, but – especially to begin with – are bound to be affected by what has happened to them as asylum seekers (in terms of where they live, their experience of the long-term community, their opportunities to start to learn English and to make their own way in the country). If they have been accommodated by NASS, they may have to resolve their housing and other problems very quickly and with little support when NASS help ends (as was noted in Chapter 6).

How have housing agencies responded?

Housing agencies have a mixed track record in dealing with asylum seekers (note also Chapter 2). Some local authorities, often acting in consortia, have responded to the dispersal demands from the Home Office. There are some notable examples of housing associations working with asylum seekers, but many associations are not yet engaged with this area of need. There are inconsistent practices between different areas in how refugees are treated under homelessness legislation, and whether and to what extent the needs of asylum seekers and refugees are considered in broader local policies such as Race Equality Schemes.

The private rented sector has been used directly by NASS, leading, especially at first, to problems of exploitation, poor conditions and little attention to the wider support that clients require. An example occurred in April 2003, when the Home Office published a summary of a report of an inquiry into problems with one such private contract in Liverpool, with Landmark (see also Chapter 2, and Home Office press release 103/2003). NASS has sometimes awarded block contracts to the private sector at 'rent' levels in excess of the average. This is not good value for money and has caused problems in the private letting market where landlords now expect higher rents, often in return for poor quality accommodation. This also causes problems with local people who view it as government help for asylum seekers to pay rents that residents themselves could not afford.

Some dispersal was successful, leading to good practice in places like Yorkshire which can now be followed. Other cases were less immediately successful, with some instances of violence and even murder in northern England and in Scotland, the use of poor quality private accommodation in places like North West England, and difficulty in securing 'sufficient' dispersal, so that places like Dover continued to suffer considerable pressures.

Constraints imposed by the present system

Where housing agencies do want to respond to the needs of asylum seekers and refugees, there are many constraints imposed both by government policy and the way it is implemented. First, as noted earlier, help for asylum seekers is strictly limited and their own ability to help themselves (e.g. by taking paid work) severely constrained. This makes it difficult for those entering the country to begin to shape their lives here. This might not matter if their cases were decided swiftly – and processing times are now improving – but if their status is unresolved for months or years it can lead to boredom, hardship and perhaps more severe problems.

Second, these difficulties are exacerbated if asylum seekers are placed in neighbourhoods ill-equipped to cope with them, for example because of the level of disadvantage they are experiencing already, or because of the burden placed on local services, or because of a general lack of local facilities. Several poorer council estates have experienced conflict or racist incidents as a response to asylum seekers being given accommodation. Even conurbations such as the West Midlands, well used to incomers of diverse ethnic origins, have experienced considerable pressure on inner city health services, leading one GP (himself from a minority ethnic group) to refuse admittance to his surgery to asylum seekers. Rural areas (where it was at one stage planned to set up special reception centres) may have few facilities of any kind. Opposition to asylum seekers – even before it was stoked up by press and politicians (see below) – came about because often there were few or no efforts to involve and prepare 'host' communities.

Third, the system fails to acknowledge asylum seekers' needs, other than basic ones such as accommodation. Take the example of mental health. People entering the UK to plead asylum will have many characteristics making them susceptible to mental health problems: a difficult and demanding journey here, separation from their family, unfamiliarity with the environment they are in, difficulties in communication, etc. As Chapter 6 indicates, many will of course be escaping traumas in their countries of origin – torture, imprisonment, and other forms of persecution – or perhaps will have been traumatised by these things happening to close family members. Their initial treatment in the UK may exacerbate these problems. Often, skilled help, such as that provided by the Medical Foundation for the Care of Victims of Torture (see www.torturecare.org.uk) will not be available. Furthermore, their needs may put extra strains on services which are already poorly provided (of which mental health is a notorious example). If asylum seekers fear that their cases might be rejected, they might seek diagnosis in support of their cases or, at worst, seek treatment before they are forced to leave the country.

Fourth, these constraints – already considerable – have been made worse by hurried decision-making and failure to communicate with the agencies and neighbourhoods whose services will be put under pressure. In the Landmark case in Liverpool, occupants of two tower blocks were moved out on a Bank Holiday weekend in May 2002 with no notice being given to the local authority or other service providers (and the Home Office investigation into the Landmark contract referred to above specifically criticised this move). In 2003, Luton Borough Council found itself an unexpected recipient of occupants of the Sangatte refugee camp in France, as part of the deal over its closure. In 2004, a housing agency reported a case of an asylum seeker pre-allocated to an upstairs flat which had no lift; it was literally only when she arrived on the bus that the housing workers discovered she was a wheelchair user.

Wider problems

Tackling issues of social inclusion and community relations also raises problems which are much wider and more intractable, and places the questions surrounding asylum firmly into the general debate about 'race' and community cohesion, which is one of this book's particular concerns.

We have already mentioned the growth in numbers of asylum seekers and the way this has dominated government thinking on the issue. But even though the numbers have grown, it is arguable that the reaction has been highly disproportionate. Politicians have portrayed the numbers as overwhelming or out of control. Credence has been attached to widely-disputed figures, such as media reporting (in August, 2002) that numbers were increasing to 200,000 annually, or assertions (January, 2003) that one in ten people in London are asylum seekers or refugees. Rather than rejecting these assertions, politicians have often responded with further promises to control numbers. Yet the truth is that, especially at current reduced levels, asylum seekers represent less than one in every thousand people entering the UK from abroad each year.

Another way in which the issue has been exaggerated is in the unfair attribution to asylum seekers in general of a range of problems that might be evidenced, if at all, by only a tiny minority. For example, *The Sun* has described asylum seekers as a '... *sea of humanity ... polluted with terrorism and disease ...*' (*The Sun*, editorial, 27th January 2003). Yet the evidence is slight. (Readers may wish to consult a useful summary of press claims and facts relating to them provided by the Refugee Council website noted in the list of useful sources at the end of this book.) A small number of asylum seekers were implicated in an incident involving an alleged terrorist cell and the death of a police officer in Manchester. Some asylum seekers need treatment for diseases such as AIDS. But a more rational response might be, rather than strengthening already strict controls, which almost oblige asylum seekers to find illegal ways to get into the UK, to open more formal access routes where asylum applicants could be screened from the start and (if necessary) monitored more easily.

Partly because claims about numbers and supposed attendant problems have not been properly addressed and, where necessary, challenged by the government and many politicians, the popular press has had a field day. On the back of claims, fed by disputed statistics such as those produced by Migration Watch UK (see www.migrationwatch.uk.com), *The Sun* in early 2003 launched a campaign to, '*End this asylum madness*'. Within a few days, 230,000 readers had signed up to the campaign, the Prime Minister responded by pledging to review asylum laws (which had already been reviewed on many recent occasions), and the newspaper was hailing its success. Even so, it called for more and quicker action: '*Blair must say **no more now**, revoke the human rights law **now** and lock up all the illegals **now** until they can be checked*'. The fact that its demands appear to have been impracticable presumably made them no less compelling to the readers who had joined its campaign.

These problems are very important in themselves, but an additional dimension is that it is difficult to separate public images of asylum seekers from perceptions of refugees, other immigrants, or even UK-born black minority ethnic people in general. Readers will recognise the portrayal of asylum seekers just summarised as having many similarities to past – or in some cases present – depictions of immigrant and even British-born members of minority ethnic groups at different times. The danger is that depictions of asylum seekers, resulting from a real yet exaggerated growth in numbers, might be – or may already have been – extended to the minority ethnic population generally. Certainly, these depictions appear to have been a factor in recent local election successes of the British National Party, often in areas which in reality have received few asylum seekers. From the perspective of asylum seekers themselves, portrayals of them by media and politicians are hardly conducive to a feeling of acceptance in the UK. Those people whose status as refugees is finally confirmed may find difficulty in overcoming this and contributing to community relations in the areas where they settle, especially if they have direct experience of racism or lack of community acceptance.

Problems summarised

The constraints on and problems faced by housing agencies in responding to these issues are perhaps wider than in any other aspect of housing practice. They range from broad and highly controversial policy issues at one extreme to matters of detailed practice at the other; at both levels changes are occurring, and responses are needed, more rapidly in this field than in others. What follows in Boxes 31-33 is a summary of these constraints and problems, drawing on earlier analysis by the author (CIH, 2003).

Box 31: The public image of asylum seekers

How the public sees asylum seekers has a major impact on their integration and also affects people from BME communities who are not asylum seekers. Some problems are:

- Negative press treatment of asylum seekers, nationally and locally.
- Difficulties caused by the high public profile given to government action to apprehend asylum seekers, making it more difficult to persuade communities to accept them.
- Low levels of material and financial support: asylum seekers may appear destitute, or cannot use local facilities, or have little to do during the day, or receive little help to learn English, which affects the way local people see them.
- Failure by housing agencies to prepare 'host' communities in some cases.
- Dispersal to very deprived areas because of pressure to accommodate large numbers. (Home Office cluster areas overlap closely with the 88 LA areas in England identified by the NRU as having the highest levels of social exclusion.)

Box 32: Support for asylum seekers

Whether housing and other agencies can offer the right levels of support to asylum seekers is affected by:

- Whether funding is available at all. This may be affected by – for example – the withdrawal of basic support in asylum cases where the person fails to apply immediately on arrival, leading to a growing problem of destitution.
- Availability of funding for wider support services.
- The state of the local housing market and whether there are sufficient dwellings available to meet the needs.
- Local authorities and other agencies (police, health, etc.) not being recompensed for the full impact of extra demands placed upon them.
- Asylum seekers' community care needs (e.g. adapted housing), which are difficult to meet at short notice.
- Slow awareness of/lack of skills or resources in housing agencies to deal with a multiplicity of needs (e.g. language needs such as the 52 languages spoken by asylum seekers in Leicester).
- In some areas, numbers imposing a severe strain on services, probably affecting services for local residents.
- Poor access to health and other services in some areas; additional health needs are not acknowledged.
- Lack of other vital services: leisure (boredom is a real problem), local transport (expensive), adult education and good legal services (otherwise must travel).

Box 33: From asylum seeker to accepted refugee

Asylum seekers whose cases are accepted may have problems making the transition, or finding their way forward as refugees. Key issues include:

- Delays in dealing with cases (although these are now reducing considerably), which delay integration of the families/individuals involved.
- Restrictions on asylum seekers working; meaning that they have to start from scratch when eventually their cases are decided.
- The short time between decisions on cases and refugees being 'on their own' (in theory 28 days, in practice often less than this).
- Delays in notifying local authorities about decisions.
- Pressure on permanent accommodation in many areas (and competition with the needs of the long-term community).
- 'Self clustering' may produce local 'hot spots' requiring extensive support (e.g. Leicester experienced the arrival of several thousand Somalis over a short period).
- Possible tensions between refugee groups, and with established BME groups (in addition to more obvious white/black tensions); e.g. when refugees arrive from both sides of a conflict, or when resources are scarce.
- The need for more widespread support services and promotion of good practice; lack of skilled staff.
- The need for promotion of good practice in 'preparing' communities to receive/integrate refugees (e.g. 'hosting' schemes, etc.).
- Inconsistent treatment of refugees by different local authorities in terms of homelessness legislation and acceptance on housing registers.
- The need for National Insurance numbers to be allocated more quickly to aid integration and help people find work.

How housing agencies are already responding

A Housing Corporation study in 1999 concluded that much housing practice in relation to asylum seekers and refugees at that time was either mediocre or bad (Zetter and Pearl, 1999). It attributed this in part to government policy, legislation and financial restrictions, but also to organisational inefficiency, poor policy, and inadequate training and resources at local level. The report argued that there were instances of institutional racism with assumptions made about asylum seekers' needs or behaviour that were not evidence based. This research is being up-dated and in looking at the current responses of housing agencies we have benefited from discussions with one of its authors. We have also discussed the issues with a number of agencies involved in helping asylum seekers and refugees in different places, including Scotland, and Wales, and English regions such as the North West, Yorkshire and Humberside and the East Midlands. In many cases in these different areas there have both been problems in meeting accommodation needs satisfactorily, and innovative action to resolve these problems. The picture is by no means universally gloomy, and there are already many examples of innovatory schemes from which lessons can be drawn to encourage change at both national and local levels. Here we give some examples which illustrate how some of the constraints and problems just summarised are, in practice, being tackled.

The most positive response has been from agencies that have set up specialist services for asylum seekers offering not only accommodation but wider support, and which have staff with relevant language skills (in some cases themselves former asylum seekers). Refugee Housing Association now operates such services in several parts of England. Two Yorkshire associations, South Yorkshire HA and Yorkshire Housing, set up a separate company, Safe Haven Yorkshire, which caters for around 3,000 asylum seekers and has a staff of 120. About 45 per cent of staff are from BME groups and together speak more than 50 languages. They manage over 2,000 properties, the majority leased from private owners (the expected response from other associations in terms of providing properties has not been forthcoming). The organisation does, however, work successfully with a number of specialist refugee groups. Staff have made a point of not just providing accommodation for NASS, but also of trying to ensure a satisfactory transition to more permanent accommodation for clients whose status as refugees is confirmed. The organisation has been prepared to make losses in order to facilitate a transition, despite the fact that NASS support (and payment for accommodation) ends very quickly after refugee status is granted.

Another form of positive response is from local authorities who have expressed a commitment to assisting asylum seekers and refugees at the political level and have followed this through in their priorities for housing and other services. Leicester City Council (along with authorities such as Sheffield, Bradford and Bolton) has made such a political commitment, and sees assistance for these groups as part of its overall commitment to community cohesion. As one of the UK cities with the highest proportion of its population from BME groups,

Leicester has become a natural focus for asylum seekers and refugees, including many (such as Somalis) who make their way there from other European countries and are not therefore officially counted as refugees. Leicester has a Refugee Housing Strategy and a specialist post co-ordinating work on asylum seekers. It has made particular efforts to encourage 'host' communities to receive refugees. One success story was the decision by one such community to pay collectively for a school trip that asylum seekers' children could not afford because of the limited financial help they receive.

Many more housing associations and local authorities have provided specialist facilities or services on a smaller scale. Bournemouth Churches Housing Association has developed a strong role in providing services for refugees and asylum seekers, through a contract with the borough council. They aim to provide a seamless service so that all housing and support issues are dealt with by the same staff, rather than people being passed from one agency to another, although more recently their services have been prejudiced by cuts in funding. Focus Group in Birmingham has a longstanding commitment to assisting refugees obtain accommodation, and also of positively encouraging grouping of refugees in the same area to provide the basis for mutual support.

Unfortunately, since the original Zetter and Pearl study (1999), although there are more good practice examples like these, many housing associations have not responded to the needs of asylum seekers and refugees to the extent needed. Although there is no comparable study of local authorities, it is likely that it would reach similar conclusions. Good practice needs to be promulgated much more widely if the kinds of approaches and services described above are to be available in all the areas where they are required. In 2005, CIH is publishing (with the Joseph Rowntree Foundation) a good practice guide which aims to achieve this.

New research findings

As work for this book was drawing to a close, a new study by Dwyer and Brown was nearing completion, focused on the welfare strategies of forced migrants, the services they encounter, and allied issues. The research (in Leeds) suggests that support arrangements are failing to meet the basic housing and financial needs of many forced migrants. There are concerns about the adequacy and standard of accommodation available (perhaps most notably that supplied through private contractors), about the problem of securing a positive housing transition across socio-legal status from asylum seeker to humanitarian protection or refugee, and the lack of a right to housing for some categories (including failed asylum seekers). Present arrangements may be contributing to hidden homelessness, while asylum seekers in general may be affected by the inexperience of NASS in managing housing, allied with emergent 'boundary disputes' between various agencies charged with provision and management. Voluntary bodies – including Refugee Community Organisations (RCOs) – may be picking up part of a burden that state services and resources do not adequately deal with. Increasingly, some tasks of supporting those without access to public welfare may be falling upon other forced migrants. Meanwhile, those migrants who experience hostility and abuse locally may find it difficult to move to other neighbourhoods. (See Dwyer and Brown, 2004, for some published findings.)

What needs to change

Many organisations have put forward proposals for change at national level intended to improve public policy and provision for asylum seekers, in response to the problems and issues identified here. Our intention in this chapter, as we have said, is to focus particularly on changes that might lead to greater social inclusion and better community relations or, at least, prevent them from being further eroded.

One response to the supposed problems is epitomised by the campaign in *The Sun*: to exclude asylum seekers as far as possible, and to incarcerate those that have to be admitted or who find their way here despite even stricter controls. This approach should be rejected, not just on grounds of principle but also because it would not work. On the issue of principle, the UK is required by its international obligations to accept asylum seekers, and this is unlikely to change significantly given the number of regional conflicts and the further pressures that may be placed on countries adjacent to conflict areas. Press reporting has indicated a government plan for 'regional protection zones' in other countries to which asylum seekers would be moved once they had been initially vetted in the UK (*The Guardian*, 5th February 2003). They would only be allowed to return once their claims had been successfully demonstrated. This plan, however, would have a long way to go before it could be implemented. In practice, the government tacitly accepts that, although the numbers of asylum seekers have now been reduced by its tough regime, significant numbers will continue to arrive both because further tightening of the system is very difficult and because of continuing conflicts in various regions.

So, if there is going to be a continuing need to accommodate significant numbers of asylum seekers, even if not at present levels, what changes in policy and practice are required? We have looked at a number of proposals by different housing and refugee organisations, which might assist in achieving greater social inclusion and improved community relations. The CIH has indicated that it wants to see a more constructive government policy towards housing and supporting asylum seekers and refugees, *positive* action to change their public image, and the development of good practice by all housing agencies, not just those who are so far committed to positive action (CIH, 2003). It has called for 'community cohesion' to be a key aim of policy on asylum, so that all new measures would be tested from this perspective as well from other policy perspectives such as controlling numbers. Carrying this through sensitively would require fundamental changes. One would be to alter the political message and stop referring constantly to asylum seekers as a 'problem' to be 'controlled'. Another would be to challenge negative media treatment and encourage positive coverage, such as reporting of successful examples of integration or stories of host communities welcoming newcomers. A further change would be to avoid highly-publicised punitive action such as the forced removal of families that have already been integrated. Changes such as these are felt by CIH to be necessary if the climate is to improve and the adverse effects on wider BME communities are to be mitigated.

The Refugee Council called on the government to drop proposals designed to deter asylum seekers but whose main effect is to make their integration more difficult, such as the denial of basic support to people who fail to apply for asylum immediately ('Refugee Council's five point plan to end asylum gridlock', *press release*, 28th January 2003). The government responded by changing some policy proposals, such as the planned building of accommodation centres in rural areas. Ministers could go further and modify the existing regime, for example by allowing asylum seekers to work whilst their cases are being decided, a measure also called for by none other than the Chief Inspector of Prisons reporting on conditions in reception centres (see *The Guardian*, 8th April 2003). The efforts which have been made to speed the decision-making system (supported by the Refugee Council) have helped, by reducing the period before asylum seekers gain proper status as refugees.

On housing issues, CIH called for NASS to develop a housing-based dispersal system, with good quality accommodation and support services in all cases, in secure neighbourhoods. NASS has now moved in this direction, and has opened 12 regional offices. CIH wants – and intends to help – the government to promote good practice on a wider scale. It wants a clearer strategy for the use of private sector accommodation, with better enforcement of minimum standards. This echoes the official report into the Landmark case (see above), which called for better performance standards and evidence of social housing management skills within private sector providers. CIH wants the wider strategic work done by local authorities – such as their homelessness and housing strategies, BME housing strategies, Race Equality Schemes and policies for supported housing – to reflect asylum and refugee housing needs. There should be more attention and resources devoted to the wider services that asylum seekers require, but also efforts to ensure that areas accepting asylum seekers gain some advantage from doing so (e.g. better community facilities) and that the effects of dispersal are carefully monitored in relation to their community impact.

Action to improve policies towards refugees is in one sense even more important than for asylum seekers, as refugees – by definition – have been accepted and will be in the UK longer or perhaps permanently. Their successful integration is crucial. A group of housing professionals advising the Home Office on refugee accommodation issues believes that accommodation should be in secure, integrated communities which have, wherever possible, been informed and prepared for their acceptance (unpublished material seen by the present author). They have already called for and even drafted a *Welcome to Britain* leaflet which they want issued to all accepted refugees. They would like accepted asylum seekers to be able to rent the accommodation provided for them by NASS if they wish to and where this is practicable. This is a measure already being investigated by Safe Haven Yorkshire. The CIH also points out that longer-term capital and revenue funding are needed if better refugee support is to be provided. For example, there are shortages of larger properties for extended families, and of appropriate adapted housing and support for disabled people. Refugee resettlement workers are needed in many more areas than have them at present. Tackling anti-social behaviour, already high on the government's priority list, is especially important in areas with refugees who may be subject to harassment. Specialist BME housing associations could play a bigger role than they do now in providing services to refugees and asylum seekers (see discussion in Lupton and Perry, 2004).

Primarily top-down policy changes such as these are very important but are not likely to be sufficient in themselves. Many more 'on the ground' initiatives are going to be needed. This will require positive action by government, such as building refugee support into mainstream funding streams, like 'Supporting People' funding. It requires bodies such as the Housing Inspectorate and Communities Scotland to include refugee services in their performance monitoring of housing organisations, so that organisations that develop them are recognised for doing so. Work on BME issues within the sector should give more attention to asylum and refugee matters. It is worth noting that they were not specifically referred to, for example, in the widely-publicised recommendations of the sector's Race and Housing Inquiry, in the *Challenge Report* of 2001 (NHF *et al.*, 2001).

There has been an important shift of emphasis by government itself, which has now recognised community cohesion as one of the main aims of its asylum policy (see for instance NASS *Newsletter*, 3, March 2004, noting the need to ensure that the dispersal programme takes into account other government initiatives to facilitate community cohesion). The government has also revised and extended its strategy for integrating refugees, *Integration Matters* (Home Office, 2004a). Although these are important steps, it will take much bigger ones to change the climate of opinion which has created so many problems for asylum seekers and refugees, and for those working with them.

Chapter 8:
Revisiting housing need

Malcolm Harrison

As we indicated in earlier chapters, there are pressures on policy-makers to take minority ethnic housing issues seriously, and to develop systematic strategies, but there is sometimes only patchy information available on the difficulties, preferences and possible housing futures of specific types of households. Consequently, interest has grown in methods for assembling information, including surveys, focus groups, consultations, and audits of provision. This chapter reviews some current issues, the topic of local needs studies, and disability, age and gender.

Defining and responding to housing need

The way need is approached varies according to time, place, economic conditions and culture. What is seen as a very achievable housing standard in the relatively wealthy UK may remain a distant hope in less advantaged countries, especially where devastated by war or disaster. Changes in expectations over time within specific countries can also be important. Within Britain, for instance, it is now almost a general norm that an adequately-equipped house should come with a central heating system, yet not so very long ago such systems were unusual. Likewise, it is assumed today that the toilet (if not more than one) should be located within the dwelling rather than in a nearby outside building. To today's younger households, previous generations may appear to have been remarkably tolerant of rather cold internal house climates, of dirt and inconvenience associated with coal heating, and of relatively primitive arrangements for cooking or washing. Our concepts of what is a 'normal' need have been shifting. On a different front, ideas about acceptable housing arrangements now take more account of the preferences and access needs of disabled people.

Realistic reviews of needs must show awareness of people's current expectations, and of how these relate to general living standards in specific societies. They must also take account of ideas about basic requirements that most households share as far as their housing is concerned. For instance, a house might be failing to meet basic needs if living in it caused some significant and demonstrable harm to adults or children. The presence of asbestos or some other dangerous material might be a case in point. Although physical housing standards are important, however, they are not the only dimensions of need. Ideally, reviewing needs should go beyond thinking about numbers of dwellings, adaptations, equipment, or physical improvements, since numerous socio-economic issues complicate what people require, how they use what is available, and their feelings about dwellings, internal facilities and localities. People may prioritise their need for affordability, security or a sense of autonomy in their homes, or easy access to kin or services.

In day-to-day practice, organisations require ways of approaching and measuring needs that are *fit for purpose*, relating to functions they have responsibility for in improving, regulating, providing or rationing housing, or dealing with costs and investment. Policy-makers will want to consider from a practical perspective exactly what is needed and why, or who should have priority and in what forms. Nonetheless, any important assumptions being made within strategies and investigations should be understood and brought into the open by those involved. Inevitably, some policy-makers may think of needs primarily in terms of their organisation's capacity to offer particular kinds of solutions, rather than through starting with households' own trajectories and wishes. For example, a provider might have prioritised new build social rented housing in the policy portfolio, and (in the absence of funding for improvement work on older dwellings) have come to see need primarily in terms of an increased supply of social rented units.

A central question to ask about concepts of need used in the policy arena concerns how far they facilitate or sustain the preferred housing pathways of households themselves. Even if it proves difficult to move from recognising local needs to policy interventions that reflect local wishes, it may be possible at least to review a range of relevant options that might be offered. In any event, obtaining adequate information on preferences remains very important. There are often no simple short-cuts, so that local surveys, contacts and ongoing consultations remain essential. Community engagement is needed, although it may be difficult to ensure adequate inclusion or communication, especially for certain less visible households (or household members such as young people) (see Temple and Steele, 2004, for issues of engagement).

Indicators and aspects of housing need

Some types of information about present conditions have been used frequently as indicators of need. Tables 2.2 and 2.3 in Chapter 2 show the situation on unfitness and poor quality dwellings, and in that chapter Deborah Phillips summarises the position on some other quality issues. Black minority ethnic people are much more likely than white households to live in 'poor' neighbourhoods, and are disproportionately represented amongst homeless people, while some minority communities are relatively more likely to lack facilities such as central heating. National data can be consulted for such matters as lack of internal dwelling amenities or problems of general dwelling quality, but available data may not necessarily measure 'relative quality' as such. We do know something about dwelling types, ages and areas, and have some data on levels of repairs needed, but comparing quality in summary terms across dwellings is inherently difficult, because there are so many variables that might be taken into account (for an introduction to some data sets see Harrison with Phillips, 2003, although written before availability of recent census data).

There are also questions of subjectivity and individuality, since perceived quality will depend upon the characteristics of the household and the weight they place on specific environmental features. Severity of conditions relates not simply to the problems of a dwelling as seen by an outsider, but to how well and how willingly a specific household can cope with them. For instance, a flat with a potentially dangerous balcony poses more threat to a household containing children than to most single adults. User perceptions of quality, furthermore, will rarely relate to physical dwelling characteristics alone. Some social rented dwellings are well supplied with services and relatively modern in constructional terms, but located in run-down or unpopular areas. Thus specific measures – concerning matters like disrepair or lack of desirable features such as damp courses – might be easier to agree upon for purposes of ranking dwellings than would a general quality measure.

Another potentially informative indicator is the level of over-crowding, which may reduce privacy and exacerbate health problems or difficulties of daily household living. At national level, over-crowding measures have shown some minority groups to be clearly short of space by comparison with white households in general (see Chapter 2). There are possibilities here of 'concealed' or 'hidden' households and an overlap with homelessness, because over-crowding may reflect the inability of some households' members to establish the separate accommodation they hope for. Over-crowding can certainly point to a need for more dwelling space, although particular occupancy levels nonetheless might be perceived differently by differing households. It has been intimated in North American contexts that higher densities might be 'explained' partly by lifestyle preferences and cultural factors associated with ethnicity (for instance Burayidi, 2003). It is important, however, to remember that over-crowding is at least partly a result of, or form of, material deprivation. We should be cautious about attributing causation of particular patterns of housing conditions primarily to culture, unless we are certain that the empirical evidence is robust, and that other potential causative variables (in this case financial difficulties, constraints on choice, or neighbourhood attachments) have been controlled for adequately in any research. Widespread over-crowding in a district expecting rapid growth in its minority ethnic population may indicate pressing needs for more accommodation space, although that will not tell us how best those needs should be met, or the relative priority residents place on space standards within the home. In any event, 'traditional' measures such as over-crowding indicators remain useful, revealing problems that in specific places remain 'intractable' (as Kearns observes for Glasgow; 2002, p. 263).

One of the most important potential indicators of priority for housing allocators is generally likely to be homelessness, but this has often presented information problems because part of the need has remained hidden or unrecognised (see Harrison, 1999; and Steele, 2002 on youth homelessness). Some people may be sleeping on the floors of friends or relatives, and be deterred by worries about harassment from being present on the street or at white-staffed facilities, while in other instances community members and networks may try to cope with things privately. Central government has been developing more positive approaches, through law, research and specific spending. Following new homelessness legislation for England in 2002, local authorities were expected to produce reviews and strategies shifting from a reactive towards a more strategic and preventative approach. Prevention implies more holistic and multi-agency responses than in earlier years, although policy still highlights selected priority categories. Scottish legislation goes further, however, moving away from a selective system focused around priority homeless groups.

Local authorities should address the needs of BME communities in undertaking their homelessness functions, including the development of homelessness strategies. Work published by Shelter has found that local strategies and reviews revealed gaps in information about particular sections of local communities, and obstacles to gathering information about homelessness for some black and minority ethnic groups who may not turn to councils for help (Siedlecka, 2004). Identifying needs here may require specific outreach practices, and appropriate staffing such as employment of women staff and those sensitive to religious and cultural issues. Interpreting and effective documentary communication may be problematic or expensive where there is great variety of languages in a district, and there may be additional complications from literacy problems. The arrival of asylum seekers can further complicate linguistic issues. One response towards improving communications involves individuals from specific communities or groups in self-help or facilitating activity on behalf of others (and Refugee Community Organisations can be important contributors).

Shelter draws attention to specific housing issues posed by the needs of Travellers, some of whom technically may be homeless, and refers to a Kensington and Chelsea site as an example of how on-site facilities (nursery, health, training facilities, etc.) can be provided (Siedlecka, 2004, p. 32). There are also more general issues of cultural sensitivity and lifestyle preferences that may be important, alongside matters affecting potential sites, such as racist hostility or affordability. The government's attempts to resolve conflicts of interests over the settlement of Travellers were subjected to fierce attack by specific newspapers in early 2005, while Gypsy groups apparently claimed that a campaign against Traveller camps by *The Sun* newspaper was '... an incitement to racial hatred' (*The Guardian*, March 10th 2005). The government seems to have been seeking more positive responses to needs from councils, while simultaneously giving new powers to force Gypsies and Travellers off unauthorised sites (*Housing Today*, 3rd December 2004). A recent commentary notes the estimate that 4,000 extra sites are required to meet current need, and that Travellers face problems of insecurity of tenure and rising homelessness; although it has been suggested that a European Court ruling may lead to improvements in security and greater recognition of government's obligations (Povey, 2004). A good summary of issues for Gypsies and Travellers is given by Niner (2004), who indicates that unauthorised encampments fail to provide adequate standards, tend to perpetuate social exclusion, and lead to friction. She notes that a network of transit sites and stopping places is needed. We can add that councils should take account of the needs of homeless Travellers for site provision when developing homelessness strategies.

Looking ahead, managing allocations, and meeting diverse needs

Data on present conditions do not necessarily inform us effectively about what people's future needs are, beyond the understanding that their accommodation should ideally be better, if this could be achieved without creating other problems for them. A chosen indicator may not actually tell us about 'need' as such, even though it may prove useful for policy development purposes. Shortfall or deficit concepts of need rest on the assumption that a person is in housing need if their present or readily-available accommodation falls below quality standards widely seen as a reasonable expectation in the UK. The need is then assumed to be for an improvement or adaptation to the existing dwelling, or for new accommodation providing the requisite standards. Yet we should not overlook questions of affordability, locality, culture, inter-personal networks, autonomy and safety. In some instances the main need a household has is for cheaper and more secure accommodation, and social rented housing has often met this need. It may well be that pressures in housing markets are leading to social renting taking on increasing importance for some BME communities. Affordability is clearly a crucial issue in making the bridge between an indicator of problematic present conditions and alternative accommodation as a means of meeting needs, but here we do not have much comparative data. We cannot say whether or how far minority ethnic households sacrifice on other dimensions of their spending in order to pay housing costs, and we do not have any broad picture of how different (or similar) their financial positions might be from white households in comparable contexts.

Equally fundamental, although there seems to be in the abstract a need for a better dwelling, we cannot determine whether social renting is the answer, or say that housing of a specific standard is required, unless we know something of a household's strategy, financial budgets and plans. Households might prefer to sacrifice dwelling quality for several reasons. These could include saving money, having a safe location, accessibility to friends, cultural facilities and kin, or being an owner-occupier rather than a tenant. In addition, they may hope that design features of a house can fit reasonably well with religious and cultural preferences. Furthermore, a snapshot of present conditions may not capture adequately the changing nature of circumstances or needs within a household, or reflect its longer-term strategy.

Over the years, local authorities have used various indicators to help manage access to social renting, and criteria have included time spent waiting as well as measures of present conditions, medical factors, and so forth. The repertoire of potential indicators of need is clearly crucial when considering priorities in allocating or providing dwellings. The experience or fear of harassment is an important example, along with situations involving isolation, or threats to children's development. Members of specific minority groups may be at significant risk. Waiting lists or queues are not necessarily a good guide to need itself, and taking account of waiting time or a local connection can be as much a reflection of moral judgements about being deserving (or of the difficulties of managing excessive demand in a way that looks acceptable to clients) as it is of relative need. In earlier periods some criteria were criticised for their potential discriminatory effects, and impact should still be kept under review. Time spent waiting, age categories, and local connections survive as measures of priority in the new era of RSL choice-based lettings (although CBL may have improved communications and attracted more interest from minorities). Today, social landlords are expected to take account of assessed housing need in prioritising applicants, and of prescribed 'reasonable preference' criteria (see Mullins and Pawson, 2005, pp. 207-209; also ODPM website). Tenancy allocation is one tool for combating homelessness (where priority need categories have been enlarged), and should also interact with programmes of support for vulnerable people. Reasonable preference categories include those who are homeless, in unsatisfactory or over-crowded conditions, or needing a move on medical, welfare or hardship grounds. Victims of violence or harassment are to be catered for, and other factors taken into account may include financial resources, behaviour, and local connections (although without discriminating here against any ethnic group). Waiting times may be used to determine priorities between households with similar levels of need. Up-to-date investigations of outcomes for specific minority ethnic groups from allocations seem rare. Pawson (2004), however, has reported a study that broadly speaking found no evidence of any systematic tendency for potentially disadvantaged groups (including BME households) to be rehoused by housing associations in the less desirable housing.

Meeting needs also requires culturally-sensitive provision and personnel, while needs assessment exercises should acknowledge issues such as gender, age, ethnicity and language barriers. Given the frequent preference for owner-occupation, support for improvement may be especially salient in some localities, but improvement policy has not had generous funding in recent years. An additional point is that planners should try to look ahead, especially when there are people occupying temporary accommodation (such as women who have left violent men). For asylum seekers and refugees, specific considerations apply (see Chapter 7), but – as with other minority groups – support for voluntary clustering might be worth thinking about and discussing with households and other participants. Considering unmet BME needs generally might also mean taking a look at the available stock and its limitations (for instance in providing for larger households). Unfortunately, as Fotheringham and Perry indicate, capital financing mechanisms for social rented housing, and approaches to density measurement, may not have facilitated the building of the larger homes needed, and there consequently might have been a bias against provision of affordable larger homes (2003, p. 6). In any case, often there is simply not enough social rented housing in good environments and safe localities.

Meeting needs by widening the choice of areas

Area choice is touched on in other chapters, and is a significant feature of household preferences. Choice about proximity and co-residence can be significant, along with a sense of belonging. There may be inter-generational changes, since housing experiences, achievements and strategies may vary not only over lifetimes but between cohorts of migrants or generations of settled groups. We might find generational as well as ethnic group differences in propensity to migrate out of established areas of settlement. While younger households might be less committed in their preferences for 'traditional' locales, youth unemployment and low incomes may constrain spatial dispersal.

Practical policy options for overcoming housing pressures in specific places focus on movement into more peripheral neighbourhoods, and possibilities for overcoming obstacles to entry to social rented housing estates outside existing areas of settlement. Whether as a transitional option or a longer-term tenure destination, social rented housing may be becoming more significant in places where previously there was under-representation, and an increasingly important housing alternative for newly-forming South Asian households in some cities, given the financial problems of access to owner-occupancy. At the same time, some BME households have a strong desire to move out of inner city areas of existing settlement, although barriers may be perceived in terms of the absence of other minority ethnic households and accessible facilities and shops, as well as from the fear of harassment. In some instances, tensions between different minority groups could also play a part in affecting attitudes to places and restricting areas of housing search (see Chapters 2 and 10). Along with avoiding harassment, black minority ethnic households may wish to distance themselves from what they perceive as a crime-prone, less respectable and 'rough' (generally white) estate culture, exactly as many white people do. More attractive 'white estates' that might suit some minority households, however, may be located further from core areas of settlement, and present problems because of having few existing BME tenants. Housing association accommodation (especially when run by BME associations) sometimes seems to have a better image than council housing has had, but BME landlords may possess too few appropriate dwellings located away from established areas of settlement.

It should also be remembered that because social rented housing already plays an important role for minority ethnic groups, policy-makers need to be alert to issues of access for these existing tenants into relatively sought-after estates and higher quality dwellings. Although concentration into lower status areas within council housing was revealed by investigations in the past, we have little recent information about minority ethnic access to areas of strong demand in social renting, or about locational options and constraints for specific groups (such as homeless people, female-headed households or 'newer' minorities).

Comments in other chapters touch upon strategies for assisting change, but any particular proposal requires careful evaluation in its local setting. Possibilities include promotion of new areas of residence, closer inter-organisational working (including the police and community development workers), improving housing-related services, supporting provision of cultural and religious amenities, providing 'race' awareness training for outer area residents' groups, and providing better public transport links to inner city locations. The idea of block or co-ordinated housing allocations might be connected up with management and ownership structures facilitating involvement of black-run collective or representative housing organisations (whether within independent or federal organisational structures). The Bradford report, *Breaking down the barriers* (Ratcliffe *et al.*, 2001), identifies actions that might help increase access to outer estates. These include improving the standard and cultural sensitivity of service delivery, more joined-up policy-making between organisations, developing appropriate property types/sizes, including houses for shared ownership and outright sale, information provision, developing community support networks, aiming for linked lettings where families are rehoused together to improve security, and exploring the potential role of BME housing associations. One feasible strategy in the short term was seen to be to increase access to housing locations between the more congested urban areas and outer estates.

Strategies should relate not only to areas but to household categories and issues of dwelling type, space and tenure, and to potential for adjusting the stock itself. Elements tailored to community needs could, in appropriate cases, include conversions to create larger dwellings (or re-conversions of sub-divided properties), adaptable housing where units can be combined or sub-divided later, and (if viable) opportunities for low cost home ownership. Programmes attempting to encourage minority ethnic households into areas of primarily white settlement are unlikely to be straightforward, even with good planning and supportive community development strategies. Unfortunately, research by Phillips and Unsworth (2002) found that the resources and political will to devise and implement institution-led initiatives to widen locational choices for minority ethnic groups were often lacking (see Chapter 2). Of course, this is not easy policy territory, especially without adequate information on the changing dynamics of local demand and preferences, or the varying implications these might have for very specific neighbourhoods containing private or social rented dwellings (and where, in some cases of low demand, selective demolition may remain appropriate).

Community cohesion and needs

Chapter 7 noted the importance of the needs of asylum seekers, where issues of planning to facilitate integration and reduce tensions will be crucial for a cohesion agenda. More generally, however, policy-makers in housing may be tempted to consider 'cohesion indicators' alongside needs ones. As well as being aware of pitfalls noted in Chapter 5, practitioners should distinguish here between individuals' housing needs and concerns derived from more collective or managerial goals. Any decision to prioritise socio-economic or ethnic mixing in social rented housing allocations (or within market renewal or urban regeneration) would have to be clearly justified, especially if it deprived demonstrably needy households of opportunities. (For discussion of lettings and community cohesion see Fotheringham and Perry, 2003.) In earlier years it was feasible to offer council dwellings to certain key workers because they were people upon whom other jobs might depend, and today's official guidance allows space for essential workers such as nurses, but this in principle is different from arguing a case in terms of urgent individual need. Creating mixed communities is likewise concerned less with immediate household needs than with management or political goals. If it rests on the basis of reliable local information about likely effects, and accommodates the preferences of disadvantaged households and opens up choices for them, then it could be acceptable. If not, then it may undermine needs-orientated strategies.

In any event, community cohesion indicators or 'measures' of integration have no place within a needs study unless they reflect concerns clearly expressed from within disadvantaged communities about barriers to housing choice or participation. Well thought-out measures and investigations of exclusion, however, could be useful in shedding light on urgent or neglected needs. Thus, the under-representation of particular groups or categories of households in better types of housing, or in specific types of allocation process (transfers, consideration on medical grounds or as a disabled person, etc.) might deserve investigation in case there was an underlying problem of unfairness in the meeting of needs, or hidden difficulties and problems of take-up. Similarly, any effects would need checking from over-representation in a particular channel (such as the homelessness route). Strategies of linked or block allocations (as noted above), into an estate with previous under-representation of minority ethnic households, might be appropriate for an area with strong demand if they helped bring the range of opportunities open to such households closer to those of comparable white groups, although other households' rehousing claims would also need to be considered and weighed up.

Local needs studies

Local authorities have a duty to assess housing needs, and are expected to pay attention to those of black and minority ethnic households. There is a wide choice of targets which a local needs study may address, going well beyond an evaluation aimed at facilitating strategies for social renting. Immediate goals might include assessing the housing difficulties of households with particular characteristics, assessing physical deficiencies of dwellings, measuring failures of supply or affordability, discovering people's preferences, assessing claims to priority for support, adaptations or accommodation, analysing broader issues linked to collective notions of need (such as those implicit in ideas about community regeneration), or examining equality of opportunities, fairness in service delivery, and cultural sensitivity of treatment. When it comes to using the information gathered, it may:

- help in discussions of housing development or improvement plans;
- underpin bids for funds;
- aid the rationing of accommodation via allocation;
- give pointers for services improvement;
- or increase the input of 'user' views.

On the other hand, critics may see surveys and consultations as ways to provide apparently technical justifications for a particular way forward, or as an aspect of delaying tactics.

The two boxes which follow highlight possibilities for productive targets and potentially poor practice.

Box 34: Some of the diverse and inter-connecting goals of local needs studies

- To assess housing difficulties of households with particular characteristics or experiences.
- To assess physical deficiencies of dwellings.
- To analyse or measure barriers or 'shortfalls' affecting supply or affordability.
- To discover households' experiences, preferences, satisfactions or worries.
- To help determine (or test with users) specific immediate priorities for investment, services and development.
- To help analyse broader issues linked to collective notions of need (such as those implicit in ideas about community regeneration). Groups may have preferences and views about needs that are shared or go beyond individual households.
- To review or audit equality of housing opportunities, fairness and 'reach' in service delivery, or cultural sensitivity of treatment. This could embrace private sector agencies as well as public and voluntary ones.
- To gather information and test support for specific bids for funds.
- To inform the rationing of accommodation and finance.

Box 35: How critics sometimes perceive the goals of 'top-down' needs studies

- To provide an apparently technical rationale for a particular way forward that has already been decided upon.
- To demonstrate that consultation has been carried out, or that there is support from users or communities, for a strategy or bid that has already been decided upon or over which little choice will be offered.
- To justify or paper over delays in progress.

Whatever their other aims, local needs studies may well reveal evidence of relatively poor housing conditions. For instance, a Sheffield study found that 11 per cent of respondents shared a living room with another household, 12 per cent a kitchen, 11 per cent bathroom/toilet facilities and 8 per cent a bedroom. Twenty per cent of owner-occupiers in the study reported rain coming through their roofs, 33 per cent problems with damp, 42 per cent with condensation, and 21 per cent with plumbing and drainage (Gidley *et al.*, 2002, p. 68).

The Housing Corporation has been proactive in encouraging local needs studies in England, and many local organisations – not just councils – have played important roles. Local needs studies have often provided useful new information, and have sometimes generated ideas to feed into the policy agenda or to help with target setting. As well as official encouragement for such studies, there has been guidance on methodologies. Methods range from social audits of existing services and practices through to focus groups and substantial household surveys, and quite a few studies have dealt usefully with specialised issues such as housing for elders, aspects of impairment, or circumstances in particular minority ethnic communities (for coverage see Matthias, 2001 and Sodhi *et al.*, 2001, 2001a). Unfortunately, some types of investigative strategies inevitably reveal more about the people that use services than about those who do not. For instance, practical considerations may make it tempting to turn to local service or community centres for sampling purposes, or when assembling focus groups, but this could give us an incomplete choice of informants. With the passage of time, awareness has grown of differentiation within broad minority ethnic categories (and of potential problems when drawing boundaries between households on grounds of ethnicity). Alongside local studies there have also been various investigations carried out over more than one geographical area, a good recent example being a study of Somalis which sought to fill gaps in knowledge related to this less visible group (Cole and Robinson, 2003).

Key points about BME needs studies

To summarise the situation on needs studies we now emphasise nine key points. After this there are brief comments on gender, age and disability. Box 36 and our discussion draw partly on our study for the ODPM (Harrison with Phillips, 2003).

Box 36: Needs studies: the record and prospects summarised

1. There have been a large number of local studies of black minority ethnic housing needs and associated topics, and these have enriched the understanding that policy-makers, researchers and local communities have of problems. Inevitably, however, many studies are primarily 'snapshots' taken at a particular moment, and there may be no research capacity to revisit households later, or to assess the responses made by agencies to findings. After some initial impact, a study might well end up 'gathering dust' on a shelf.

2. Studies have highlighted both the diverse needs of different communities and the commonality of housing experiences across some groups. There are frequent income and affordability problems affecting housing, and access problems in terms of social housing. Low-income white households may share some of the problems with black minority ethnic people.

3. Studies have often focused on specific issues or groups, and there is a strong case for continuing such work, especially where it has policy relevance, or connects with previously neglected or hidden difficulties, preferences and experiences. More knowledge about particular religious groups and their needs might be helpful when dealing with design or community development issues. Local investigators should try to be inclusive in relation to disabled people, illness, gender and age, taking account of the potential diversity of preferences, conditions, problems and opportunities within as well as between households if relevant.

4. In many instances it is desirable to conduct research in co-operation with local communities, and to ensure that local people share in any financial benefits that the research exercise itself can bring. Local people might be offered training, or be drawn into consultancy or mentoring roles, and community-based organisations might have roles to play in research. 'Option appraisal' (looking into alternatives for meeting needs) should be an inclusive process involving local people.

5. The methodologies, measures and indicators available for needs studies are varied, and there is potential for disagreements about how far a specific type of information is actually a good guide to needs in a particular locality or community.

   For instance, 'traditional' measures of households' relative needs may under-value isolation or potential harassment, or perhaps even over-crowding, while minority ethnic households could be under-represented amongst groups taken as 'urgent' categories, such as recognised medical priority cases.

   At the same time, some BME households have been prepared to forego higher dwelling quality to achieve more security from harassment, to avoid perceived dangerous localities, or to become or remain owner-occupiers.

6. The auditing of practices and performance is a useful adjunct or component of needs studies, capable of highlighting under-provision or low take-up, and other issues affecting minorities. It is important to up-date the focus in line with changes in law and practice, and to consider private as well as public and voluntary sector housing providers. Monitoring ought to ensure a regular flow of useful information that can feed into needs studies and statements when appropriate. Findings from periodic monitoring should be reported and discussed as standard practice, with firm officer and committee responsibilities to appraise progress and respond.

   (For the range and detail of monitoring tasks to be considered, see Blackaby and Chahal, *Black and Minority Ethnic Housing Strategies: a good practice guide*, 2000.)

→

The impact of stock transfers to new social rented landlords should be scrutinised, checking for any implications that possible fragmentation of council stocks might have for offering an integrated service, or for differentiation of choices between ethnic groups. The advent of new priorities or systems for social renting (such as choice-based lettings) should generate prompt auditing and monitoring responses. It is important to evaluate effects for different categories of households. Investigators should check the impact of criteria used for priority and weightings, and the role of waiting time and age categorisations in determining outcomes. Reports suggest some positive results from recent changes in lettings practices, including increased numbers of applications from minority ethnic households, and effects achieved by increasing the points available for over-crowding (see Robinson *et al.*, 2004, p. 29; Blackaby, 2004, p. 57).

7. Attention needs to be given to the possibility that there may sometimes be an ongoing mismatch between available policy levers on the one hand, and the preferences or needs revealed for minority ethnic groups on the other. One argument is that insofar as policy and investment preoccupations continue to emphasise social rented housing rather than the private sectors, there presently may be too few means of responding to housing and allied disadvantages for some of the communities whose needs are being researched. This issue of mismatch deserves further analysis, and has potential implications for policy.

8. The issue of local needs studies should be kept under review nationally and regionally, with attention paid to indicators that have been under-utilised, to possibilities of social audit approaches being developed further, and to the question of whether in the longer term any more dynamic notion of needs would be capable of being operationalised. For local and regional practitioners, it would be useful to check how far needs studies have been acted upon, and on factors affecting the responses to them of provider organisations.

9. Autonomy, a degree of self-management, and opportunities to influence decisions can be important aspects of housing need, but have been inadequately monitored both in the context of social renting and specialised provision. Needs studies might seek to audit participation and representation in a variety of contexts. For insights into relevant issues, readers may consult findings recently published by the ODPM on involvement of BME tenants and communities, relating particularly to stock investment options and planning for meeting government's Decent Homes Standard. A guide has been produced by a team from the Centre for Urban and Regional Studies at the University of Birmingham, and the work highlights barriers that need to be assessed, effective consultation, increasing trust and engagement, option appraisal, the roles of Independent Tenant Advisors (including BME organisations), and recruitment onto boards and steering groups.

(See Mullins *et al.*, *Empowering communities, improving housing: involving black and minority ethnic tenants and communities*, 2004, at the ODPM's website, or in hard copy.)

Disability, age, gender and specific needs

Investigations into minority ethnic housing needs have indicated the importance of disability and chronic illness (see for instance Kearns, 2002, p. 252), and needs for services, support or adaptations are likely to grow. Law noted from a Leeds study of the 1990s that minority ethnic households were under-represented amongst households with medical priority, and that at least in this particular city a low percentage of minority ethnic households were then receiving Disabled Facilities Grant (Law, 1996). Begum has referred to the '... *dual impact of race and disability*', highlighting how people may be placed thereby in a unique, and '... *particularly disadvantaged position*' (1992, p. 13). Older disabled people from BME communities living outside extended households may well face problems of extreme isolation and very low incomes, and there have been indications of considerable and growing need for sheltered bed-spaces, very sheltered units, aids, adaptations and residential care among elders in some places (see Harrison with Phillips, 2003, pp. 55-56). Chamba *et al.* have noted that institutionalised racism, lack of consultation with black minority ethnic communities, and stereotypical beliefs about black families are all problems that have been identified within service provision to black families with a disabled child (1999, p. 1). Parents here may face financial hardship and unsuitable housing. Radia's study in London (1996) showed that Asian mental health service users experienced problems of inappropriate housing, difficulties with neighbours, burglaries, racist attacks or harassment, and fears for their personal safety. Users lacked adequate support to be able to take charge of their own lives, and services were not culturally-sensitive. Radia indicates ways forward, including offering a range of quality supported independent housing and residential care, specialist housing, and trained outreach support workers to service both residential projects and those people living more independently in the community.

It has been argued that BME older people are more likely to face a greater level of poverty, live in poorer quality housing, and have poorer access to benefits and pensions than white older people (JRF, 2004a). Yet it is important to avoid stereotypes about the needs of elders or disabled people. Different minority ethnic communities may have differing and changing expectations about service provision, and about the structures of family life and inter-generational patterns of support. Policy-makers should be wary of over-estimating the preparedness of service users' relatives, extended families and social networks to provide informal care. A South Asian community might well use housing differently from white households, and thus have less present need for separate elders' accommodation but more need for large family dwellings; but this should be verified in specific localities. People may be 'left out' of kinship arrangements. Furthermore, lack of explicit demand for a service will not necessarily imply absence of need, since problems of communications or cultural insensitivity of provision may diminish take-up. Aiming for culturally-sensitive services can mean rethinking matters ranging from the personnel employed on a specialised scheme (and the skills required of them, such as community language abilities), to dwelling design (see Penoyre and Prasad *et al.*, 1993). Valued aspects of sensitive services could include empathy and understanding, culturally specific and identity-conscious practices, and safe and empowering environments where negative stereotyping is limited (see Chahal, 2004, p. 8).

Looking ahead, a predicted steep increase in numbers of elders within certain communities, taken alongside an altered ratio of younger to older people, is likely to increase needs in many places for community services, and may reduce the potential for households to arrange informal care. Practitioners keen on making accommodation appeal to elders might aim for low risks of harassment and crime, culturally-sensitive staffing, outreach or support services that respond to the desire for respect, design that takes culture into account, proximity to family, and closeness to community, shops and places of worship. A group of interviews by Comrie in Leeds showed that African/Caribbean elders lack knowledge and awareness about renovation and repair grants, want more information about sheltered housing, residential and nursing homes in their area, and want something done about the level of crime and anti-social behaviour in their neighbourhood. Those from all tenures wanted to continue living independently in their own homes or to be housed in a bungalow or sheltered accommodation (Comrie, 2004). Other recent findings from the same city for the Chinese community show elders increasingly in need of improved housing, social care and health services provision (Law, 2004).

To reinforce the point made above about different minority groups having differing expectations, we can refer to Manchester research by Karn *et al.* (1999). This found the needs and preferences of elders apparently rather different for each ethnic group studied. African/Caribbean informants emphasised independence and had positive views of sheltered housing, although finding inadequate cultural sensitivity in the way specific sheltered schemes were run. For South Asians it seemed that good domiciliary services and flexible forms of housing (allowing older and younger generations to live with or near each other) were likely to be most effective. Nonetheless, over-crowding might put severe strain on arrangements for families caring for their own elders, who could themselves favour greater space and privacy. Adaptation of their own (or family's) homes remains one useful model for meeting elders' needs, while (given a shortage of larger dwellings) acquisition and allocation of adjacent properties might be useful, perhaps with consideration given to possibilities such as a connecting door, or simply members of an extended family living next door to each other (see Karn *et al.*, 1999, p. 134).

Local needs analyses may benefit from distinct coverage of the experiences of women from minority communities, illuminating issues such as unacknowledged (or hidden) homelessness, limited choice and problems of quality in social renting, and stigma associated with separation from families, partners or communities. There are also difficulties in private markets because of low incomes, and hazardous housing pathways linked to domestic violence or abuse (cf Gill, 2002). Gender is potentially significant for housing destinations, interacting with other factors (including income, age, and ethnicity) to give complex patterns of experience. Interestingly, in a recent review of studies, Kusminder Chahal notes that the differences between the experiences of men and women were often sharper than the differences between different ethnic groups (Chahal, 2004, p. 2). In any event, relative disadvantage has been experienced by female heads of household, whether single persons or heads of families, and social rented accommodation features very significantly when households are female-headed. A recent report on Muslim households' housing indicates that, contrary to received opinion, census levels for one-person and lone-parent households within this group are approaching levels similar to those for the total population (Housing Corporation, 2004a).

Refuge and support services can play important roles, as they may for white households. Black minority ethnic women needing assistance may prefer a refuge outside their local area for reasons of safety, but want accommodation in places with substantial minority ethnic populations, to be able to have access to culturally specific facilities and avoid racism. Needs may be especially acute for women facing a '... *dual problem of racism from the wider society and rejection from their own communities*', while the '... *specific needs of children of mixed parentage often remain unrecognised*' (Rai and Thiara, 1997, p. 9). A study by Ahmed and Sodhi (2000) found that few black and minority ethnic women in Rochdale knew about supported housing. Service providers identified a range of provision in terms of accommodation type and levels of support to meet the diverse needs of women, and highlighted specific gaps in service provision for women with high support needs. Very few Asian women identified a need for supported housing, but many identified a need for support, and some wanted to be close to cultural facilities. Ahmed and Sodhi also point to a need for greater provision of women-only, age- and culturally specific schemes, and more discrete provision for those escaping domestic violence (p. iv).

There are many other specific groups of housing users for whom information might be valuable, but some needs remain very under-researched. It would be useful, for instance, to know more about housing trajectories, barriers and opportunities for younger men, and to review prospects for enhanced interventions here to manage risks or facilitate constructive options. We also have surprisingly little detailed empirical research on housing conditions focused primarily around the perspectives and circumstances of children in BME households and communities. Potentially, insights into children's housing and neighbourhood experiences might be set within an understanding of a wider range of factors enhancing or inhibiting their development and opportunities. The topic of children's housing needs seems urgent in view of what we have noted earlier in this book about the impact of poverty.

Some conclusions

Housing needs for black and minority ethnic households should be reviewed regularly, but a needs study should not become an end in itself, to meet formal performance expectations, or something which is filed away and not acted upon. Investigation, monitoring and audit activities should be connected systematically into ongoing mainstream processes of policy review and development. At the same time, needs studies can offer means for helping communities improve their knowledge about conditions, trends and services through participating in research, consultancy and audit. To avoid this being perceived as tokenism, research budgets should cover employment of local people as well as experienced professionals, and the research itself should be more than an isolated 'one off' enquiry. Although communications problems may remain obstacles to discovering or fully reflecting people's views (and some voices may be missing when community representatives are invited to come forward), community engagement is important. Carefully targeted surveys and consultations remain good ways for checking that practices are going in the right directions, and hitting the best targets for households in terms of aspirations and expectations. This should sit alongside well-established processes of regular data collection, monitoring and audit. Consultation and participation for elders, women, youth, and disabled people from minority communities will be important in relation to ongoing research focused on improved provision and services. For disabled people, participation in running of specific enterprises deserves attention, with emphasis shifting from care and containment to helping participants develop choice and independence, since these may be crucial aspects of need.

We noted in Box 35 the criticism that needs studies can become a means for justifying delays, but systematic work on needs does not have to stand in the way of rapid positive responses to known problems. Practitioners can pick out points for swift action, sometimes acting as advocates for the needs of people who are not themselves well represented politically. An example from a Midlands city in the early 1990s, on tackling harassment, illustrates how a great deal can be attempted through a committed approach to immediate better practice, involving individual officers (Box 37).

Box 37: Getting involved to generate swift action

'In 1990 the Housing Department decided to make racist incidents one of its highest priorities. We decided that the six members of the directorate would themselves be on call outside office hours, be in radio contact, etc., and be linked to the police, so that when an incident occurred one of us would arrive with or soon after the police. All staff could see that the issue was being taken seriously and they gave priority to the follow up work needed with both the victim and the perpetrator. People who experienced regular problems, but wanted to stay where they were, could have an emergency call system like the elders' call system, which worked 24 hours. This worked well for some time and was eventually integrated with day-to-day work and the special arrangement ended. It was also very good for us as senior managers, as we experienced the problems directly and could discuss them at our weekly meetings, sorting out any problems quickly.'
(Former senior housing officer)

Practical actions for landlords here might also include providing specific 'defensive' adaptations, fittings or equipment promptly at people's homes. At the end of the 1980s Leicester City Council's plan to install emergency buttons at homes of tenants who suffered racist attacks (backed up with 24-hour call-out support) was sufficiently innovative to reach the national press (*The Guardian*, April 3rd 1989). A crucial point is that innovation and discovering 'what works' should be continuous processes, to which systematic needs studies could contribute regularly. At the same time, proactive individuals can make a difference, despite the importance of entrenched patterns of exclusion. This potential has long been acknowledged in phrases like 'equality champion', 'equal opportunities champion' or 'equality and diversity champion', and roles of this kind can sometimes be catered for explicitly within staffing structures.

Pathways, trajectories and assets

To understand people's longer-term housing needs more fully, analysts should probably move in the direction of a pathways concept, catering for a more dynamic account of households' circumstances, constraints, strategies and prospects. Alongside data on the present, this would require knowledge of routes and paths over slightly longer periods, from the past and into the future. Ideally, a reasonably holistic perspective would be sought on people's strategies and needs, taking some account of matters of finance, employment, religion, ethnicity, health, social support, educational plans and so forth. Insights might be accumulated on key processes of change across neighbourhoods, or for particular groups or cohorts.

Unfortunately, there are many obstacles to developing dynamic and holistic accounts. It could be problematic trying to unravel strategies, histories, and future prospects within quantitatively-framed interviewing exercises carried out under tight resource constraints. There might be mixed feelings from informants about some options (such as the prospect of older persons continuing to live with younger relatives), while people may lack adequate information about a proposition such as shared ownership, so that it forms no part of their effective range of choices. Even if informants are interested in revealing their hardships or plans, questions might arise about how seriously felt a problem or need is. Nonetheless, local investigations of needs and expectations certainly may go beyond reviewing specific immediate conditions or preferences, and seek more speculative information about longer-term changes for households. At the same time, it may be possible to take note not only of affordability and physical housing quality issues, but also cultural concerns, security, and constraints arising from harassment. If there is a general answer that goes part-way to dealing with problems of uncertainty and depth for investigators, it may lie in a mix of methods: scanning a good range of opinions and data, holding ongoing discussions about the practicality and costs of options, and learning as much as possible about relevant trends and experiences in particular neighbourhoods.

As indicated in Box 36 (9), autonomy is an important aspect of housing need. This may be affected by landlord/tenant relationships and tenant participation rights, as well as by rights derived from user control of property assets. We have argued elsewhere (Harrison with Phillips, 2003, 10.2) that one route for policies might be to develop in the direction of 'assets based' concepts of welfare, in which support might focus more on helping people (individually or collectively) establish or sustain a stake in housing property, and on diminishing or covering some of the risks encountered. This approach does not seek to put tenure preferences or arrangements ahead of urgent needs, such as adequate sanitation or settled accommodation for homeless households. Rather, the argument is that autonomy is an important need that can be met in a variety of ways, and that rights of ownership or control will often play a part in these over the longer term. In reviewing possible BME household pathways, analysts might investigate the potential for collective forms of ownership or equity acquisition (through co-ops, self-builds, estate transfers to tenant ownership, community land ownership, etc.). Perhaps there may be more potential than has been acknowledged for transferring ex-local authority stock into the ownership of black and minority ethnic-run organisations, including housing associations and co-ops, or for involvement of black-run bodies in joint ventures and federal structures for taking control or collective ownership as transfers occur.

Turning to policies focusing on individual ownership, we suggest that to be effective these should take account of potential constraints relating to financial viability and affordability in specific places. Prospects for owning vary geographically and shift with trends in house prices and labour markets. Policy-makers seeking to develop specific schemes may need an up-to-date overview of the local potential for low cost ownership, alongside an awareness of any barriers implicit in interactions between costs, available public funding, rules, availability of sites or dwellings, and household incomes. Existing owners also deserve attention. Burrows has shown not only that half of all people living in poverty in Britain today are home owners, but that being from BME groups is one of the factors associated with those owners more likely to be in poverty (JRF, 2003). Karn *et al.* (1999) ask to what extent the preference for owner-occupation is likely to be undermined by realities of poor conditions and repair costs, and what steps can be taken to ensure the viability of home ownership or alternative tenures in older terraced areas, especially where grants are not available. Unfortunately, local policy levers remain limited as far as 'down-market' owner-occupation is concerned, although sustainability might be enhanced through improvement grants and other types of support. Given more funds, we might see expanded use of a range of tactics such as extensions or loft conversions for large families, adaptations, equipment and enlargement related to impairment and chronic illness, 'knocking through' of dwellings, and so forth.

An important option when considering needs strategies might be to build more often on the existing 'gateway' roles BME housing associations play in relation to tenants contemplating social renting, by developing in the direction of a broader range of functions connected with ownership, shared equity, community investment, maintenance, social support and sustainability (see also Chapter 4). The right to buy might be handled more explicitly as a possible component in local authority or RSL strategic planning for minority ethnic choice, although benefits would need to be weighed against any potential disadvantaging effects for low-income households. While tenure preferences are open to revision in the light of specific changes (in family, jobs or incomes), access to social renting may form part of a longer-term strategy for some tenants looking to buy a dwelling at a feasible price (although the impact of family circumstances on this route to ownership should not be overlooked, especially as regards single parent households on low incomes). Shared ownership is a potentially important field for further policy development, overlapping with regeneration policy and with planning for greater choice in outward movement.

Box 38: Could we work towards more dynamic and holistic needs analyses?

To engage fully with households' needs, policy-makers and researchers could try to develop more dynamic accounts of circumstances, constraints and prospects. This would combine data on the present with knowledge about people's housing pathways over slightly longer periods, from the past and into the future.

In ideal circumstances a holistic perspective would be sought on people's strategies and needs, taking some account of finance, employment, religion, ethnicity, health, social support, educational plans and housing across a neighbourhood. This might reveal how people's housing strategies fit in with their other circumstances and intentions.

Both the above goals might in practice be very hard to achieve for a needs study, and perhaps the more sophisticated an understanding of specific groups became, the more difficult it could be to generalise. On the other hand, the two ideas do suggest some ways of thinking about need that might be useful when designing a study.

Issues of autonomy, ownership and control are relevant to people's housing pathways, and a genuinely holistic approach to longer-term needs would encompass tenure, assets, participation, and minimising of risks.

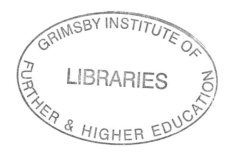

Chapter 9:
Racist harassment and anti-racist strategies

Kusminder Chahal

As we have indicated in earlier chapters, racist harassment involves far more than spontaneous insults or mindless physical acts in the street or playground. It can restrict people's choices of housing locality, jobs or schools, and affects the ways in which they plan and conduct their daily lives. Harassment can range from isolated and apparently personalised incidents of expressed hostility, to pre-arranged individual or collective campaigns of aggression. This book highlights the contemporary challenges of the community cohesion debate and the issue of asylum seekers, but (as other chapters have already made clear), that should not mean downgrading the concern to combat harassment. Indeed, it can be argued that a serious approach to community cohesion must include at its heart the kinds of anti-racist strategies and procedures that help diminish the incidence of this unacceptable behaviour. Households should not have to live under threat, and inclusion or integration into the wider society require firm rules, really effective and visible inter-organisational working, and well-resourced practices to prevent intimidation and abuse.

Following recent changes brought about by a European Community Directive, the Race Relations Act itself now states that harassment on the grounds of race, ethnic or national origin is unlawful (for comment on the Directive see Ahmed Iqbal Ullah, *Race and Housing Research Briefing 9*, 2003). In the past, harassment has been treated very much as a public order offence (being covered, for example, by more general provisions on threatening, abusive or insulting words, behaviour or display within the Public Order Act 1986), but more specific legal coverage has developed recently. The Protection from Harassment Act of 1997 dealt with threats, verbal abuse, written abuse, distressing behaviour, non-violent physical harassment, damage to property, violent behaviour, and following, standing or parking a vehicle outside someone's house. Additionally, the Crime and Disorder Act 1998 tackled a number of racially aggravated offences that now carry higher penalties than the equivalent 'basic' offence. Complementing criminal law provisions, social housing providers may use tenancy agreements and their authority as landlords to limit anti-social activities including harassment.

Racist harassment is officially defined as occurring when someone's actions or words, based on race, ethnic origin or national origin, are unwelcome and violate another person's dignity or create an environment that is intimidating, hostile, degrading, humiliating or offensive. It should be understood that racist harassment may differ from certain other types of incidents which are also perceived as matters of conflict or tension, but which may not be part of a pattern of denigration or racialisation. Thus, there are differences between tackling racist harassment on the one hand, and defusing localised inter-ethnic tensions or unplanned outbreaks of street conflict between white and non-white people on the other. Furthermore, as one of the early reports on harassment in housing observed, racist harassment should not '... *be regarded as just a rather nasty type of inter-tenant dispute*' (London Race and Housing Forum, 1981, p. 5). Racist harassment is rooted systematically in the labelling of people as 'different', and as outsiders who are apparently open to intimidation on a day-in, day-out basis. The outsider may be blamed for having resources, rights or opportunities that the racist may feel he or she has been personally deprived of, or should not have to share.

Not all racist attacks are against people who are seen as being non-white, but black minority ethnic people are far more likely to experience such harassment than are white households. The British Crime Survey results of 2000 indicated that the chance of being a white victim of a racially motivated incident is considerably less than being a black or Asian victim and that people of Pakistani and Bangladeshi origin were far more likely to be victims than any other group (Home Office, 2001). Some perpetrators may simply attach racist abuse or intimidation to their angers that have arisen out of relatively small local grievances. Although the most appropriate response here may be a relatively mild one such as mediation or a civil remedy (for example an injunction), these kinds of harassment may easily become part of a damaging pattern if not checked. For the more active racist, however, the outsider is a potential permanent 'target' who may be kept from becoming a full mainstream citizen with normal rights of movement, interaction, access, and participation. The perpetration of 'hate crimes' may be towards this end.

Racist victimisation turns normal, daily activities into assessments of personal safety and security. This analysis may apply to some degree not only in the racialisation of black minority ethnic groups, but also to harassment across religious divides amongst white people (as in Northern Ireland). Steps have been taken recently through UK legislation to limit the scope for discrimination against workers because of religion or similar beliefs (including subjecting someone to harassment), and it should not be forgotten that non-white people may be targeted overtly in terms of their religious affiliations although the attack may actually be a racist one aimed at them because they appear ethnically different. Since hate crimes may also be targeted at people who are 'different' in terms of sexuality, disability or gender, there can be households who are under threat for these reasons at the same time as for ethnicity.

This chapter builds on some previous research involving the present writer, and supported by the Joseph Rowntree Foundation (see Chahal and Julienne, 1999; Chahal, 2003), but is also informed by the ongoing work of other key researchers in the field (see especially Lemos, 2000; and JRF, 2000a). The focus below is primarily on harassment and its implications, and on direct ways of reducing it, but one must recognise that the wider context has to be one in which there is a range of anti-racist strategies in place. At the start, however it is essential to remind readers that those who experience harassment should not be viewed as inactive people who simply receive ill-treatment and do nothing in response. Households experiencing harassment adopt strategies, plans and tactics to deal with the problems, and may resist the perpetrators or handle the effects in varied ways. This points to the significance (noted elsewhere in the book) of good communications and consultation with households, both for policy-makers and for employees at the community level.

Experiences of harassment

Not only is harassment a widespread phenomenon, but it is a very serious and longstanding one. Nonetheless, it was probably not until the late 1970s and early 1980s that the subject really began to get some of the official attention that it deserved. By this time the evidence was mounting that the problems might be widespread and serious. For good reason, the CRE's 1987 report on racist violence and harassment in housing appeared under the title *Living in Terror*. That report showed the severity of some events (including arson attack resulting in deaths), and illustrated the humiliating methods that may well have reflected the characteristic mindset of perpetrators. For example, in a cited South London case a woman and her family began to experience harassment three months after moving into a flat in 1983, with doors slammed in her face, and abuse and attacks on her children when they went outside to play. The children were sometimes tied up or had their heads banged against walls by white youths, and were even put in the large communal dustbins and left there, their clothes having been removed first. As time went on, harassment became very frequent, with her milk bottles being smashed and pushed through her letter box almost daily, her door urinated on, and lighted material or broken eggs put through the letter box. The tyres of her car were slashed and other damage was done, and stones and bottles were thrown against the windows late at night (CRE, 1987, p. 12).

Even after 20 years of reform efforts, such incidents still happen, so that this is a field where constant vigilance and support remain essential. Indeed, recent media treatment of asylum issues has probably increased the likelihood of severe harassment incidents for minorities. In the 1980s attention was drawn to a big agenda of issues needing consideration in housing contexts. They included:

- the under-reporting of the problem;
- the importance of improving policies, monitoring and procedures;
- the significance of support systems for those who wanted to 'stay put';
- effective action against perpetrators;
- liaison between agencies; and
- good communication of policies locally.

Quite a few of the issues discussed in earlier periods still remain salient two decades later. Recent reports have drawn attention to the slow and bureaucratic responses to harassment by housing departments, the need for more sensitivity to victims and their families, and the limited feedback and support infrastructure to help those making complaints. For housing practitioners it is important to appreciate that a substantial body of evidence and experience has shown harassment to be a major problem in or near to the home. This will be where many of the incidents occur. Thus staff involved with housing management and neighbourhood anti-social behaviour are potentially in the front line when it comes to dealing with 'hate crimes'. A central point to understand is the continuity of incidents and adverse experiences over time, and the limitations of tackling this through focusing only on isolated reported incidents.

'We can't all be white'
(Chahal and Julienne, Joseph Rowntree Foundation, 1999)

The above sentence was the title chosen for the 1999 report written by the present author with Louis Julienne, and was spoken by one of our informants. We drew on fieldwork in four areas across the UK to explore experiences of racist victimisation in and around the home for people who had reported incidents, and to establish how people articulated experiences of racism, regardless of whether they had reported them or not, their location and time-frame. A depressing and regular feature in people's responses was that interviewees evidenced the 'routine' nature of racism. Racisms had become part of every-day experience in a variety of social situations, not just in and around the home but in shops, in the street and at school. Various encounters had made informants aware of their apparent 'difference' as perceived by white people, and there had been a variety of types of incident. The most commonly mentioned had been verbal abuse, but intimidation and attacks on property took second highest place. It is worth noting that unpleasant 'bodily offences' or animal excrement may form regular parts of harassment technique, as perhaps they sometimes may within what is perceived currently as 'anti-social behaviour' more generally in housing areas. Thus one victimised person described how the perpetrators had '... *threatened me, called me names, puked, peed and shat on my stairs*', and another observed that the perpetrator '... *threw dog shit at my daughter*'. While some assaults formed part of an obvious behavioural pattern, others could be sudden, ferocious and entirely unexpected, as in the case of an informant whose attacker had knocked on the door, come in, and made an attack (breaking nose and cheek bones), while the victim was cooking the Sunday dinner. One general effect of more regular abuse and violence is to restrict movement and social interaction, instilling caution or fear amongst adults, both for their children and themselves.

We found that the impact of racist victimisation had a profound effect beyond the actual events or incidents, affecting all those being targeted. Family relations between spouses were affected by the stresses, health and well-being were compromised, and there was an increased sense of social isolation because relatives and friends were less likely to visit, or reduced the numbers of their visits in face of threat or fear of perpetrators. Children were perhaps the most affected because they were not allowed to play outside and in some cases were having problems at school too. There was a heightened preoccupation with escorting children to and from school, and not leaving them to play outside unsupervised. Generally families seldom ventured out at night. Harassment also extended on occasion to friends of the children, as was described in reference to a three-and-a-half years old child who played with a family's daughter. He had been *'... headbutted by their* [the perpetrators'] *older son and called a "Paki lover"'*. The continuing routinised character of harassment was indicated in comments such as those in Box 39.

Box 39: Racisms as regular and ongoing parts of every-day life; some views from the grass roots

'I think everybody has been here for such a long time that they have learnt to adapt to their environment. You have been conditioned throughout your life to accept this as normal. You can't change it. It is not ... good for your self-confidence or self-esteem.'

'... to some extent you see discrimination and harassment as every-day life. For example, being called names.'

'Just because your colour is different or you look different you are either a "Paki" or a "Chinky". ... So many people have called me "Paki".'

'Young people have thrown stones at my windows and broken them. This always happens. I have wooden boards behind my windows to stop the glass from flying.'

'It happens all of the time. I cannot remember a particular incident. You don't know what time or where it is going to happen but it does happen.'

When harassment occurs, verbal racist abuse will often not be reported on its own, perhaps partly because (and however hurtful it may be) it is difficult to prove clearly. One of the problems with harassment is that an accumulation of apparently small or relatively minor incidents may build into a more damaging situation for an individual, and this could apply with shouted insults, graffiti, and similar acts. The threat of violence to persons or property, however, may be more likely to evoke a specific active response. People in our study made reasoned decisions on whether to report incidents, basing this on the extent of the threat, the likely response of agencies, and potential recriminations from those being reported. The particular context was significant for the response that was chosen (see Box 40).

Box 40: How contexts may shape responses people make to harassment

'If I experienced verbal abuse in the street I would not report it. But if I had it from a colleague I would report it because you face that person every day.'

'There are reasons why some people won't report ... [there is] the fact that they will face recriminations especially if they live in certain estates. ... There is not much that can be done, the police can't protect them.'

'People have lost confidence in the police, and in their landlords and housing associations. They tell you "what is the point of going there [to a reporting agency], they won't do anything".'

Importantly for analysts of housing, the 1999 report confirmed (in line with other studies in this field), that the home itself remains a prominent target for racists. As we mentioned earlier, the location of racist harassment is often close to or aimed at people's dwellings (see Chahal and Julienne, 1999, p. 4). Just as in the 1980s example mentioned above, our study showed that there might be eggs, rubbish thrown, offensive materials pushed through letter boxes, graffiti, vandalism, and so forth. A harrowing common experience for those with children was the reality and fear of racism when the children were going to and coming from school. In the majority of cases studied, the victims of harassment lived in areas occupied largely or entirely by white people, while being a woman and having children seemed to be relevant to being victimised. Other factors linked to victimisation seemed to include being new to the area, skin colour or cultural/religious identification, having a white partner, and gangs of young people 'hanging around'. We can note from the general literature that the issue of neighbourhoods of predominantly white residence has long been important with the development of 'no go' areas for non-white people at various points over the years (a matter mentioned earlier in this book). The maintenance of boundaries excluding black people has depended to some extent on harassment. Thus the clustering of minority households in specific areas of established minority ethnic settlement is often highly rational from a safety perspective (see Chapters 2 and 10). In any event, in our survey the main targets of racist perpetrators were mainly women where the spouse was seldom present during the incidents (usually because he was at work), while children and young people were often key factors in the victimisation process (both as perpetrators and as victims). When children or young people were the main perpetrators, this was often with the tacit or even explicit approval of their parents (although we should remember in any case that perpetrators tend to be drawn from both sexes and all age groups: Lemos, 2000, p. 8). It is probable that matters have got more difficult since 1999, especially for those people who appear to have visible Asian cultural affiliations, or who may be labelled by potential perpetrators as supposed asylum seekers. (There has also been an impact on Muslims in particular since the events of September 11th 2001 in the USA.)

One of our key findings concerned the array of strategies that households developed to prevent or minimise the harm of harassment. People acted as positively as they could, and tried to prevent victimisation from re-occurring or escalating. Their strategies ranged from trying to ignore, avoid or limit the possibility of racist victimisation, to challenging the perpetrators or the perpetrators' families, or reporting to an agency in hopes that some form of action would be taken. Even the simplest tasks, such as hanging up the washing or putting out the rubbish, became strategic events to be planned in advance. Thus, racist victimisation helped create strategists who acted to try to create or recreate some normality despite an oppressive environment, even if – in worst case scenarios – normality was restricted to life inside a heavily defended home. Families changed routines to prevent victimisation, and some protected property with security measures or physical deterrents (such as new fencing). In effect, racist harassment was managed and responded to in the specific circumstances in which it arose, within a more general context where there was a lack of direct support provided to people experiencing campaigns of victimisation. People who anticipate experiencing danger or threat may make an assessment of the risks to their safety or security, and in our study this had influenced perceptions both of neighbourhoods and of public events. On the latter, as one informant put it (referring to avoidance of the chance of violence), Asian people '... *do not go to football matches*'. As far as choice of housing locality was concerned, there were resonances with the views revealed in other studies and noted elsewhere in this book (see especially Chapter 10). Real choices of where to live are restricted for minorities by the anticipation of the kinds of negative experiences demonstrated by our informants. Indeed, in our records there were accounts of people having had to leave specific estates in the face of harassment, sometimes at considerable cost. Meanwhile (as is also noted in Chapter 10), the racisms that might be present in middle class or 'respectable' areas could seem less visible and overt than in working class estates, and thus less threatening and more manageable. Examples of observations are given in Box 41.

Box 41: Examples of comments on the character of neighbourhoods and the pressures of harassment

'I think if you live in a nice sort of middle class area, I'm not saying people are not racist but at least they might be polite to your face. But if you live in a rough area it is a known fact that there is more violence and crime. I'm not saying it is all racist but you are more likely to experience it. All the incidents I have heard about have occurred in these types of areas.'

'People in deprived areas do physically attack ethnic minority people. But that does not mean that people in the so-called nice areas are not prejudiced. And they have power as well. The power they show is not speaking to you, or belittling you, not mixing with you. The power people have in deprived areas is the power of force.'

'There was a Pakistani family who really got on well with their neighbours. They were so happy living in the area. But from a couple of streets away there were children who used to come and they were the only Pakistani family living in the street. They started to get frightened from the abuse and finally moved out from the area.'

→

'We hate living here. We are always under strain. You are always under pressure. ... You are always watching for something.'

'My children did not want to go out any more and they hated so much the area that they asked me all the time to move out from there. They could hardly sleep at night.'

'It was a nice property [that we previously lived in], it was central heated and me and my husband had spent so much money doing it up. I told the council I was only taking this property [the present one] because I was desperate and having a breakdown.'

'I was going to move but my child is settling. ... I thought what shall I do? I haven't done anything. I'm perfectly happy here. This guy [the perpetrator] is pushing me out.'

Policy responses: the gap between households and official anti-racist practices

There was something of a gap between the policies and procedures that had been developed to challenge racist victimisation and the experiences of those who were the principal targets of racism, suggesting a need for better listening, outreach and more effective responses by agencies. People often tried to cope without reporting an incident, perhaps hoping that matters could be resolved, but this might fail. One informant described how she and her husband had put up with many things (including dogs' excrement put through their letter box), but that it eventually became too much. As she put it, *'I had a miscarriage last year. We took the verbal abuse for four years'*, and then *'We went to the police and they said "you should have written this down, everything that has happened to you"'*. Unfortunately, making an official complaint to the police or local authority generally resulted in dissatisfaction with the organisation's response, although GPs proved a valuable source of help. The interviewees in our study felt isolated and abandoned, and there was not much to suggest an effective and systematic multi-agency response looking beyond the individual reported incidents.

Interpreting the situation, we would suggest that the service-led approach was not a good match for households' needs, which would have benefited from fuller efforts to handle the routinised continuities of racist activity as perceived from the grass roots. The 1999 report noted a frequent sense that independent, community-based agencies should exist, with capacity to monitor and support complainants, while there was a need for the opening up of access points for people to report, and to receive sympathetic treatment where the consequences of racist victimisation would be understood. Where minority ethnic organisations or other potential contacts might be available in an area, an improvement was needed in awareness and networking by police and white-run housing organisations, in order to channel people appropriately, sensitively, and swiftly. It is clear that slow or reluctant action by public bodies can leave households vulnerable, pushing them into moving home in situations where there are few safe destinations to choose from. Sometimes they may become homeless in an environment where ideas for temporary 'respite' provision or refuge accommodation for victims are under-developed or unheard of.

Developing better anti-racist practice and supporting those who are victimised

The study commented on above was distinctive in highlighting the issue of household strategies, but its findings nonetheless matched up well with material from other sources. Of course there will be local variations to monitor in the future, and new or less visible problems associated with specific circumstances or groups (such as asylum seekers in particular places). In addition, policy-makers will need to understand the broader housing market situations into which harassment experiences fit for minority ethnic groups and communities. Yet the main features, techniques and effects of harassment are certainly well enough known to provide strong indicators for policies and actions. The biggest weakness in current knowledge probably concerns the drivers and motivations of racist incidents and patterns of behaviour, including the attitudes and causes of aggressive activity from younger (mostly white) people. Improving ways of tackling this might require a considerably improved knowledge of socio-economic and cultural contexts, lifestyles and deprivations. In the long term, action on this front is probably essential in any effective plan for enhancing or building genuine community cohesion.

In fact many of the features which constitute good practice for housing providers today have been recognised for a very long time, and it is useful to list some basic ones from the 1980s to show the continuity.

Box 42: Policy recommendations in the 1980s

These included:

- Monitoring of all reported incidents.
- Clear designation of officer responsibilities (and where appropriate the appointment of specialist staff).
- Racial harassment as grounds for eviction in tenancy agreements.
- High priority transfer for victims where necessary.
- Prompt removal of graffiti.
- Work with tenants' associations, and regular consultation with local community groups.
- Regular liaison with police.
- The need for a sympathetic response to be built into staff training.
- Regular reporting of issues and progress to relevant committees.
- Informing all tenants of the council's stance, and encouraging victims to report incidents.

(See CRE, *Living in Terror*, 1987, p. 14)

Despite the recognition of many appropriate best practice principles so long ago, change has unfortunately not been quite as productive or fast as might have been hoped. Consequently the thrust of much of the recent constructive writing or discussion in the harassment field is still towards trying to suggest or develop better methods for tackling abuse and violence, bearing in mind the kinds of experiences that we have been illustrating. There has been, however, an increasingly sophisticated understanding of exactly what to focus on, so that debates about responses look much more developed than in earlier decades (and issues such as multi-agency working have more prominence). In parallel with this type of debate, there is a need for more investigations of the effectiveness of specific actions, and a better sharing of knowledge about what works or does not work. Amongst the most important positive steps taken recently has been the development of the innovative *RaceActionNet* by Lemos & Crane. This is a web-based action network dealing with racist harassment in the home and neighbourhood. It has over 1,000 members including local authorities, the police and criminal justice agencies, social landlords, and black and minority ethnic voluntary and community organisations. Members can access databases of action being taken in areas across the UK, download learning materials and legal guidance, take part in discussions and exchange ideas. Since its launch in March 2001, the network has highlighted a range of new and emerging problems and solutions (such as identifying alternatives to eviction as a result of racially motivated anti-social behaviour), and has brought together members to work on practical solutions through action research.

The development of the *RaceActionNet* was underpinned by a very substantial investigative exercise (see Lemos, 2000; JRF, 2000a). Researchers from Lemos & Crane interviewed 250 contacts from agencies tackling racist harassment in 67 local authority areas where the majority of black minority ethnic people live in England, Scotland, Wales and Northern Ireland. Respondents were asked to describe the types of action being taken by their own organisations and other agencies. Five main topic areas seen as keys to good practice formed the basis of the interviews.

These were:

- prevention and publicity (including multi-agency working);
- reporting and monitoring;
- support for people experiencing or witnessing racist harassment;
- action against perpetrators; and
- training for staff.

Informants were asked about a list of types of action under each of these main heads. The investigation revealed that most agencies felt under-reporting still to be a problem, and that, even when incidents were reported, they were not always recorded as racist and did not always generate an appropriate response. Multi-agency forums existed in most areas (although the larger cities outside London appeared to have the greatest difficulty sustaining them), but some experienced conflict or lacked resources. Efforts to establish 'third-party' reporting centres were patchy, as were reporting arrangements outside normal working hours other than to the emergency services. The term 'third-party' here refers to independently-based locations such as a medical clinic, mosque, community centre, and so forth, where complainants can present themselves.

As far as support for victims was concerned, this was more likely to be available in areas where there was a specialist agency working on racist harassment. When provided, support might include advice, counselling for victims (in one-third of the areas), personal alarms and mobile telephones, and home security improvements for social housing tenants. Alarms were provided for vulnerable tenants in most areas, being seen as offering frightened tenants reassurance. They could be linked to a local council's careline for older and disabled residents. Twenty-four hour helplines, however, were only available in some areas. Few areas had in-depth counselling by trained staff familiar with harassment, and in many areas what was on offer could be more accurately described as advice rather than counselling. Very few social housing tenants were transferred as a result of racist harassment, while many social landlords felt that the priority was dealing with perpetrators rather than moving victims. Yet action against perpetrators still seemed to be rare. The research found that 10 to 15 per cent of reported incidents resulted in a prosecution, and only a tiny proportion of cases reported to social landlords resulted in possession action. The use of injunctions to stop harassment was rare, while anti-social behaviour orders by this time had only been used in three of the areas surveyed. Most frontline staff in police and housing services had received some training in equal opportunities or 'race awareness', although specific training on racist harassment was less common. A few areas were developing schemes to change the behaviour of perpetrators, and examples here included work with racist offenders by probation officers and community justice schemes for young offenders. Even so, programmes of this sort were rare.

As well as researching the existing situation in overall terms, Lemos & Crane produced several recommendations and located many instances of good practice. Box 43 notes some examples of innovations, and readers may find a fuller account in the Lemos report itself.

Box 43: Examples of innovations noted by Lemos & Crane

- Use of lay advisors to the police in racist incident panels.
- Restorative justice in harassment cases, where a trained police officer may chair a meeting between the perpetrator and the victims, confronting the offender with the impact of the harassment and agreeing on the amends to be made. A 'restorative caution' can be taken into account if the perpetrator re-offends. The approach is thought suitable for cases involving neighbours or people living near each other, but not for the most serious crimes.
- Self-help groups for victims of racist harassment (enabling isolated people to meet at a safe place away from home).
- A witness mobility scheme.
- One-stop shops and information hotlines for reporting racist incidents.
- Appointment of an anti-racist harassment worker in a private sector housing unit, providing advice and assistance to private tenants and owner-occupiers.

(See Lemos, *Racial Harassment: action on the ground*, 2000, pp. 28-46, etc.)

RaceActionNet has developed guidelines on how to interview people who have been racially harassed and who may be offering evidence against alleged perpetrators. The guidelines are instructive in how to undertake an interview following a victim-centred approach (see *Interviewing victims and witnesses: guidelines for housing practitioners, Part One and Two*, at: www.RaceActionNet. co.uk). These guidelines, organised in two parts, offer, for example, advice on key stages of the interview, information on effective listening skills, questioning and use of interpreters. The document is particularly relevant to local authorities and housing associations because the way a victim is interviewed has a critical impact on their perception of the support that they are getting, their ability to make decisions about what is in their best interests, and whether they co-operate in any legal action that follows. (For Lemos & Crane and *RaceActionNet* contact details, see the guide at the end of the book.)

Taking the right steps locally

It has long been clear that what is required is a sensitive, swift, co-ordinated response to hate crimes and harassment, coupled with mechanisms that encourage people to come forward. The DETR (now ODPM) code of 2001 (*Tackling racial harassment: code of practice for social landlords*) sets out action that all social landlords should take to prevent racist harassment under the following headings: working with other agencies; prevention and publicity; encouraging reporting; supporting victims and witnesses; and action against perpetrators. The Home Office *Code of Practice on Reporting and Recording Racist Incidents* (issued in 2000; see 2000b) highlights the expectation that victims should be treated in a sensitive and understanding manner. Among the good practice guidelines given for dealing with victims are those shown in Box 44.

Box 44: Good practice in responding to incidents (Home Office, 2000b)

- The agency that has the first contact with the victim or witness reporting an incident should respond in a sensitive way that shows an understanding of how victims of racist crimes may feel.
- Training should be provided for those who will make first contact with victims of racist incidents.
- If the victim wants the case to be referred to the police or another agency, this must be done as soon as practical.
- A locally agreed protocol should ensure that someone is responsible for keeping the victim informed of progress, whether that is the police, the agency that took the initial report or another agency.

(See Home Office, *Code of Practice on Reporting and Recording Racist Incidents*, 2000b, pp. 10-11.)

One important key to generating better responses from victims' perspectives (and to meeting general goals such as those exemplified in these Home Office statements) is likely to be the development and resourcing of specialist agencies, especially ones that have strong connections into local communities and networks. Their potential relevance in assisting victims was made clear both in our own 1999 study and in the subsequent report from Lemos & Crane (cf also Argent *et al.*, 2000, p. 60). Even on basic issues like encouraging the reporting of incidents, access to places where people feel safe and comfortable (or 'third-party' reporting centres unconnected with the police station or housing office) may be very important. Ideally, development through specialist agencies should take place in tandem with improvements in mainstream services, where dealing with racist incidents should be securely integrated into regular practice and inter-organisational planning. At present, however, the patchy capacities of that mainstream have to be acknowledged, reinforcing the case for specialist agencies playing an enhanced role in many places. (For an instance of what could be attempted in a proactive local authority, see our example in Chapter 8, Box 37).

As a result of a dearth of published information about community-based support projects, a specific investigation was undertaken by the present writer, with results being published in 2003 (Chahal, 2003; JRF, 2003a). The research involved eight case study sites, and its aims were to discover how such support projects responded to victims, and the difference they made to the lives of people experiencing racist harassment.

The research found that racist harassment support projects exist unevenly across the country. Some developed as a political response to racist attacks (including murder), in localities where minorities live, and others have grown out of a perceived need to better co-ordinate a range of agencies to respond to and raise awareness about the issue. They all offer assistance and support to victims of harassment through casework, and such casework intervention has a positive impact on the quality of life of the clients. Caseworkers offer direct support, validating the clients' experiences through sympathetic listening and assistance, and helping to re-build the confidence of individuals, families and communities. A number of projects offer a 24-hour service for their clients and potential clients. The focus of a dedicated agency with experience of racist harassment cases can make victims feel supported, and confident that they have somebody on their side. It can also add independent weight to complaints from victims, thereby helping encourage other organisations to respond effectively. A central aim of the projects (explicitly or implicitly) is in effect to empower clients, and this implies achieving good and purposive relationships.

Four key tasks were identified as crucial to effective casework:

- offering help;
- creating an intervention;
- reducing the immediate impact of the harassment; and
- aiming to resolve the complaint.

Comments from informants for the research showed the valued attributes of a successful casework role (and this applied for white as well as black clients).

For instance, one person said that the agency '... *understood what I was saying*', and that they '... *don't judge you like the guy at the council did ...*' Another remarked that the caseworker '... *knew how I felt, you know, what prejudice is like, you know how much it pains*', and that this '... *was the first time I felt somebody was listening, somebody that was taking it in*'. As far as possible the workers seemed to be promoting people's rights (and awareness of these), putting clients swiftly in touch with other contacts and services, acting as advocates when appropriate, and being accessible. There was also emotional support. One informant illustrated this when she explained how a worker saw how depressed her mum had been and how her health had deteriorated because of the harassment, '... *but they picked her up and talked to her on a one-to-one basis and in Punjabi as well*'.

Community-based racist harassment support projects engage in a variety of activities. Some work with local schools and pupils to raise awareness and/or conduct local monitoring. A number have developed training and other resource materials to challenge harassment, while some co-ordinate campaigns around specific incidents. As has often been the case with many other kinds of innovative projects that lie outside the public services mainstream, such support projects can seem poorly funded, and caseworkers are over-stretched in their day-to-day work. The number of racist harassment caseworkers varies from project to project, with caseworkers sometimes managing over 80 cases at a time. There may well be a frequent need for more solid support and access to training and further opportunities for these workers themselves, given the emotionally challenging nature of their role. Casework could be improved by developing national guidelines on racist harassment casework, offering an accredited course for existing and new caseworkers, and developing a network of caseworkers to disseminate information and offer peer support. Like clients, some caseworkers might benefit from access to counsellors. Unfortunately, projects have experienced regular funding crises often resulting in a reduction of (or withdrawal from) direct casework. The author is managing a national network of racist harassment caseworkers to improve practice with victims.

Clearly, the capacity for the community and voluntary sectors to provide appropriate support for victims in particular districts could be strengthened by more adequate and secure funding streams (and perhaps community cohesion initiatives might be a useful source here). Given more funding and support from partner organisations, some projects would be well positioned to expand their work, reaching across geographical boundaries, as well as contributing more broadly to conflict resolution. It would also help if there was full recognition of the needs of caseworkers for structures of support, and more development or enhancement of community-based solutions to providing support and assistance. One possibility worth exploring more often would be to engage those familiar people to whom victims disclose, and others in a local community, to act as a network of support. Building local coalitions of this kind could help strengthen the community-based approach to victim support, perhaps challenging the perpetrator and reducing prejudice in a more co-ordinated manner. Many projects already co-ordinate local racist harassment multi-agency forums.

In some ways the development of a community-based approach might appear to be about filling damaging gaps in existing services, but there is also a strong case for seeing such an approach as an essential or central component in any genuinely client-orientated methodology involving inter-agency collaborative working. A number of questions can be asked of managers and senior officers within housing organisations, who need to take account of this issue. These questions are set out in the next box.

Box 45: Questions for housing organisations that are keen to see better support for victims

- Is there a clear set of guidelines on how to support and interview victims? If not, can one be generated?
- Are staff trained and aware of the guidelines (if these exist in an adequate form)? If not, can training be prioritised?
- How will such guidelines be monitored and evaluated? Clear lines of communication, responsibility and reporting back are needed.
- What does good practice in racist harassment casework and support mean in housing organisations, and is what is offered responsive to the needs of victims in terms of advice, information and potential resolutions? Can existing practices be tested or improved through consultation with other contributing organisations or with victims?
- Is there a need for a dedicated racist harassment support worker?
- Would racist harassment cases be better dealt with by an independent organisation, and (if so) how could it be set up within a local community? Is there a local racist harassment support project in the area already, or (if not) is this an option for development?
- Are there clear lines of communication between the victim, the reporting organisation and other agencies? Have the perspectives of victims and of partner organisations been sought here, to see if there are deficiencies or if things are working well?

Conclusions

Deterrence or punishment of perpetrators remain indispensable conditions of success in dealing with harassment (Lemos, 2000, p. 2), while encouraging people to voice their experiences and complaints is as important today as it has always been. As comments elsewhere in this book indicate, however, things have moved forward in some ways in housing policy and practice, and in line with this the understanding of issues and potential strategies related to hate crimes seems more sophisticated than in earlier years. Yet progress on the ground by social landlords and other agencies has often remained inadequate, and it may be even harder to restrict harassment outside areas of social rented housing (where levers used by public and voluntary sector landlords may not be available). Many examples of good practice that have been widely endorsed have not been fully taken up.

Supportive work within the right kinds of organisational settings with those who have experienced harassment is an essential part of the response that agencies and policy-makers need to bring about. This way forward has been a constructive focus for parts of the chapter, and something that can be worked towards immediately. Furthermore, given enough resources, community-based organisations might have the potential to play larger roles in the reduction of tensions and handling of disputes across districts. Of course, the further development of independent support organisations should not be taken to justify any lack of urgency within mainstream service providers. Effective mainstreaming remains important, and partnership with community organisations, referral arrangements, and joint protocols should aim to ensure that victims get a response and that services are geared to their needs. Although there may be too few RSLs with dedicated officers, and a patchy staffing response across councils, there have been valuable innovations and people who have shown considerable commitment (see examples in Chapter 8, pp. 149-150).

In any event, local support services can only be part of the answer, because preventative strategies and broader long-term efforts to tackle causes of the harassment phenomenon are also required. It is important to deal with offending behaviour itself, seeking to change this and perhaps the social environments within which it develops and is sustained. The more general containment of serious forms of anti-social behaviour is an allied issue for housing providers and other bodies, connecting both with the control of harassment and with apprehensive attitudes to particular housing areas. Multi-agency work on harassment thus becomes part of the approach to wider crime and disorder strategies. Policies such as deployment of estate wardens or rangers, concierges, and other personnel may help, especially where they can assist people in practical ways as well as dampening overt expressions of hostility and criminal activity. It remains important to consider cultural sensitivity and training when schemes and projects are staffed up. Furthermore, properly-resourced community development work of various kinds might be focused usefully on localities where changes are under way, where minority households are moving in, and where education, youth work and community engagement might help if handled well (for an interesting account of proactive interventions see Lemos, 2000, p. 43, on work by Ashiana Housing Association of Rochdale). Appraisals of risk through discussion with households or larger groupings may be worth undertaking, with a view to setting up preventative action and monitoring, especially when tenancy allocations involve access into neighbourhoods occupied predominantly by white people.

Yet there is a long and difficult road to be travelled, not least because harassment and 'race' hate are sustained and encouraged by many of the events and trends happening elsewhere in society. Media reports that excite popular opinion against asylum seekers may have multiplier effects, providing a stimulus or excuse for a wave of actions against many other minority ethnic households, even though these may have been long settled in the UK. Hostility to Islam or other religions in the political context of the perceived threat of terrorism may have similar effects.

Thus, it is important to take as holistic a view as possible, ensuring that anti-racist approaches become more genuinely mainstreamed and proactive, and that anti-harassment goals secure a prominent and regular place in neighbourhood planning, urban regeneration and community cohesion strategies. Indeed, there will often be a strong case for placing anti-harassment and allied preventative work right at the centre of a community cohesion strategy, if such a strategy is to connect successfully with the most urgent issues.

Chapter 10:
Perspectives from the grass roots: a Bradford case study and its implications

Deborah Phillips and Malcolm Harrison

Debates about the problems of multi-ethnic societies need to be better informed by detailed knowledge, and by an appreciation of realities at the grass roots. In this chapter we offer specific case study insights into how people approach their housing circumstances and needs. Drawing on material collected in West Yorkshire from 1999 onwards, we present perspectives as far as we can in the form they were provided to us by minority ethnic informants. The material touches on living arrangements, housing itself, and relevant social issues and trends. One important focus concerns how people feel about localities in terms of 'community', neighbourhood environments, harassment, and anti-social behaviour. Another issue is the relationship with local authorities and housing associations. A crucial component for any realistic debate about community cohesion must be an understanding of complexities and outlooks amongst households, and of their perceptions of neighbourhoods and interactions. We hope, therefore, that this chapter will show the kinds of understandings that are essential to make the debates more meaningful.

The research

Our 1999-2000 fieldwork involved seven focus groups convened in Bradford to explore housing aspirations, expectations and experiences. The groups included young Bangladeshi women, young Bangladeshi men, young Pakistani men, tenants of a local BME housing association (some of whom were retired or in ill-health), young African/Caribbeans, and an older group of the latter. A white inner city council tenants' group was also convened to see if additional issues might surface (and this included some people with children of mixed ethnic heritages). Our fieldwork at this time connected with high profile questions about access into social rented housing in contexts of apparently faltering general demand in parts of northern England. The findings helped contribute to two reports; *Breaking down the barriers* (Ratcliffe *et al.*, 2001), and *A question of delivery* (Tomlins *et al.*, 2001), both of which have been cited earlier in this book. For neither of these, however, did we fully present the richness of insights offered by our informants. Consequently the present chapter goes further with the material and interpretations. As well as local facilitators who helped us generously, 61 people participated directly in the study.

We have supplemented and up-dated the 1999-2000 picture by referring to more recent West Yorkshire research by a team led by Phillips. This investigated housing and neighbourhood aspirations and experiences of people of Indian, Pakistani and Bangladeshi origin living in the inner city and outer areas of Bradford in 2001-2003. The findings drew on a survey of 146 households (most of whom were home owners), and shed light on the complex interplay between growing minority ethnic empowerment and widening housing options, and the bounded nature of minority ethnic housing and area choice. Recent census data have also been noted, indicating the significance of minority communities, as well as providing background on suburbanisation. The 2001 Census indicates that Bradford's Muslim population, mainly of Pakistani, Kashmiri or Bangladeshi origin, numbers just over 75,000 (16 per cent of the city's total). Smaller groups of Indian Sikhs and Hindus make up the remainder of Bradford's 88,400 South Asians. The fairly small African/Caribbean population constituted 0.6 per cent of Bradford's total population in 2001. Census data from 1991 and 2001 show evidence of increasing consolidation of Pakistani and Bangladeshi Muslim populations in core settlement areas, whilst numbers of Indians living in the suburbs have grown. Significantly though, Pakistani movement into outer areas has also been evident, although on a relatively small scale. Ten per cent of Pakistani Muslims in Bradford were living in outer areas by 2000, compared with 35 per cent of Indian Sikhs and 28 per cent of Hindus. Even higher proportions of Muslims (22 per cent) were living in outer areas of the neighbouring city of Leeds, although this was still below the 45-50 per cent of Hindus and Sikhs in the suburbs of that city. Differences in levels of South Asian suburbanisation in the two cities probably reflect the greater economic opportunities available within the more buoyant economy of Leeds, as well as differences in resources and housing preferences of Asian households in Leeds and Bradford.

Our locality-based case study has limitations. Using focus groups proved a good way of revealing relationships and issues, but there may have been views that were under-represented. Furthermore, situations elsewhere may be different, and it would be useful to have comparable material on experiences from parts of the Midlands, Lancashire or London. Perhaps there are some places with fewer problems of economic disadvantage and restricted housing choice, although housing markets may be very tough for consumers in the South. Nonetheless, several issues touched on below may be important in other parts of the country too, and our key messages have general applicability. The chapter is divided into sections covering important topics, but these overlap. It should be noted that stock transfer to new landlord organisations and the advent of choice-based lettings have somewhat changed the housing practice environment to which some of the focus group comments related in the 1999-2000 study.

Family, 'community' and housing

Housing concerns tend to relate closely to the kinds of households that people are in, and to the social and economic situations they are dealing with. Our informants in 1999-2000 came for the most part from inner city areas, and were in rented accommodation. Family circumstances varied, with focus groups including some participants who were heads of households or jointly running a home, and others who were young men and women still residing with older relatives. Informants spoke at length about experiences and needs, linking housing to such issues as kinship, children, financial circumstances, and neighbourhood preferences. One key issue for the future concerns the pressures for separate formation of new young households, and how attitudes to this connect with matters of family and locality. In regard to these connections it is important to refer to outlooks in Asian households (see below), since these are often assumed to emphasise the extended family. African/Caribbean participants in our research included more single people or single parent heads of households in their own accommodation. Nonetheless, it was pointed out that some African/Caribbeans also want to live as extended families, while particular young participants said they had little choice but to continue to live with parents, given the financial constraints.

South Asian perspectives on family, continuity and change

Much has been said about the strengths of culture and kinship within UK Pakistani, Indian and Bangladeshi households, and these factors may affect housing perspectives. Within the South Asian groups in our 1999-2000 study there was some tendency for young people to express a preference for moving out of the parental home to form autonomous households, but family links, interdependencies and obligations generally meant a desire for not moving too far away.

Insights from younger female informants are valuable when trying to get a feeling for change and continuity. It was clear at the outset that women may play an important role in household housing choice, and that their understandings of future family life and networking could be crucial. For those in the Bangladeshi young women's group (most of whom were married) there were strong feelings about involvement in household decisions. Various factors affected this. Among those living in the parental home, one felt that earning an income gave her some power as a contributor. For those women who were married, the fact that some husbands had grown up abroad gave them by necessity a greater role in decision-making. One explained that her husband didn't know the language or 'the system', so that in a sense she made more decisions. A key issue on which the women were firm concerned living arrangements on marriage. Although parental approval and contact remained important, a preference for separate accommodation following marriage was evident. Several saw potential difficulties in living in the same house as parents, relating to conflicting roles and a lack of privacy as a couple:

> '... are you going to act as a daughter or a wife? In your own home you're a wife or a mother. You're a person.'

> *'It's very difficult to be your own person* [in the extended family set up] *... for instance you can't stay in with your husband and watch television, or you can't get close to him because it's something that's taboo in our culture.'*

> *'As a married person, my husband's not married to the family he's married to me so therefore in order for me to work on my marriage I need to move out.'*

There was recognition that views and expectations were different amongst their parents' generation, but that the situation now reflected having grown up in the UK. One explained that *'... because we are in this country we would have ... grown up expecting to have our own house'*, and *'... realising that a husband and wife relationship needs to be worked on'*. Even so, the right decision might depend on particular circumstances (size of family, etc.), and parental views could still count:

> *'When I moved out, my father had some say ... when I went to view a house ... before he even said anything about the house he said "no, that's too far away".'*

> *'Although I make decisions with my husband, we both have a joint decision, I do want to get the approval of my father, well my parents.'*

Housing availability may be important in facilitating or inhibiting choice, and getting things right at the outset is important. As one participant indicated, *'... housing is one of the biggest things that helps the marriage to work well'*.

In any event it was clear that the wish for separate living arrangements did not mean a desire to weaken family ties and move away. There was recognition that parents expected their children to stay close to provide support in their old age, but benefits did not run in only one direction. As one informant explained, *'I need the support of my parents ... it's stability isn't it'*. The general ideal was summed up in the reference to *'... not living in the same house, especially on marriage, but nearby'*. Apart from the social and emotional support of family, many identified a number of practical benefits for themselves of living near to the support of parents: in terms of babysitting, help when running short of money, or the convenience of nearby facilities (such as a drive in which to park the car). It was also evident that while there were strong feelings that women should leave the parental home on marriage, there was no indication that the group felt this was sensible before then (although one young woman living at home nevertheless indicated aspirations for independence). Recognition of the reluctance of parents for children to move out of the family home (and the consequential protective effects) was evident in a comment about the risk of homelessness (or rather the lack of it):

> *'Because our families want to get hold of us ... don't want to let go ... that's why ... they don't kick us out.'*

Most in the young Pakistani males' group anticipated moving out of the family home in the future to form separate households, but there was strong agreement about not wishing to move too far away. This was put in terms of not wanting to move '... *right far away from my parents and all*', and wanting '... *to stay nearby*'. There could be a sense of obligation:

> '*I think it's important to stick with your family no matter what ... even though you move out you're still supposed to be a family. You're supposed to, you know, me personally as a Muslim, I think I should stay not that far away from our parents and look after them as well. As the eldest, I think I've got a responsibility in a way.*'

One young man living with his widowed father '... *couldn't imagine*' leaving him. There was general agreement that the strongest responsibilities rested with the eldest. Problems were discussed, however, of having parents come to live with them in their own homes, references being made to problems of mothers-in-law, and to things not always working out because of generational differences. On the question of family decision-making, the young Pakistani men pointed to what they perceived as male heads of households having the final say in housing decisions, but also to the role of women being important, making suggestions and finding out about options. As one put it, '*My mum, she comes up with the ideas*' although '... *ultimately it's my dad who makes the decision*'.

Participants in the young male Bangladeshi group were mostly still single and living with extended families, and therefore perhaps held less definite perspectives about independence than the Bangladeshi women. Nonetheless, most expected to move out at some future stage, despite awareness of financial constraints and a preference some retained for staying with the family. For the present, certainly, they might be very willing to defer to parents or to stay as part of their parents' households:

> '*I'd like to live on the outskirts, but my personal choice doesn't really matter 'cos my dad, he likes to stay close to the mosque, he'd like to stay near a community where he's familiar with ... he wouldn't want to go into a white estate or a white community.*'

> '... *the last thing I want to do is leave my family. I'll always want to live with the extended family ... that's the norm in our society ... unless in exceptional circumstances: where there is no space or the house is falling to bits.*'

Turning to the question of inter-generational change, one young Bangladeshi man emphasised flexibility in his own generation, pointing out that, '*For me ... I could live anywhere if I had the money*', while another said:

> '... *we're growing up and we can drive and we know our way around ... I could live on the outskirts and it would take me ten minutes to drive in.*'

*But for my dad to do it would take him half a day, catch a bus, walk down ...
an' the Mosque as well ... three or five times a day ... people like to stay near
the mosque so they can always go and pray.'*

Mutual respect between generations did not necessarily mean shared aspirations or
orientations. On housing, differing aspirations were linked to changed life
experiences. It was felt that in the 1970s when the community was smaller, and
many couldn't read or write, there was a need to be close together. The parents'
generation had grown up retaining that need for group security, and didn't feel
alienated or threatened in their own community as they would in another area:

*'When they first came to this country there was only a small number of people
so they liked to stay in small groups ... at one time in the seventies there were
14/15 people living in the same house cooking downstairs, purely because
they worked in similar places, communication was a problem, they couldn't
read or write, they weren't very literate ... Dad tells stories about the
seventies, about the eighties, how they used to go out and be dominated by
white people so there is still that fear ... living in this area I feel there is more
stability* [for] *him.'*

As might be expected, the BME housing association tenants' group confirmed the
significance of living near to family indicated by younger informants. Family
were valued for providing support and security, although this desire for closeness
did not necessarily mean a wish to live in the same street. (When this was
discussed there was a comment, *'No! Oh no!'* followed by general laughter.)
The needs of the older generation were acknowledged, however, given their
dependence on the community and strong reluctance to move out. Language
barriers could be important for some people with regards to a decision on where to
locate.

Clustering clearly remains very significant, because of constraints as well as
practical positive reasons. Analysis of distinctive Asian names on the Bradford
Register of Electors showed that there are some areas of intense residential
segregation between Asians and non-Asians. Some streets were occupied
completely by Asian households and some enclaves (defined through clusters of
enumeration districts) within the Manningham district were about 80 per cent
occupied by Asian people. This degree of clustering, however, is very localised.
Contrary to the popular myth of Asian segregation and the image of ethnic
separation presented in the Ouseley report, there is a considerable degree of ethnic
diversity within inner Bradford.

Communities, localities, collective needs and social divisions

It is not enough to talk of family alone, since broader collective concepts were
also drawn upon in discussions. The young Pakistani informants, for instance, felt
the importance of living together as a Muslim community, and agreed that

proximity to the Mosque, halal meat shops and community facilities were important. Although mixing with other groups was perceived to be desirable, and living in the midst of the Pakistani community not always a good thing (a more ethnically mixed environment perhaps being seen as better), the Pakistani community was of great significance to them. One observed that Pakistani Muslims were '... *community type people'*, although amongst Pakistanis there was also some feeling that they could '... *get stuck'* in specific areas even though many might like to move out to nicer environments. Amongst the BME housing association tenants, remarks clearly indicated a sense of community associated with locality. For instance, one said of the Manningham area, '... *there are certain areas ... it might be a bit run down, but there is a strong Asian community'*. They were alert to the loss of valued community traits, sometimes contrasting this with perceptions of the home area where '... *we're looking after each other, keeping an eye open ... not only a sense of friendship, it's like being in a family'*.

For young Bangladeshi men and women there were negative implications not only from the stigmatising and stereotyping of the community, but also from gossip and lack of freedom or privacy. On the other hand, again the importance was perceived of living together as a Muslim community, and of nearness to appropriate facilities. Positive comments on community in focus groups could be hedged about by very specific qualifications or interpretations. For instance, a number of Bangladeshi female participants, who had already experienced independent living, argued that it was preferable to be near to but not in the centre of that community. Distinctions were drawn here between the generations:

> '... *they* [older members] *are living to the culture ... culture dictates how their life style is ... I was born in this country, I've been brought up in this country, I've had all my education in this country. I don't want the culture to dictate how I am to live my life.'*

> '... *he* [my father] *wanted me to buy a house in this community and the reason he gave was that it's like a village, and that's the very reason why I don't want to buy a house in this community ... because everyone knows your business.'*

It was felt that younger people had more flexibility and mobility (and the car could affect locational choice), albeit within limits and taking account of parental influence. The impact of traditions was referred to from time to time. For instance, one woman explained that it was the cultural norm to have an 'open' house. This could have positive aspects, but was also felt to put great pressure on women to maintain expected standards, and there was talk of a claustrophobic culture (as with '... *it's nice ... but not all the time'*). Another, who had bought a house in a street on the edge of Manningham, particularly valued the privacy afforded, and the ability to go home and put on jeans and t-shirt without being judged by the neighbours. She observed that, '*I don't have to be presentable all the time ... my house doesn't have to be vacuumed all the time'*. Nonetheless, a key criterion affecting locational choices for informants remained the need to retain easy access to family and facilities such as Mosques and shops back in the Asian community. One woman pointed to the dilemma of wanting to be away from the core area, yet needing to stay close to its services and support. The Mosque sometimes appeared of particular importance:

> *'You can't really move that far if you want your children to actually be brought up religiously, that's the main restriction for most people I think ... especially if you haven't got any transport.'*

One young woman wanted her children to be able to attend a Bengali Mosque, rather than one serving the Pakistani community. Although another speaker suggested her rule of thumb was to be within a half hour walk of such facilities, having access to a car was seen as a key liberator. A speaker in the tenants' group stressed the pull of the Mosque for elders, and this might outweigh considerations of physical housing need. Seen from the perspective of one older participant in this group, however, there was a generation shift. Thus, *'... with the older generation, they want a Hindu or Sikh temple'*, but the younger generation *'... would rather have a restaurant, a shopping centre'*.

The term 'community' has many meanings, and may have defensive functions when groups feel hard pressed. Perhaps unsurprisingly, some concerns about tensions between minority communities surfaced in discussions. In the women's group strong feelings were expressed over the noise apparently made by the Pakistanis in their area (e.g. at weddings, or during World Cup cricket), and Pakistanis' attitudes and supposed lack of care towards the local street environment. Some informants seemed quite hostile. Given that the Bangladeshi community is a relatively small group within a larger Asian population, this perceived division has implications for the ease with which Bangladeshi housing preferences and other needs can be met, as when parents are seeking to be near a Bengali Mosque. There was agreement over the need for more interpreters and for people in the housing services generally to be more culturally aware, and the group felt disadvantaged relative to Pakistanis in this respect. Subsequent research shows that similar sentiments may be found amongst Punjabi speakers of Indian origin (another small minority).

For the African/Caribbean groups, the issue of community emerged clearly in the context of safety concerns and in relation to the availability of support, but also against the backcloth of being another 'minority within a minority' in Bradford. Some participants looked back to a recent past when many African/Caribbean families had lived in an area which has since been developed, and when they felt things had in some ways been better as far as community was concerned. The safety issue was a real one, as one woman's comments illustrated clearly:

> *'... three white guys stopped me and told me "you don't belong here" ... I had no-one to shout at to help me, and that wouldn't have happened* [in the area in

which African/Caribbean families were at one time clustered]. *So we do need somewhere like that.'*

Several young women in particular were keen to be able to live within walking distance of their families for support purposes. More generally, there was a substantial sense of loss when participants referred to local history. There was wide agreement that the African/Caribbean population had lost something extremely valuable when there had been a breaking up of the community in a specific area because of council redevelopment:

> *'We did have pockets of communities and they're* [the council] *the ones that broke that up ... there was support there for the African/Caribbean community and that's what the council did, they tore it apart.'*

This was paralleled by negative general feelings from some of the younger participants about family and community change:

> *'People had to move out of the areas that they were brought up in ... that support system went. It costs more now for babysitting, for nurseries. Before it wasn't costing the government any real money because it was all being passed on and we were looking after each other ... we were all brought up by other people around us. We were all brought up by each others' parents.'*

> *'The issue is that people wants a community. Our parents came here from the Caribbean and they has something in common ... but us today, our generation, we haven't got anything in common ... People of colour have people around them, especially with people of African descent, people then tend to say it's a ghetto. I think young people today want some sort of community.'*

It was clear that there was a strong preference for having a definable community base in the city, so that people would at least have the choice of living in a distinct neighbourhood rather than being dispersed, and that issues such as supporting older people could be facilitated. The feeling was that, *'You feel more comfortable around your community'*. One additional factor mentioned was the loss of black professionals from the community at a grass roots level, linked with the feeling that *'... a community of people isn't just poor people'*, although alongside an awareness that there are not many communities (black or white) with different classes living together. There was a strong feeling that the social rented sector had neglected the African/Caribbean population's needs as a community. The planning process had apparently given little attention to 'community spirit' and social amenities:

> *'There was no thought put into how's this community going to live communally ... there's nothing to do with human social interaction of how communities are going to live.'*

While the issue of the possible ghettoisation of the African/Caribbean population was raised, most participants wanted the choice of being able to live in a distinct African/Caribbean neighbourhood and community, rather than being dispersed across a number of areas as at present. The value of social contact, trust, safety and support were all stressed in much the same way as in the South Asian focus groups. One participant urged a stop to '... *pepper-potting us around different areas where we can't actually link up with our own people'.* The importance of children being able to relate to their African/Caribbean identity by having people of similar origins around them was also referred to. As one woman put it:

> *'I would be fine living in an all black area. I wouldn't be comfortable in an all white area. I want my children to see their image around them. I think that's very important.'*

Discussions with Bangladeshi and African/Caribbean informants highlighted how notions of community can be woven into a picture of collective history or identity, and provide potential resources or foci for common cause in seeking facilities. On the other hand, a politics of need based strongly around community, religion or cultural affiliations might appear at grass roots (rightly or wrongly) to have negative exclusive outcomes as far as small groups like these are concerned. This is a reminder of the importance of not allowing an ethnicity or 'difference' agenda to push equality of opportunities into the background. It echoes the dangers felt by some observers about strategies of 'ethnic managerialism' (see Harrison and Law, 1997). The interplay between a sense of community and the actions of public bodies also needs to be kept in mind, in that solidarities may emerge or be re-confirmed partly in response to threats or opportunity spaces created in policy domains. Some perception of a potentially negative impact from institutional behaviour was evident amongst informants. Along with a view that the city was segregated (albeit with patterns of settlement changing), there was a feeling from some respondents that the council were responsible for reinforcing or even creating a divided situation, in which some benefited more than others. As one informant put it:

> '... *you control property, you control people. A lot of people realise that and you can choose who lives in what area and how you want to raise an area or sink an area, and that's what's always gone on ...'*

This perception resonated with a rather different account coming from a white tenant, who talked about a specific area where she had lived since she was born, and which she felt had always been '... *a divided estate',* because '... *the council won't do anything about it'* and '... *keeps it separate'.* Views from this focus group showed suspicions that, along with locality divisions, specific areas were treated less favourably than others. The housing literature covering earlier periods in Britain suggests a long tradition of segmentation or separation between and within some estates, derived in part from management practices of housing departments. A degree of geographical separation arose in some places between the 'respectables' and 'less respectables', partly through the process of housing allocation and management, and as time passed this incorporated ethnic divisions alongside others. Although much has changed, this tradition still seems present in the consciousness of some housing consumers, although how far and in what form it might live on in allocation practices is uncertain. Beyond it, however, is a perception of a more generally divided city, and its consequences, positive and negative.

In referring to divisive official strategies, some informants commented bleakly on the social consequences, indicating a strand of thought attributing tensions to segregation and lack of positive contact with other groups. One such participant suggested a need for people to grow up in mixed ethnicity areas, and strong argument followed in his focus group about the practice of naming estates with distinctively Asian names. It is easy to overstate issues like this, although they may be significant between minority groups as well as with the larger white communities, but perhaps they reflect wider sensitivities to potential for conflict over rationed material resources and group political impact. Within one of our African/Caribbean focus groups the issue of a particular nice group of houses having an Asian name came up in a negative way, being treated by the group rather humorously as an indicator that these particular dwellings were thought unlikely to be available for African/Caribbean tenants. On the other hand, it is the resources and their availability that are really the important matters rather than the name, and some young Bangladeshis felt naming served an educational and cultural purpose, retaining heritage for the second generation, and creating a feeling of belonging. Of course, the naming of streets and blocks has always been an outlet for cultural, political, aesthetic or proprietorial aspirations and sentiments, with English street names embracing all manner of associations, some of which might feel uncomfortable to specific households living there today.

Box 46: Community and community cohesion

Relating our material to the community cohesion debate, we emphasise three points:

1. It seems likely that many people in minority communities would in principle welcome a more inclusive city, and there is little evidence of inward-looking attitudes.
2. Potential tensions between groups deserve attention when services and investments are being planned and delivered, but divisions should not be exaggerated. Minorities within minorities should be considered.
3. Strong community affiliations perform very important positive and practical functions, but expectations and interactions are far from static. Neither are they uniform across a minority ethnic group.

Locational issues

Comments about location reflected the realities of patterns of constrained choice. Despite a desire for privacy and independence, aspirations to live outside the inner city or preferences for newer houses amongst some young people, and a preparedness to move to certain of the more mixed areas a little further out, there was recognition of the ongoing need for close contact with family and community. Nonetheless, a powerful theme concerned the difficulties within present areas of residence.

Over-crowding and poor quality dwellings in home areas

There was awareness across all focus groups of over-crowding, poor quality dwellings, and other problems associated with the inner city. This came into play alongside the family and community issues as a serious consideration when people reflected on present living circumstances and possible change. Collective housing history and its consequences were recognised, as illustrated within the Bangladeshi young men's group:

> *'Our parents bought houses round here because they didn't have a choice ... close to factories where nobody else wanted them, they were cheap houses which were given to our parents and that's just the way it went.'*

Insufficient space and numbers of rooms were clearly major problems for large families trying to live together:

> *'The biggest problem is over-crowding at the moment. We're all living in over-crowding but we don't realise that we're doing that ... we're used to living in that condition, it's the norm now, we've accepted it now.'*

One Pakistani participant, now occupying his own flat, had previously been sleeping on the floor for eight months because of over-crowding. Less dramatically, most of the young Pakistani group identified problems relating to over-crowding in large households, affecting such issues as privacy and space to study, or ability to get away from family demands. In the Bangladeshi young men's group strong feelings were expressed on the stresses and health risks of living in such conditions, sharing toilets (which was seen as a hygiene problem), or bedrooms. Some houses were problematic internally, being *'... so bad, damp ... that people come out with asthma'*. The lack of space put pressure on a family receiving visiting relatives, with everyone *'... being really nice to them'*, but thinking *'I can't wait til they've gone'*. Despite pressure on space, the level of actual homelessness was perceived to be low, although over-crowding may represent a form of hidden homelessness as families or the wider community try to give members a roof to sleep under. One person thought that this was *'... where our families are very good'* in that *'... we all support one another'*. Perhaps this may conceal problems of people who no longer fit into the networks and informal support systems, or have turned their backs upon (or been rejected by) the community, but this did not emerge as an issue in discussions. Social renting landlords should nonetheless keep this topic in mind. Mention was made, however, of hidden homelessness when elders got into difficulties after having sold their Bradford homes (perhaps intending to move abroad or elsewhere), and ended up having to live in Bradford with someone else. Homelessness was a more overt issue in discussions amongst the African/Caribbean participants. One informant had worked in a hostel, and knew of many young homeless people, and comments ranged from '... *abuse ... at parental homes*' to '... *rebelling adolescents*', to '... *alcohol abuse*' and '... *nowhere suitable*'.

In any event, living in over-crowded conditions was clearly not a desired state, and comments were made by Asian informants about possible broader implications. One argued that housing conditions were a major factor in other social problems such as petty crime and vandalism, under-achievement at school and poor health. Another referred to the effects on children through being on the street:

> '*Over-crowding at home ... people want their own space, they're going out, kids want to spend more time on the streets because of the over-crowding ... out and about nothing to do ... see a car, kick it, and been charged with criminal damage ... Haven't got their own space to do homework ... so under-achievement ...*'

One expressed the view that the community had grown up to consider poor housing and local environment and poor service as the norm. He suggested a lack of expectancy and of power contributed to low standards, and highlighted the decline of financial support for private sector housing ('*They've taken away the grants*', etc.). In this focus group the discussion continued with comments such as:

> '*There should be a system to keep housing up to standards ... where people can live without falling in or catching something or rats crawling about.*'

> '*I'm sure a white person walking into my house would think "do people live here?" ... I'm sure they'd do that on every other house on my street.*'

One argued their area needed more help in the form of block grants, but the group lacked any confidence in the system by which block funds were allocated. A participant felt that strategies to improve the inner city were misdirected at re-building rather than maintaining and looking after what was already there. It was put that a major problem was people's difficulty in standing up for their rights, and that they needed to be educated about this. For elders, the problem was exacerbated by language problems, since '*Everything comes out in English*', but '... *not everyone reads or understands English*'. One argued that choices were constrained by a more general powerlessness related to lack of education, and that this was something affecting some white households too. Within the tenants' group the stresses of the broader environment for elders were noted, following a comment that the neighbourhood was '*... over-crowded, over-crowded everywhere*'. Another of the participants explained that this perspective related to the speaker suffering asthma and having had a stroke. Thus:

'*... lacks open spaces ... too closed in for him especially when he's such a poorly man ... had the same with my father who had a stroke and he found the rooms very* [claustrophobic] *... [and there were] too many kids on the street ... knocking the balls and windows.*'

The aspiration for a quieter and more protected environment in older age may well be very cross-cultural in Britain, but its achievement is frequently impossible, although specific new build designs in urban settings can seek to create a sense of protected or enclosed space if circumstances are right. A Bangladeshi informant from nearby inner city Leeds indicated during related research work, the sense of dependency that may be felt by some elders. She felt helpless, three daughters having left the area (apparently because of harassment and disturbances), and dependent on a particular community worker because of her lack of English language.

Other features of inner city life

Critical comments sometimes crossed the boundary between those physical features of environment that were viewed unfavourably (including empty dwellings, lack of play space or drab views), and the social, health or behavioural issues associated with the same areas. For Bangladeshis, discussion included concerns ranging from prostitution, drugs, poor health, or the proliferation of dogs on the street, to littering, vandalism and racist abuse (sometimes connected with proximity to the football club). Members of the Bangladeshi women's group noted that efforts to improve the local environment (for instance by developing gardens) were frustrated by local youths or children. The proliferation of cats and dogs on the street was seen as a particular problem.

Both women and men spoke of the stigma of living in the inner city, where the postcode might affect a person's chances of obtaining employment. One informant from the white focus group indicated that it could be important how you stated your address when applying for a job, since using a particular estate name might mean no interview. For Pakistanis there were some ambivalent attitudes towards the inner areas where they lived. Most saw these as their preferred areas of residence for the future, given familiarity and the issue of proximity to their community, while older residents in particular stressed the positive connections and valued facilities. On the other hand, members of the Pakistani groups were critical of the inner city areas' poor status, run-down appearance and litter, and showed some preparedness to consider certain areas that were further out. Although tied to the locality, informants might feel that this was not through free choice. There was a feeling that Pakistanis get stuck in areas of this type, and that some would like to move, even if not very far. Preferences were bounded by limitations: Pakistanis might tend to talk about moving, but '... *can't really do anything about it'*. The problems of continuing pressures on land and space were acknowledged. As one informant put it:

> *'In the beginning the Asian community was very afraid of getting out. Now that they realise the inner ... area is very tightly spaced, they've got to live somewhere, one or two have made a big stride and moved over to* [an area some way off], *which they've liked.'*

Police in the area were seen as a problem rather than a support, with a feeling that people's rights were easily abused. Suspicion of the police parallels some points made about the council and other landlords, with critical comments reflecting a gap that is bound to be hard to bridge from either side. Yet there is plenty of recognition of the importance of crime. Drugs were seen by the young male Bangladeshis as a major problem for the area, although one suggested also that there were actually drug problems everywhere but that they were especially visible in the inner city. The true picture was subject to distortion by area stereotyping (and not just of Asian areas). A participant felt that getting people into good housing and providing support might help.

Like the South Asians, the African/Caribbeans viewed inner city areas with ambivalence, perceiving advantages in terms of accessibility and proximity, but also problems associated with social and physical decline:

> *'On the whole, the inner city parts of* [the city] *where the majority of black people live are not attractive, they are not that good.'*

There is some perception that certain areas in the inner city are treated as destinations for specific people and facilities that would not be encouraged into more peripheral areas. Informants noted facilities for, or the presence of, alcoholics, people needing mental health rehabilitation, those on probation, and drug addicts. It was felt that people were dumped in specific inner areas because of lack of organised opposition:

> *'... it's not about them themselves being there necessarily, it's about the fact that nobody else would take them. ... it's not that group who cause the problem, ... but why in such close proximity have you got all these people with very high support needs when already in that area you've got a lot of people with support needs that aren't being met?'*

Perspectives on other areas of the city

For the young Bangladeshis there were limits on the areas that they would consider moving to. Views were shaped by experiences of prejudice and racism, and unsurprisingly neither the Bangladeshi men nor women were happy about the idea of living in 'all white' areas. Concerns were voiced about isolation and racist harassment, and some informants identified specific white estates where they would not consider living. One young Bangladeshi man recalled an incident from going to school in childhood:

> *'I went to* [a particular white area] *and this woman turns round and says you black bastard what are you doing here … and I still remember that, every time I go into* [that area] *I remember that, so I've got fear.'*

While one woman, who had bought a house on the edge of Manningham, valued the fact that her street included non-Asian households, she did not wish to move right away from the Asian areas. Illustrative comments in the young women's group included:

> *'… you don't want to be the only Asian family living on the block.'*

or

> *'The white people living there … you do get a lot of stick off them.'*

Perceptions of social rented housing areas were sometimes very negative. One of the young Bangladeshi group commented:

> *'… every time we had to go there we had to move the junkies out of the way … you go to the next man's flat he's got the same problem … you go to all the estates in Bradford and they've all got the same problem … because the council's not willing to sort it out.'*

People's perceptions are affected by their responsibilities, particularly if they have children, and racisms may powerfully affect both members of minority communities and white people who have children of mixed ethnicity. One such parent from our white tenants' group complained about harassment in schools within a particular predominantly white estate. The young Pakistani men (thinking ahead) wanted to live where their children would not be in danger:

> *'I'd prefer to live somewhere that's clean where my kids can stay away from trouble.'*

The issue of an apparently changing social world, in which 'youth' signifies problems as much as family continuity, manifests itself in home areas as well as further afield. Informants related negative reactions received when telling off local children. Yet the notion of unruly children was also potentially divisive, since some informants were concerned about the difficulties that their children faced, one saying *'If they're not going to play within their own community where are the children going to go?'*

This kind of issue, however, becomes part of broader and definitely negative perceptions when it comes to reflecting on people in more distant neighbourhoods.

Crucially for Pakistani participants in our 1999-2000 study, there was a reticence about considering living in what were perceived to be rough, white areas (cf Bowes *et al.*, 1998). Isolation, insecurity, racist harassment and the risk of falling into trouble (for young people notably via fights and drugs) were concerns discouraging moves to specific areas or estates. Some places were seen as 'bad areas', and the negative image of council estates in particular was linked to worries about anti-social behaviour. Amongst the BME association tenants' group there were some very hostile reactions when particular estates were mentioned:

> '... *a very rough estate ... you're sat there in your living room and you see people outside peering in.*'

> '... *all I've heard is bad things about that area.*'

What seems to have been happening is that a negative perspective has developed – distinguishable to some extent from concerns about racisms on the street – with regard to life within low-income white estates. For some informants council housing was thus '... *more or less ... last choice*' when '... *stuck*'. Household members might be wary of what they saw as a damaging working class youth culture (the word class actually being mentioned by participants), which might draw in or influence Asian youth, and therefore they expressed the kinds of reservations about behaviours that might equally have been expressed in the past (and could be today) by 'traditional respectables' within white working class and lower middle class communities. One speaker in the tenants' group brought this out very clearly:

> '*I'm not trying to degrade anyone ... it's just that most of the Asian people which came over ... were quite well to do families ...* [I'm] *not saying very rich ... but well to do – I mean how the hell did they get the money to come to this country – so, well to do, middle class ... but when they come to this country they have to live with the working class ... that's when the trouble started ...*'

By contrast, the UK middle class offered less threat:

> '*If you go 10 or 15 miles ... you could be walking on the street and nobody's going to call you a black git are they? ... because they're all middle class, they're all educated ... the trouble with us you see, with us being workers, and our older generation ... they weren't educated ... so they had to take any kind of job ... and they had to live with the working class.*'

The same informant saw this exposure as a reason for a decline in morality and behaviour amongst younger Asians. Another, however, put it differently saying '... *all the children, 17, 18 ... it doesn't matter where they're living, they could be on a posh estate, but they all move to town to get pissed or whatever ... LSD and everything*'. The terminology deployed in focus groups was sometimes illuminating, as when one young Pakistani informant referred to '*... squatters and scruffs, and people like that*'. Particular concerns included drugs, litter, neighbours and problems with dogs in council estates. This overlaps with the serious worries about racism, and the practical concerns of distance, language problems, and community contact. One participant for instance referred to having been offered houses elsewhere, including ones further from the inner city, but had felt that his wife '*... wouldn't find it easy*', and thus had come to the established area of minority ethnic settlement. Attitudes to areas might be affected by whether other Asian households had already been moving there, alongside estimations of the presence or significance of specific social problems or general bad reputation. At the same time positive 'pull' factors for established areas of settlement work alongside the negatives about places further afield.

Certain outer areas were seen as desirable by some of the African/Caribbean participants, who valued the cleaner, quieter environments and better schools, and (if opportunities arose) would like to move there in the longer term. Issues around crime, unemployment, drugs and disorder were important, affecting how areas would be seen as possible destinations, as well as reservations about present locations. For instance:

> '*... the root of the problems is two things: unemployment and crime ... it's the crime element which is driving people out of areas, not necessarily the housing.*'

Given satisfaction on this score, preferences might sometimes look very similar to those we might expect to find expressed by many of today's aspiring white households:

> '*... near the* [outlying] *town centre, ... that kind of area. You're close enough to the countryside, it's not as densely populated as other parts ... and it's better facilities ... I think some of the schools are better over that side and I think some of the social problems are probably there but they're a lot less visible than in other parts of* [the city].'

The Asian tenants' group also acknowledged that prosperous people were moving out to attractive areas further afield, one suggesting that Indian households had been less entrenched than the Pakistani ones and had begun to move sooner. By contrast, one African/Caribbean participant recounted an unpleasant experience of moving to a large town beyond the main city areas:

> '*Yes, there's racism and the fact if black people start moving into certain areas in certain numbers there's concern ... and some of that concern shows itself in terms of local people increasing the amount of racism against you as a way of stopping other people coming there or make you feel unwelcome. I've certainly been in communities where that's happened ... I was in Keighley and during the day it's fine, really nice people, but you go to the pubs in the evening time ... it's a different story.*'

This had something of a parallel with comments by one of the participants in the Bangladeshi women's focus group, on the difficulty for Asians of moving into mainly white areas. A friend of hers had been relocated to Pudsey (some way distant) during redevelopment, but had been unable to deal with '… *all the racism*', and had felt that until she had gone there she '… *didn't know* [she] *was black*'.

For the African/Caribbeans, it was felt that an area's reputation would affect the ability to sell a house bought under the right to buy, and that an area might affect other life chances. In general terms, the main areas identified for avoidance were the 'densely populated Asian areas', 'rough' council areas characterised by anti-social behaviour, and places with a history of racist harassment. Although on the whole the groups felt that the city was 'not too bad' for racist incidents, there was an unsurprising awareness of what might happen in specific localities. Parts of one area, for instance, were thought to have '… *problems where the white tenants don't like black people'*. Even so, there were some younger African/Caribbean participants living on that estate who were fairly positive about it. As one young man explained:

> '*A thing that is really getting good now is that we are getting a few more black families moving on to the estate … They've just done it up so it's more attractive than what it used to be.'*

Perhaps this is a reminder that things aren't static, and that matters can improve as well as deteriorate. As regards perspectives on ethnic mix, African/Caribbean participants expressed a range of opinions. Some said that they would prefer to live in a mainly 'black' area, but most were happy to live in mixed areas. Many indicated that they would not want to live in an 'all white' area because of racism (although not everyone felt the same way). As one put it:

> '*But I've certainly been in all white areas where racism plays a big part in the culture of the people without them even knowing it, and I wouldn't particularly like that.'*

Things sometimes might be less direct, but still oppressive:

> '*There is covert pressure … Children will throw things at your door because you don't fit into the stereotype of what blackness is supposed to be and you don't fit into the stereotype of what working class is supposed to be …'*

There may be rather refined understandings of local geographical distinctions in terms of relative danger. Thus, one woman stated:

> '*I've lived in* [a specific estate] *and been racially harassed …* [speaking directly to other participants who had suggested that this area was OK] …

it's not the side where you lot live on, but it's [a particular part of the estate].
I lived on [this part] *and* [it] *is definitely a 'no black zone'. I lived there
eleven months and that was eleven months far, far, far too long.'*

In her focus group there followed some general agreement over this, and
discussion identified two sides to this area and a divide within it. Feelings about
potential isolation and the importance of the African/Caribbean community
reinforced this kind of worry. Parents were concerned about their children
having bad experiences in areas with predominantly white or Asian populations.
There was a worry about the possibility of a son or daughter being the odd one
out, or open to victimisation. This was not solely a matter of white racism in the
culture of the neighbourhood.

Thus, as one person explained:

> 'It is an issue and people may not want to talk about it, but if you are in a
> school where 99 per cent of the people are Asian you'd feel threatened for
> your children because you don't want your child to be the odd one out,
> rather than the fact that they are all Asians ... you might feel your child is
> going to be dominated by ... or victimised because of that, in the same way if
> it was 99 per cent white, they're probably going to get something similar ...
> and the areas are going to be like that as well.'

Some indicated that neighbourhood preferences were not simply a matter of the
ethnic composition of an area, but that 'social class' was important as well.
Echoing some of our Pakistani and Bangladeshi informants, they aspired to live
alongside 'decent people'. An indication of what was to be avoided was given in
a description of one person's experiences with a classic 'neighbour from hell'
situation, where the landlord had finally acted. One might guess that
perspectives on anti-social activities could also be influenced by directly
experiencing racisms from specific white working class groups with whom parts
of the city and daily life may be shared, and with whom there may be
competition from time to time for resources or jobs. 'Decent people' may mean
those whose standards would include not condoning racist behaviour as well as
other anti-social activities, which in turn might be given a conscious or
unconscious link (correctly or over-optimistically) to preferred groups of higher
status. An informant in an earlier Leeds study (with which the present writers
were involved) had suggested that middle class people were likely to pose less
overt problems, since being privileged already they apparently felt less
threatened by black people (Harrison and Law, 1997, pp. 291-292). There were
further concerns from the Bradford study about Asian youths, and threats it was
thought they could pose. When class was directly mentioned by some
African/Caribbean informants, there was also reference to the loss of middle
class members from their own community.

Adding to the picture of attitudes to outward movement

Material from our later research included additional information on attitudes to areas and on suburbanisation, and embraced owner-occupier households that had been able to afford a move. The main reasons given by Bradford's Pakistanis and Bangladeshis for moving to the suburbs was the need for larger housing (48.1 per cent of respondents), better quality accommodation (40.7 per cent) and a better area (37.0 per cent). Levels of satisfaction with the outer localities were high. Half of the suburban respondents could find nothing bad at all to say about their neighbourhood. A few said that the Mosque or temple was a bit far away, but we received mostly positive comments. These related to such matters as quietness, friendliness, good reputation, good schools and privacy. Of those living in the suburbs, 69.2 per cent had maintained links with the community in the inner city, both through visiting friends and relatives and through use of shops. Asian respondents were asked whether they felt that Asian families would move into areas with fewer Asian residents in the future. Here there were slightly different responses from people living in inner and outer areas of Bradford, but the general message was the same; they thought that Asians would gradually move into more mixed areas (although not generally into white areas). As one young Pakistani man put it:

> 'They will probably not move to a strictly white area. As you earn more you want to move into better area, but will always look for an ethnic/ Asian mix.'

Eighty eight per cent of those living in more ethnically mixed areas believed more outward movement would occur in the near future, particularly amongst the young and the better-off. People living in the heart of the inner area Asian community were less sure; many (both young and old) stressed the benefits of community living. Nevertheless, 60 per cent still said that they thought there would be more outward mobility in the future. Better housing and more independence for the young were seen to be important motivating factors for suburbanisation, but some respondents also commented on the positive benefits of greater mixing for community relations in the city. A Pakistani woman felt:

> 'Yes, it's better to have a good healthy mix of people. You learn a lot. It's a much better environment. If I moved, that is what I would want.'

Nonetheless, 73.1 per cent of respondents said that there were certain areas of Bradford that they would avoid. The main reasons given were racism, high crime levels, and fear of racist harassment. 'Rough' council estates, with a predominantly white working class population, were particularly likely to be perceived as areas to avoid. The other big constraint on outward movement is the limited access to private sector suburban living facing numerous inner city households without adequate financial resources.

Outlooks on tenure and access to good housing pathways

Perceptions from Bangladeshi and Pakistani informants

There was a strong aspiration for home ownership amongst young Bangladeshis, although with qualifications such as recognition of financial constraints. All the Bangladeshi women's group favoured the idea of buying a home rather than renting, one saying, *'It's cheaper to buy'*. Many wanted the flexibility of owning their own house, the freedom to decorate, etc. The following comment sums up many of the perceived practical advantages of buying over renting:

> *'I'm buying a house because of the fact that I'm paying £223 rent which is more than I can afford ... it's not going to go to my benefit in the end. I can't decide what I want to do with the house, what it's going to look like ... and I can't dictate surrounding issues like school or what shops are so that's why I've decided to buy a house, fitting the criteria I want and in the end, in 25 years, the house is going to be mine. It's something I can leave to my child.'*

Another speaker highlighted the importance of cultural reasons:

> *'I'd like to own a house for my own reasons ... but my dad would like me to own a house because I have a land and a house that belongs to me and that's similar to the feelings he has, a Bangladeshi man, from Bangladesh, of owning land of being proud of land.'*

Although none of this group expressed a desire to rent, one respondent did give a more cautious view on buying, arguing that the relative ease of buying a house masked considerable difficulties of maintaining it (in terms of mortgage repayments and repairs). Another said *'... it's easy to buy, but ... to carry on paying on the mortgage is really hard'*. There was acknowledgement that in certain circumstance (such as for those on benefit or in difficult financial circumstances) renting made sense, or was unavoidable. One stated *'I'm better off renting a place than buying my own house'*, because *'I only have to pay £10 out of £70'*. Others noted that those unemployed do not have choice, and the advantage of not paying for repair work. The latter positive advantage, however, was qualified by the thought that getting the repairs done *'... takes ages'*. The experience of one woman, forced to move when her landlord had decided to sell, illustrates that decisions can be very pragmatic when under pressure:

> *'I didn't look at what area it was ... I didn't look at what community ... I just needed a house.'*

Most of the women's group seemed aware of the concept of right to buy and thought it could provide tenants of social housing with a cheap way of buying a house. One, however, alluding to the stigma of council houses (and areas), questioned how easy it would be to sell the house on in the future, as '... *a lot of people don't want to buy in council areas'*. Others argued that withdrawal of tenant incentive schemes had had negative effects. One woman keen to buy her rented home noted that her housing association landlord were not going to give her the opportunity, saying '... *we are not going to become like the council'*, who sold so many houses they don't have good ones left.

There was a preference for ownership amongst the young Pakistanis and most of the housing association tenant group, but several felt renting could be an important stepping stone or the only realistic choice. Alongside the financial obstacle of unemployment there could be an Islamic issue related to paying out interest for mortgages. One of the tenants thought that renting was better, but this was partly shaped by previous experiences when he had lost his job and consequently given up his home. Some Pakistani young men had little knowledge of social renting, but most agreed that they might consider council housing in future if unemployed or on low earnings. This was despite negative images. There was some perception of social renting as a transitional stage, one informant seeing a housing association as a place '... *where you can establish yourself and then probably move on and then if you've got enough money you can buy your own home'*. A possible generation shift in attitude was suggested in which renting had started to be seen as more acceptable. Some Bangladeshi informants also felt that social renting could play an important role in early stages of new household formation, but there was some perception that social rented dwellings were of poor materials and in some ways less satisfactory than parents' older homes, despite the problems of the latter. For Bangladeshis, knowledge of how to get access to council housing (as it then was) was partial, although better amongst the young women than the young men, and there was concern about lack of interpreters and the need for more cultural awareness. The Bangladeshi young men had little knowledge about how to apply for housing association accommodation, and barriers (and delays) were perceived in the applications process, but there was some positive comment on the local BME association. Generally, the Bangladeshis were negative about council housing because of how they perceived the quality and location of the stock and the associated service.

Amongst Asian informants, while advantages were recognised of cheap rents and responsibilities being taken on by the landlord, there was opposition to paying out rent for what was seen as undesirable housing. Suspicions existed about allocation practices, one view being that the council had sought to house Asian households into undesirable areas. Male participants disagreed over the extent to which the failings related to racist prejudice or just a bad system, which in the eyes of some encouraged dishonest claims about relative urgency. The young Pakistani men believed that the allocation system did not care for young people at all, and there was a claim that the council catered essentially for white people, with perhaps two children, '... *and a dog and a cat and a mum and a dad'*. The issue of honesty also emerged from white informants, where comment was offered on the need to lie about circumstances in order for a woman to get accommodation for herself and her children, and the advantages that could arise for people who could 'play the system'. Furthermore, comments were made here on problems of access for young people. There was some perception amongst Bangladeshis of perceived stigma attached to being a council tenant, and concerns about the small sizes of dwellings. Housing association dwellings were generally regarded as a better option than council houses (somewhat more favourable impressions being held similarly by young Pakistani men), with a higher reputation in terms of appearance and less of a drugs problem, although high rents drew complaints from all minority ethnic groups (see for instance Box 47).

Box 47: Critical perceptions of RSL rents

'Councils are not so bad … it's the housing (associations) … it's £70 a week for a three bed … they're robbing.'

'… they say they're serving the community … but I don't think they're serving the community, they're serving their pockets.'

(Views from female Bangladeshi informants)

BME housing association tenants

The BME housing association tenants' focus group had good knowledge about many issues and about how to obtain information. They showed a strong appreciation of their association's approach to serving the community's needs, and satisfaction and pride was expressed by those living within an area covered by a specific housing association's mutual aid arrangement. This meant that the tenants were expected to make a commitment to the area and other people there. Those covered by this scheme appeared to take an active and very positive approach to it, feeling it was important for closeness, support and harmony. It appeared to be reinforcing what was presented by them as a local situation where there was considerable co-operation between residents on matters such as keeping the area tidy, and pride in care of their estate. One participant noted a '… *sense of family, a sense of community*', and observed also that '… *we tend to have religious meetings*'. There was clearly some pride in the tidy and clean environment achieved and maintained in the area covered by the scheme, in contrast to other areas where '… *people will bother with their gardens but they're not bothered about what's outside on the footpath and they never educate their children round to that system*'.

The main practical issues for this group were to do with dwelling size, cultural sensitivity and rent levels. Houses with four (or more) bedrooms were important, as were big rooms catering for large families, and the capacity for the separation of men and women downstairs. Design problems were seen in one case to concern the lack of separate rooms, which was '… *not culturally friendly*'. As far as the dwellings were concerned, however, only a few in the group found very much to criticise about their landlord, and the new stock clearly had an appeal by comparison with run-down private sector housing. People were attracted to this BME association by both the locations in which it held stock and the perceived suitability of the housing. One made clear that he felt at home with the landlord, referring to it approvingly as an *'Asian firm'*, and other comments included *'They've been good to us'*, and *'They've been alright with us'*. Even so, there was comment on allocation practices and allied issues where suspicions had developed for some participants. In discussion, however, difficulties of managing the situation were acknowledged:

> *'What they* [some people from the community] *don't realise is that there are other people who are really urgent to be rehoused. They think that as soon as they put in an application you can get a house straight away. That's not the case ... it's obviously first come, first served, and you've got to wait in line. But I think our people expect, they want to jump the queue, but they can't do that ... They* [the association] *look at everybody's reasoning, they look at emergency cases ... and people tend to lose patience ... I think it needs speeding up.'*

On the whole there was a positive impression of their landlord, qualified by the worries about long waiting lists and delays and by some lack of understanding of allocation practices (and occasional fears of patronage). High expectations pointed to some degree towards 'Housing Plus' activities going beyond traditional housing management tasks. The perception of the management responsibilities of the association extended in one instance into the idea that the association should compel people to keep an area clean, and in effect control behaviour, although it was also explained in the group that the RSL did not have enough powers to do this.

African/Caribbean informants

There has been a significant tradition of social renting amongst the African/ Caribbean population of Bradford as elsewhere. Most informants aspired to home ownership but did not necessarily regard it as a realistic option. Although the right to buy was viewed favourably, many were dubious about the merits of exercising this in a poor area, and doubts were expressed about shared ownership, where a property might 'never be your own' (and where some participants felt they lacked information). The point was also made that some people who had purchased had missed out thereby on subsequent council modernisation of stock. On the other hand, one participant made very clear the frustrations that can arise from being dependent on social renting. Although he apparently had been able to offer valuable labour market skills as a trained car mechanic, appropriate work had been hard to get, and his preferred housing pathway seemed denied to him. He expressed a sense of being trapped in a specific social rented dwelling. Low incomes and limited job prospects inevitably formed part of the backcloth to problems in getting mortgages, although younger informants indicated aspirations for ownership that they felt might differ from those of their parents. Some believed that they had different housing needs and expectations from the previous generation, most obviously in relation to quality.

All of the African/Caribbean focus group participants had experience of council housing, when living in parents' homes or as tenants in their own right. Some had moved on to housing association accommodation and some had used private renting. Given their familiarity with council housing, the social rented sector might seem a more obvious option to them than to most Asian informants. All agreed that council housing (as it then was) was cheap, contrasting with housing association accommodation, and if a house could be obtained then the garden might be of better size than in private renting. Many felt that it was not possible to live in housing association dwellings unless in receipt of benefits. It was recognised that in some areas council modernisation programmes had given rise to better accommodation than in much of the private rented sector. Even so, there were reservations because of the areas targeted for modernisation. As one informant put it:

> '... the areas where they've developed, it's predominantly white areas.'

There was awareness of the loss of available stock through the right to buy, and issues about access and allocation, including a feeling that ease of access was determined by the type of property and housing area that applicants were prepared to accept. The problems of difficult tenancies and places were well understood, and could lead to people deciding against social renting:

> 'I used to live in council property but the problem with that is the quality of the housing and also the security of the housing ... the fact that if you live in multiple occupancy housing, you've got no control over whether there is alcoholics or drug addicts living next door to you. If you've got children then you have to put up with that and I don't agree with that ... That's why people flee from them blocks because they want to be able to control at least some of the environment when they're coming.'

Perceptions have long existed in cities of hierarchies or distinctions when it comes to social rented housing areas. So it was no surprise that one informant referred to having received offers in the past in '... *really undesirable places'*. Views on relative desirability, however, may well vary according to ethnicity and other household variables. Alongside criticisms of the treatment of young single people (one person having been allocated into a flat in a vandalised and partly abandoned block), there was some sense that unfairness or negative racist or other discrimination persisted in allocation practices. An informant referred to people's difficulties in getting housed in relation to relative needs:

> 'The council they don't house people according to their needs ... in my block of flats ... there'll be elderly, ex-mental patients up on the 12th floor, children, dogs, all kinds of situations in those high rise flats, it's not right.'

It may be that the subsequent stock transfer and introduction of choice-based lettings in Bradford has begun to affect attitudes, although it is uncertain that impressions will necessarily change very rapidly. Clearly, suspicions voiced by our informants need to be set alongside positive appreciations of social renting. Given the grass roots feelings about social landlords generally, however, there is undoubtedly a need for landlords to maintain very good lines of communication, to avoid misunderstandings by making clear and sticking to transparent procedures, and to keep priorities under review. There is little research material on working practices and priorities following stock transfer, although it seems that age categories are being used as a discriminator that may work against younger people in terms of limitations placed on potential allocation destinations.

When it came to the help and information provided by the council, there was a degree of approval in the African/Caribbean groups, but qualified with reservations about the unresponsive behaviour of some officers. Participants suggested that the council should apply rules on anti-social behaviour more strictly, support black elders, establish a drop-in centre for African/Caribbeans, and provide more support on bad estates. People on estates faced many problems associated with unemployment, loss of pride and lack of community spirit.

African/Caribbean views on housing associations reflected the fact that eight informants were living in association accommodation, while most others were aware of what was on offer. There were favourable comments on a local white-run association with a long history of commitment in this city, positive reference being made to consultations with tenants, property and garden maintenance, and the properties themselves, but high rents and allied costs were clearly negative factors. As one woman said:

> '... beautiful flats, love to live in them, but can't afford them, they are so expensive to heat.' (Heating costs were cited as a problem during our study by other informants too.)

As noted above, the rents issue arose in other focus groups. The white tenants' group felt that council rents were reasonable but none were interested in moving to housing association accommodation because of the higher rents. African/Caribbean informants expressed the feeling also that specific needs of their population had been neglected by RSLs as well as the council, and that associations should be targeting the African/Caribbean population as well as Asian households:

> 'I'd like to see housing associations cater for African/Caribbean people ... they should listen to the minority in the minority.'

There was resentment that large houses developed in a specific area had been allocated to Asian households, participants feeling that the African/Caribbean minority always lost out to the Asian population in the city. This kind of outlook needs to be set against the situation of rationing that might operate for the larger or more desirable properties in preferred areas. Both amongst African/Caribbean and Asian informants there was criticism of the limited amount of larger family housing available within the social rented sector, and an awareness of the difficulties people experienced.

Some comments reinforced a point also arising in relation to Bangladeshis, that it is unsatisfactory to think in crude 'black/white' terms for many policy development purposes, or when considering needs. There may be minority ethnic communities whose needs differ from each other, or who feel overlooked or even overwhelmed by the presence and apparent political or cultural strength and voice of neighbours from larger groups. When it came to perceptions of specific housing associations, the local BME association attracted more sceptical comment from African/Caribbeans than from our South Asian informants, perhaps because of its strong association with the latter, and the sense amongst the African/Caribbean groups that their needs had in some way been by-passed. Some were aware of the potential of the idea of co-ops, in terms of managing their own properties, and were interested in thinking further about this.

Conclusions

This chapter has tried to convey the complexities of housing experiences and preferences, and the nature of choice as a bounded and contingent process. If the community cohesion concept is to be useful, its exponents must engage with the complications and realities of interactions, restrictions, opportunities and hazards that affect households. All focus groups expressed strong attachments to local areas, and participants often might prefer homes to be upgraded rather than having to move. Young people from the minority communities frequently expressed preferences for being accommodated in independent households outside the parental home, but did not want to go too far away because of family links. In effect, a key issue that emerged in relation to preferences for the future concerned connections; with families, communities, localities and facilities. This makes the process of outward movement complex, and means that the inner city is likely to remain a significant focus of people's preferences, or of their realistic constrained choices (although the spatial tie could be relaxed with increasing car ownership amongst the young). Putting this in terms of its negative side, fear of isolation and other disadvantages helped restrict locational preferences. Young Pakistanis and Bangladeshis were generally prepared to consider living in areas a short distance away from the main communities, but informants generally did not want to be the only Asian or black families in a street or area. As far as policy implications were concerned, this indicated probable merits of strategies that might facilitate new or emerging settlement clusters.

There was not much in the way of evidence of specific desires to be separated off in some way, and there seemed to be general approval for genuine multi-culturalism in some senses or contexts. Indeed, from time to time individuals expressed strong feelings against segregation by colour, ethnicity or disability. Rather, it was practical concerns about daily living that seemed predominant when geographical locations were considered. It was generally understood that some families or communities had begun moving further afield, and that although specific areas might pose problems racism was not necessarily always the central issue. For financially better placed households, suburbanisation seems likely to continue to proceed in the owner-occupier sector, although no doubt more easily in some places than others.

None of this meant that people were satisfied with present housing or environmental conditions. Little positive was said about the inner city environment in general, and critical comments ranged widely across issues of physical standards, lack of recreational facilities, abuse of the environment through littering and vandalism, pollution or intrusion from industry and other activities, and behavioural matters such as the presence of drug dealers or anti-social behaviour. Participants were aware of the impact stigma could have when insurance or jobs were being applied for from within an area that had a poor reputation. They experienced directly or through relatives and friends the sharp edge of bad housing. One tenant vividly described his sister's house, indicating that he thought the poor health of his nephews might be linked with the conditions: '... *if you go into her house you realise it's got damp, it's got rotting floorboards, the sink is leaking, nothing at all, no amenities, sockets hanging out the wall'*.

As is probably the situation in many other communities elsewhere (white or black minority ethnic), aspirations to become owner-occupiers appeared widespread, but were modified or qualified by financial and other considerations. The aspiration for ownership was supported by arguments about its real cost being cheaper than renting, practical advantages in decision-making about the house, cultural pressures in favour, and passing on an inheritance. Yet choice of moving further out to attractive areas was constrained financially for would-be owners, just as it can be for low-income white households. As one young Bangladeshi put it:

> *'I went to look at a house last week, £135,000, on my salary – am I dreaming – I've got to be realistic ... for me to move out from the inner city area I know I'd have to work another ten years without spending a penny.'*

There was some awareness of the right to buy and its potential as a route to ownership, but also of its impact in reducing the stock available for later entrants to social renting. It was regarded with mixed views, with awareness that there could be problems if one bought what was a poor quality unit in an unsatisfactory place. There was concern from some housing association tenants about not being allowed to purchase. One said *'Why am I paying £80 or £90 a week for a house I can't own?'*.

Even in social renting, housing costs could be an issue. Housing association rent levels seemed to be problematic, perhaps especially for larger dwellings. It was these rent levels that often drew the main complaint. Some saw them as too high for the service on offer, with participants feeling that the system of setting rents was inflexible, and that there should be a fairer way of means testing. There was also concern about housing difficulties facing young people (who might need not just a home but other support too), long waiting lists, allocation practices, and shortage of larger dwellings. On the latter, some mentioned cultural dimensions including the issue of separate room space for men and women. On the other hand, the point was also made that over time families would become smaller. Furthermore, new good quality dwellings were much appreciated, particularly where there was a favourable contrast between housing association properties and surrounding housing of other kinds and standards.

When it came to communications and knowledge about housing practices there were three main significant points, although these might need up-dating in the light of the recent large-scale transfers of stock in the city to new landlord organisations. First, social landlords appeared to have had a patchy impact in making housing routes and options known to households, and there had been limitations in offering culturally-sensitive services, although the local BME housing association (Manningham HA) had a somewhat different (and positive) profile within the Asian communities. In the tenants' focus group meeting relating to this landlord, its 'mutual aid' scheme was firmly supported (as we noted above) by tenants who were experiencing it, and proved of great interest to tenants renting in other streets who were also present. One tentative conclusion was that the former tenants seemed to have become better organised collectively (perhaps partly because of the scheme), an issue that apparently prompted the latter participants to use part of our discussion time to plan for getting a better collective way forward for themselves! Unfortunately this focus group lacked female participants, so we were unable to say how far the positive view of the 'mutual aid' scheme crossed the gender line. An additional point from those not in streets covered by the scheme was that their area in any case had more tensions, and was believed to be adversely affected by the presence of non-housing association properties. Thus, it was felt that in an area bordering with private housing, trouble '... comes in'.

A second issue about communications is that there seems to be a mixed set of perceptions and beliefs across communities about landlord practices and behaviour, sustained by accounts of past events, knowledge of recent positive or adverse experiences, and some possible myths or mis-interpretations. It is a mistake to dismiss allegations about unfair practices without analysing them carefully, since they need to be confronted and tested where possible. In any local authority area some may prove true while others rest on misunderstanding or incomplete information. Councils and other bodies should make sure that policies and practices are more widely understood, should look for ways of ensuring that equality and fairness remain 'up front' as visible concerns, and should keep detailed outcomes under review, perhaps in collaboration with other local partners. It was clear from the young participants in our study that the role of women was important in making suggestions and finding out about housing options, so it is important to ensure good access to information for women.

A third issue was that residents themselves should be treated systematically as potential participants in decisions, and as valuable sources of knowledge about things that need tackling. The white tenants' group made several critical observations about participation and consultation, and also commented on the inadequate quality control over builders doing modernisation work. There were complaints too from African/Caribbean participants about repairs services. The perennial problem for officials of being accused of being out of touch was evident in some of our discussions, and can only be overcome by better communications in both directions. This does not mean that landlord performance was always viewed negatively, or unappreciated when it was good.

There is dissatisfaction with housing and environmental conditions in the inner city, and many people have aspirations for better accommodation. The theme that a person's address can affect opportunities in life ran through all the focus groups. On the other hand, prospects for outward movement amongst minority ethnic groups are clouded by concerns about the unpleasant reception that households might well receive, and the loss of valued contacts and facilities. Although there was no universal condemnation of council housing amongst Asian informants, negative images of white working class estates generally over-rode doubts felt about present areas of settlement in old and over-crowded housing. Even though knowledge about outer areas of Bradford was frequently sketchy, many participants had clear views on the specific areas that they wished to avoid. Our focus group informants were not seeking to 'self-segregate', and indeed were prepared to consider a range of areas outside established areas of settlement, if conditions were reasonable and there were enough people from their own communities living there. During the subsequent research to which we have referred, some Asian informants lamented the fact that it was difficult to achieve ethnic mixing, because white people seemed to move out as Asian households moved in. No neat dividing line was drawn between housing quality issues and choices on the one hand, and questions of behaviour, neighbouring, and social stresses on the other. Minority ethnic participants' worries about anti-social behaviour were endorsed in the white tenants' group, where there was dissatisfaction about the level of action from the council and police in respect of drugs and drug dealing on estates, on vandalism by youth, and on enforcing requirements in tenancy agreements. Perhaps it is only to be expected that there might be an underlying wish that outside organisations would step in, to share and tackle the problems that residents feel they encounter on a regular basis. Furthermore, issues raised about estate reputations by the white participants had strong parallels with the social class issues raised by the Asian groups when they were explaining their negative views of many council estates. It seems likely that most residents would look for a range of activities related to estate life and problems from any landlord that was proactive on community concerns, and was interested in the social sustainability of areas where it was renting out properties.

A general lesson for social landlords everywhere may be to seek to combine three things. First, a determined effort to plan constructively and innovatively, with an eye to the wide range of issues that concern households. Second, good consultations, sometimes seeking out hidden needs and voices or 'minorities within the minority'. Third, an ever-present concern for equal opportunities and good communications about this. Both fairness and inclusion must remain 'up front' so as to ensure that they are understood and kept under review, and that smaller groups and less visible problems are not neglected. The issue of how to reconcile the fair treatment of individuals with the wishes of larger groups remains a difficult one that may depend for its resolution partly on local circumstances and priorities. The need to demonstrate fairness is heightened by the increased significance of asylum seekers.

Chapter 11:
Key conclusions

Malcolm Harrison

Many messages in this book have been fairly optimistic, although hedged about with reservations. As we have indicated, equality of opportunities remains firmly on the UK agenda, and there is more acknowledgement of cultural sensitivity and institutionalised racisms than in the past. Progress is patchy, but valuable changes and innovations have occurred. Nonetheless, continuing problems need to be acknowledged. Some difficulties for black minority ethnic people are shared with low-income white communities, but others are distinctive because they derive from racisms linked to perceptions of colour. Barriers to progress remain, with particular groups encountering severe problems, and the complexities and hardships are exemplified in our two chapters devoted to people seeking asylum. Furthermore, the climate of popular debate has been adversely affected by increased hostility to Islam, heightening dangers of violence or abuse against those associated with this religion. More generally, the threat of harassment remains widespread, large numbers of minority ethnic households have very limited housing choices, resources for positive initiatives are often in short supply, and there are still too few BME staff finding their way into senior positions in some of the public or voluntary sector organisations involved with housing. Meanwhile, lack of information makes it difficult to appraise what has been happening in those private sector organisations that finance, manage or deliver housing.

Within housing policy, crucial issues include the future of financial support for housing improvement and sustainable low cost ownership, the effects of ongoing council stock transfer, and government strategies on investment, rents and availability of social rented dwellings. Against a backcloth of high private house prices, in many places there is undoubtedly considerable unmet demand for affordable lettings located in safe environments, and sustainable in social, economic and physical terms. As was indicated in Chapter 8, information on local preferences and preferred housing pathways is essential for policy-makers. Along with the desires for ownership, or for specialised accommodation for specific types of households, there are likely to be strong demands for sensitively managed affordable social rented dwellings.

One central concern for this book has been the issue of community cohesion. Whereas some contributions to recent debates about this have denigrated supposed tendencies for 'self-segregation' amongst minorities, and implicated these as crucial causes of social division, there is little from our material or other sources to support such an analysis. In fact, tensions and divisions are most likely made or amplified by those rather conventional and very potent racist practices that are often responsible for fracturing or undermining whatever community cohesion there might otherwise be across households of differing origins. Institutional responses are still inadequate to deal with this, and sometimes make matters worse or even cause the problems. Yet despite the racist obstacles encountered, minority ethnic people's desires and tendencies for outward geographical movement and inclusion in wider society continue to shape their perceptions, plans and activities. As material in Chapter 10 suggests, these households may have a great deal in common with white households as far as aspirations and perceptions of neighbourhood environments and interactions are concerned.

In line with this, Chapter 5 recommended a path through the community cohesion agenda for policy-makers and practitioners that would strip it of its ill-informed elements and assumptions, and 'bend' the concept usefully in the direction of an 'Inclusion and Co-operation Agenda'. This can build on those practical and well-motivated local strategies that are evident already, promoting inclusion and seeking ways forward that are appropriate for specific times and places. Practitioners should be wary (and many probably are) both of grander enterprises in social engineering, and of becoming over-alarmed about residential separation as such. Strategies should connect with realities of neighbourhood living and household preferences. Furthermore, if the community cohesion agenda is to prioritise matters that are really urgent, racisms need confronting in depth, along with the environments in which they are sustained. This overlaps with the more general need for proactive, supportive and preventative strategies to deal with complex problems of crime, anti-social behaviour, substance abuse, and low incomes, affecting white households alongside minority ethnic ones. Insufficient or under-funded affordable housing provision and local services are parts of a mosaic of problems here.

Multi-culturalism and its limits

It is important to add a postscript to our positive approach to multi-culturalism and the diversity agenda, to remind readers of the limits on the accommodating of particular cultural, religious or other beliefs in public policy domains. First, a 'diversity agenda' usually cannot justify the ignoring of equality claims. Unacceptable cultural practices can exist in parts of white society and within some minority ethnic communities, and any practices that demonstrably damage specific categories of people should be challenged. It is important for policy-makers not to invoke culture as if it were a justification for downgrading the human rights claims of women, gay or lesbian people, or any other group. For example, as one recent writer makes clear, council staff should not '... *flaunt a culturally relativist position*' in which officers' stereotypes identify forced marriages as a part of some supposed minority ethnic culture, thereby excusing council inaction on the rehousing front where vulnerable women should be receiving support (see Gupta, 2004).

Second, there are limits on the degree to which religious expectations should enter public life. Although people's specific needs and wishes should be met where it is reasonable and practical to do this, there will sometimes be limits on how far preferences or beliefs of religious groups can properly be accommodated. Individuals generally deserve and should receive respect, and we should therefore try to take account of their religious sensibilities in policy and implementation contexts (including housing). It is also essential to protect people from being discriminated against unfairly in services and jobs because of their religious commitments (or lack of these). Religions, however, vary greatly in their requirements, and in their implications for non-adherents, and differing belief systems can conflict. Indeed, a strong personal belief (or disbelief) for one person may be seen as blasphemous by another. Experiences in Northern Ireland remind us of the potential for religious allegiances to fuel violence and exclusion. Certainly, in many societies believers invoke religion as a justification for actions which are threatening to others. There has recently been alarm in Britain about so-called 'faith crimes', in which it is suspected that children may have been violently targeted because they are seen by believers as being 'possessed'. Closer to our field of expertise, and writing specifically about religion and urban regeneration, Furbey and Macey indicate that while religion may be said to contribute to social cohesion and 'regeneration', some faith traditions 'resist' such engagement, and develop '... *introverted or militantly sectarian responses'* to, for instance, '... *the challenges of globalisation and social diversity'* (2005, p. 111). The implications of a militant religious stance are captured especially neatly in a recent press report referring to the US 'Christian Soldier gun shop', an emporium that apparently supplies a wide array of lethal weapons to a keen public (*The Guardian*, 13th September 2004). Bearing in mind the London bombings of July 2005, all religious fundamentalisms should be confronted vigorously.

Public policy must protect everyone's individual freedoms of thought, and no-one should be expected to respect a set of views they cannot believe in. This need not preclude action against people who focus on religion deliberately to incite violence or conflict that will threaten public order, or damage symbols or artefacts in order to hurt adherents. Nonetheless, protective legislation in this area would deserve challenging if – rather than primarily combating the stirring up of hatred against specific groups of people identified through their religious affiliations – it opened the door to a suppression of critical debate.

Third, funding of bodies providing services needs to be within clear rules, and to take account of any genuine practical constraints. Organisations run by people from minority ethnic communities have proved their worth, and have helped make policy environments more culturally-sensitive and inclusive. They should continue to be supported, albeit within the general frameworks that govern proper practice within all organisations receiving public funds or being accorded formal recognition in service delivery or participation processes. BME organisations should not be expected to achieve targets that are not imposed on white-run bodies. In some circumstances, there may be resource constraints on the extent to which separate services or facilities can be developed to meet specific cultural preferences, although this should be subject to careful exploration and discussion if important to client groups. Having a multitude of entirely separate small providers might be problematic in resourcing terms in some specialised work, although catering for a multiplicity of divergent needs within a unified service could also prove difficult (see Beveridge, 2004). When religious organisations are involved in public services, they should operate within a general framework of fair treatment and freedom of expression, and open access to knowledge or alternative beliefs. The multi-cultural agenda makes the terrain more complex than previously, and rules and standards may be re-fashioned in the light of this, but reliance on faith organisations and groups to deliver public services is not without potential limitations as well as advantages for policy-makers and politicians. For the grass roots, furthermore, it may reflect a tendency for governmental practices to co-opt cultural and religious groupings and organisations into a process for managing behaviours and dissent.

Ten conclusions from this book

Ten key points need to be kept in mind when looking into specific contexts, and these are set out in the box below.

Box 48 : Ten key conclusions from this book

1. In many situations research is still likely to uncover evidence of a persistent pattern in which burdens and penalties continue to be imposed on minority households by negative actions and practices, coming primarily from the white-dominated mainstream. Stereotyping may play a role here, alongside direct actions of harassment or deliberate exclusion, and indirectly discriminatory practices such as under-representation within consultative networks, or poor communications with minority communities. Nonetheless, detailed facts are generally needed before reaching conclusions about exactly what the problems are, or their extent. Organisations and their impact vary.

2. Although government has specific policies for asylum seekers and refugees, practices in this field cannot be evaluated entirely separately from questions about discrimination, harassment and ethnic relations. Government contributions via policy development and official statements on asylum seekers have contrasted markedly with more general strategies on ethnicity and equality, and may have helped give sustenance to some kinds of racist outlooks. Unfortunately, the tone and underlying assumptions of the community cohesion debate have also raised problems.

3. Much can be achieved by law and guidelines in modifying or controlling discriminatory behaviours and improving the sensitivity of organisational activities. Social harmony and good ethnic relations cannot really be successfully 'engineered' in the short term by policy initiatives, but equality laws and improved knowledge have helped change how we live and relate to each other. UK experience illustrates what can be done by continually pressing forward on the long journey to fairer and more sophisticated practice. Ongoing scrutiny and monitoring are needed to identify deficiencies, and we should not become complacent. →

---

4. Studying the implications of ethnicity in policy domains should not be cast in terms of a kind of 'victimology' in which the positive achievements of households and organisations are under-valued. Acknowledging diversity means taking account of the varying trajectories of different ethnic groups and cohorts, and appreciating their strengths as well as the barriers that some may face. There are many success stories alongside accounts of severe deprivation affecting certain groups. Perhaps, in some instances, minority ethnic households from certain community backgrounds appear to have achieved better positions and have stronger community resources than white households on low-income estates, and the needs of the latter should not be neglected. On the other hand, the threat of harassment and the impact of being perceived as 'non-white' adversely affect even those households who have achieved a measure of economic success. Issues of 'colour' have a distinct characteristic, in that the pattern of hostility and discrimination tends to persist strongly even after a degree of integration into UK lifestyles, and applies across a wide range of minority ethnic groups.

5. It is a mistake to become preoccupied with spatial patterns of residence for different groups, and to build upon a combination of these with cultural distinctiveness an image of socially divided cities, or of 'threats' to community cohesion. What matter are: (i) the behaviours of institutions in providing or facilitating housing; (ii) good communications and interactions between groups, households and organisations in an ongoing environment of learning and collaboration; (iii) fairness; and (iv) real choices that households can safely exercise when choosing where and how to live.

6. Other dimensions of difference need to be kept in mind alongside ethnicity, including age, disability, gender, sexual orientation, and socio-economic status or class. One of the underlying problems for many minority ethnic households is that they are economically disadvantaged, as well as being seen as different from the mainstream. This may be associated with being dependent upon specific labour markets, being a single parent household, living in an area where affordable housing is in short supply, being a disabled person excluded from well paid work, being treated as a non-citizen while an asylum seeker, or coming from a community which has a high incidence of poverty and low levels of capital.

7. Ethnicity is a complex topic, and categorising people into broad groups on the basis of perceived origins or backgrounds may not always fit the realities of identities and affiliations of individuals. Cultures are not fixed and unchanging, and increasing numbers of people have complicated and mixed heritages. It is also easy to miss the needs of smaller or newer groups. New stereotypes about cultural practices and commitments should not be drafted into service too readily as successors to earlier ideas about supposedly distinctive groups of white people and those of African or Asian origins.

8. A preoccupation with the ethnic diversity (or faiths) agenda should not be allowed to deflect attention from equality issues and socio-economic disadvantage. Diversity and ethnicity should not be highlighted so as to be used as a basis from which to manage communities and try to condition behaviour within them in a top-down manner, or through particular forms of hierarchical political representation. At the same time, government should encourage progressive rather than fundamentalist tendencies whenever public funds are made available or participation occurs.

→

9. The increasing complexities of organisational and inter-organisational environments need to be confronted in an ongoing way within professional practice. Progress through enhanced regulation and performance measurement is not cost-free, and commitment has a price within service provision. This may include everything from the costs of data-collection and monitoring to the staff time devoted to consultations. Perhaps one lesson might be that organisations need to put equal opportunities strategies and responsiveness to diversity close to the heart of their regular planning, so as to avoid marginalising equality work into separate compartments where resources become key constraints. Meanwhile, central government needs to keep under review the impact of its regulatory systems, not just in terms of outcomes for services, access and employment, but also in respect of their effectiveness, demands, strengths and weaknesses within practice environments. There are substantial costs as well as gains from our transition towards an 'audit society', and we need to bear these in mind (and perhaps target the reduction or better management of some of them) when seeking improved ways of evaluating and handling organisational and inter-organisational performance. It may be desirable to challenge the priority given to some of the other kinds of goals that drive organisational practices and individual personnel, if we genuinely want proactive approaches to equality, diversity, participation, partnership and community development. Perhaps the issue of local empowerment and 'ownership' will turn out to have been one of the crucial factors in the longer term.

10. Those who seek improved community relations should press for more resources and understanding for dealing with problems within disadvantaged white populations, and for tackling racist outlooks and the climate in which they prosper. The latter is perhaps the hardest task of all, since some national events have been undermining prospects for common sense and improved understanding. Negative factors include: the widened gap between rich and poor and the accompanying pressure on those services and resources allocated to disadvantaged areas; media and politicians' treatment of asylum and migration; and some of the side-effects of recent overseas military commitments and hostility to Islam.

List and summary of some useful websites

Compiled by Kusminder Chahal and Lisa Hunt

http://www.ligali.org
The African British Investigative, Monitoring, Equality and Complaints Board (LIGALI) is a non-profit making organisation that uses the Internet to expose the current policies of UK based organisations who refuse to support the ideology of equal rights for all.

http://www.amrnet.demon.co.uk/
The Association of Muslim Researchers is a group of people following research and religion. They are looking to identify gaps in knowledge and find ways to fill them, and develop solutions to the issues of racism.

http://www.asylumsupport.info/
Asylum Support Info focuses on all matters that concern people seeking asylum, together with a directory of hundreds of online resources relating to: conflict, country data, court cases, deportation, detention, discrimination, funding, gender, government, human rights, trafficking, law, media, migration, and policy.

http://www.audit-commission.gov.uk/
The Audit Commission is an independent public body that aims to ensure that public money is used efficiently, effectively and economically. This site offers links to Audit Commission reports.

http://www.blink.org.uk
Black Information Link. An interactive site for black communities.

http://www.carf.demon.co.uk/
The Campaign Against Racism and Fascism (CARF) is an independent anti-racist site and also a magazine. It documents resistance against racism including issues concerning black and refugee organisations, monitoring groups, anti-deportation campaigns, football fans and similar issues.

http://www.warwick.ac.uk/fac/soc/CRER_RC/
The Centre for Research in Ethnic Relations (CRER) is based at the University of Warwick and deals with research into the experience of people from minority groups. It focuses on the process of racial discrimination, issues of citizenship, political participation, cultural identity, refugees, ethnic mobilisation and nationalism.

http://www.cih.org/
The Chartered Institute of Housing is a professional body of people working in housing with the aim of contributing to the well-being of communities and influencing housing policy. This site has links to publications plus information about training and conferences.

http://www.citizensadvice.org.uk/

The Citizens Advice service helps people resolve their legal, money and other problems by providing free legal information and advice, and influencing policy-makers. This site has links to various publications.

http://www.c21project.org.uk/

Citizenship 21 was inspired by a series of bombings targeted at minority groups that took place in London in 1999. They help with harassment of all kinds including racist, disablist and sexist.

http://www.cre.gov.uk/

The Commission for Racial Equality is a publicly funded, non-governmental body set up under the Race Relations Act 1976 to tackle racial discrimination and promote racial equality. It helps victims of racial harassment and discrimination by providing information. It works with public bodies and businesses in order to ensure equal treatment.

http://www.magenta.nl/crosspoint/uk.html

Crosspoint Anti Racism UK. A good gateway to other anti-racism/anti-fascism sites.

http://www.ethnicminorityfund.org.uk/html/index.asp

The Ethnic Minority Foundation (EMF) is a charity organisation aimed at building capacity within minority ethnic community organisations, influencing policy, and stimulating participation in regeneration and neighbourhood renewal.

http://www.fbho.org.uk/site/

The Federation of Black Housing Organisations works to eliminate racism in housing. They provide information, advice, research and training services on housing management and race equality.

http://www.btinternet.com/~thegypsycouncil/

The Gypsy Council for Education, Culture, Welfare and Civil Rights is involved in a wide range of support, liaison and lobbying work. It publishes a newsletter, *The Hub*.

http://www.irishsocieties.org/

The Federation of Irish Societies aims to make a comfortable Ireland which is participating in a multi-cultural Britain. They promote the interests of Irish communities, to continue Irish cultural history, to help develop the youth movement and to represent the voice of Ireland in Britain.

http://www.furd.org/

Football Unites, Racism Divides aim to bring together people from different racial backgrounds. They use football as a way to spread racial awareness, working with various football clubs in order to promote anti-racist education in schools, colleges and youth clubs.

http://www.fairuk.org/

Forum Against Islamophobia and Racism (FAIR) is an independent charitable organisation that seeks to raise awareness and combat Islamophobia. It monitors specific incidences of harassment and violence and advises the relevant agencies on how to deal with such issues. It also keeps watch over such media as print, radio, television, Internet, fashion, music and local events.

http://www.gara.org.uk/
The Glasgow Anti-Racist Alliance tries to combat racial harassment by supporting the minority groups in its area and providing help with social, educational, and domestic aspects of life. It works on research as well as organising a work-shadowing scheme to stop racial harassment in the work place.

http://www.homelesspages.org.uk/index.asp
Homelesspages provides information about publications and training on homelessness. It has links to a wide range of organisations as well as links to all local authority sites.

http://www.homeoffice.gov.uk/
This site offers information about all the different Home Office departments: Community and Race; Crime and Policing; Immigration and Nationality; Drugs; Terrorism; Passports; Justice and Victims; and Research and Statistics. It provides links to various reports, for example the Cantle review on Community Cohesion: (http://www.homeoffice.gov.uk/comrace/cohesion/).

http://www.hact.org.uk/
The housing associations charitable trust (hact) aims to develop and promote solutions for people on the margins of mainstream housing. They work at a local level supporting individual projects, and at a national level influencing policy and practice.

http://www.housingcorp.gov.uk/
The Housing Corporation invests in housing associations to provide homes that meet local needs.

http://www.dmuracetoolkit.com/main.asp
The Housing and Race Equality Toolkit is funded by the Housing Corporation and comprises management tools for housing organisations to conduct race equality audits. The toolkit also provides an additional resource for Housing Corporation regulators investigating race equality issues.

http://www.irr.org.uk/
The Independent Race and Refugee News Network provides individuals in the voluntary sector, activists and students with information on issues such as government policies, police and criminal policies, violence and harassment, asylum seekers and refugees, education and employment.

http://www.icar.org.uk/
The Information Centre about Asylum and Refugees (ICAR) is an independent information centre aimed at promoting understanding of refugees and asylum seekers in the UK. This has links to a number of publications as well as information about research that is being carried out in this field.

http://www.jcwi.org.uk/
The Joint Council for the Welfare of Immigrants (JCWI) is an independent voluntary organisation that campaigns for justice and aims to combat racism in immigration and asylum law and policy. This site has links to publications, training events and campaigns.

http://www.jrf.org.uk/
The Joseph Rowntree Foundation (JRF) is one of the largest social policy research and development charities in the UK. It also engages in practical housing and care work through the Joseph Rowntree Housing Trust.

http://www.lemosandcrane.co.uk/
Lemos & Crane conducts research on various social policy issues including race equality; supporting vulnerable and homeless people; and communities and neighbourhood renewal. The site has links to publications and events.

http://www.torturecare.org.uk/
The Medical Foundation for the Care of Victims of Torture provides care and rehabilitation to survivors of torture and violence. It is particularly relevant to those working with asylum seekers and refugees but has also links to a number of other sites.

http://www.metoo.org.uk
Me Too rejects violence against minorities of any type. They provide anti-discrimination aids for teachers and encourage people to make a stand via a petition style movement.

http://www.monitoring-group.co.uk/
The Monitoring Group (TMG) is a charitable organisation offering legal, moral and practical support to those suffering from racial harassment. They monitor the responses of institutions when they are confronted with these issues and provide information and training to those dealing with victims.

http://www.monitoring-group.co.uk/TMG%20services/minquan/
Min Quan is a branch of TMG providing support to the Chinese community.

http://www.naar.org.uk/
The National Assembly Against Racism produces leaflets and newsletters concerning issues to do with all aspects of racism. They run a number of campaigns in order to combat racism.

http://www.wales.gov.uk/index.htm
National Assembly for Wales.

http://www.housing.org.uk/
The National Housing Federation is an organisation that represents the independent social housing sector. It has 1,400 no profits organisations in its membership and seeks to promote its members and provide affordable homes.

http://www.nrdf.org.uk/
The National Rent Deposit Forum (see Chapter 2 for reference to this organisation).

http://www.nawp.org/
Newham Asian Women's Project provides support to Asian women and children experiencing violence. They offer advice and support on a number of topics including safe housing, welfare or income benefit claims, health concerns and legal advice such as non-molestation orders or injunctions.

http://www.odpm.gov.uk/
The Office of the Deputy Prime Minister is responsible for policy on housing, planning, devolution, regional and local government, and the fire services. It takes responsibility for the Social Exclusion Unit, the Neighbourhood Renewal Unit, and the Government Offices for the Regions. This site has links to various publications.

http://www.raceactionnet.co.uk/
Race Action Net is made up from hundreds of organisations including government, housing, public services, police, criminal justice agencies, community and volunteer organisations. It aims to provide information on prevention, support, witness aid and help dealing with perpetrators. It also provides a self-assessment framework for organisational performance in tackling racial harassment, racist attacks and anti-social behaviour.

http://www.r4rj.org.uk/
The Race for Racial Justice site aims to unite communities across Britain against racism by organising high profile sponsored events in order to raise funds for anti-racism groups and charities. The website contains information about the racial justice charity, the world's major religions, religious calendars, discrimination and the law and definitions of race.

http://www.refugee-action.org.uk/
Refugee Action is an independent national charity aimed at helping refugees build a new life in the UK. Their work includes campaigning, refugee volunteer projects and community development work.

http://www.refugeecouncil.org.uk/
The Refugee Council is a charity organisation that helps refugees and asylum seekers in the UK. Their work includes giving advice and support; working with refugee community organisations (RCOs); offering training and employment courses; and disseminating information on worldwide issues. This site provides links to Refugee Council publications and other related sites.

http://www.refugeehousing.org.uk/
Refugee Housing Association (RHA) was created nearly 50 years ago and is one of the country's leading providers of housing and support for refugees and asylum seekers.

http://www.runnymedetrust.org/
The Runnymede Trust is an independent voluntary organisation that acts as a 'bridge builder' between minority ethnic groups and policy-makers and fights against social injustice and racial harassment. They have a number of practitioners' handbooks, briefing papers, and research reports.

http://www.ruraldiversity.net/rural_race_equality_project.htm
The Rural Race Equality Project provides a range of information concerning rural cases of racism. It includes a list of key organisations which can help deal with race issues in the South of England.

http://www.scottish.parliament.uk/home.htm
The Scottish Parliament.

http://www.england.shelter.org.uk/home/index.cfm
Shelter battles to end homelessness and bad housing in Britain by campaigning for new laws, policies and solutions. This site provides links to a number of publications.

http://www.twafa.org.uk/
Tyne and Wear Anti Fascist Association (TWAFA) is one of the longest running anti-fascism groups in Britain. They work with local communities and the police in order to combat fascism by spreading a message of tolerance.

http://www.unhcr.org/
The United Nations High Commissioner for Refugees leads and co-ordinates international action to protect refugees and resolve refugee problems worldwide. This site has links to various publications, research and statistics.

http://www.victimsupport.org/
Victim Support is an independent support charity, which helps people deal with the effects of racial crimes. They provide someone to talk to in confidence, information on court and police procedures, compensation and insurance, and links to other sources of help (including every Racial Equality Council).

Bibliography

Ahmed, A. and Sodhi, D. (2000) *The housing and support needs of women especially those from ethnic minorities*, Commissioned by Rochdale Women's Housing Aid Group, Rochdale: Rochdale WHAG.

Ahmed Iqbal Ullah Race Relations Research Archive, Race and Housing Research Briefings, in *Race and Housing Quarterly Newsletters*, and *inHabitus*, Manchester: the Archive.

Allen, T. (forthcoming), 'Private sector housing improvement in the UK and the chronically ill: implications for collaborative working', *Housing Studies*.

Ambrose, P. (2000) *A drop in the ocean*, Health and Social Policy Research Centre, Brighton: University of Brighton.

Ambrose, P. and MacDonald, D. (2001) *For richer, for poorer?*, Health and Social Policy Research Centre, Brighton: University of Brighton.

Amin, A. (2002) 'Ethnicity and the multicultural city: living with diversity', *Environment and Planning A*, 34, 6, pp. 959-980.

Andersen, H., Munck, R., Fagan, C., Goldson, B., Hall, D., Lansley, J., Novak, T., Melville, R., Moore, R. and Ben-Tovim, G. (1999) *Neighbourhood images in Liverpool*, York: Joseph Rowntree Foundation.

Anthias, F. and Yuval-Davis, N. with Cain, H. (1993) *Racialized boundaries*, London: Routledge.

Argent, K., Carter, S. and Durr, P. (2000) *Facing reality: evolving responses by London boroughs to racial harassment*, London: London Housing Unit.

Atkinson, R. (2004) 'The evidence on the impact of gentrification: new lessons for the urban renaissance?', *European Journal of Housing Policy*, 4. 1, pp. 107-131.

Attwood, C., Singh, G., Prime, D., Creasey, R. and others (2003) *2001 Home Office Citizenship Survey: people, families and communities*, Research Study 270, London: Home Office Research, Development and Statistics Directorate.

Back, L., Keith, M., Khan, A., Shukra, K. and Solomos, J. (2002), 'New Labour's white heart: politics, multiculturalism and the return of assimilation', *The Political Quarterly*, 73, 4, pp. 445-454.

Bagguley, P. and Hussain, Y. (2003) 'The Bradford "riot" of 2001: a preliminary analysis', paper for *Ninth Alternative Futures and Popular Protest Conference*, Manchester.

Baker, C. (2004) 'Pathfinders' cash rolled out', *Planning*, 9th April, p. 8.

Beazley, M. and Loftman, P. (2001) *Race and regeneration: black and minority ethnic experience of the Single Regeneration Budget*, CURS, Birmingham and CPPUC, Central England; London: The London Borough of Camden and the Local Government Information Unit.

Begum, N. (1992) *Something to be proud of: the lives of Asian disabled people and carers in Waltham Forest*, London: Waltham Forest Race Relations Unit and Disability Unit.

Ben-Tovim, G., Gabriel, J., Law, I. and Stredder, K. (1986) *The local politics of race*, Basingstoke: Macmillan.

Beveridge, M. (2004) 'When tabloids attack', *Housing Today*, May 7th.

Birmingham City Council Housing Department (1998) *Black and minority ethnic communities' access to outer city housing*, Birmingham: Birmingham City Council.

Black Housing (2003) *Tenant Inspectors*, 131, November/December, pp. 12-13.

Blackaby, B. (2004) *Community cohesion and housing: a good practice guide*, Coventry: CIH.

Blackaby, B. and Chahal, K. (2000) *Black and minority ethnic housing strategies: a good practice guide*, Coventry: Chartered Institute of Housing, Federation of Black Housing Organisations and The Housing Corporation.

Blackaby, B. and Larner, D. (2003) *Equality and diversity*, Good Practice Briefing, 26, Coventry: Chartered Institute of Housing.

Bloch, A. (2000) 'A new era or more of the same? Asylum policy in the UK', *Journal of Refugee Studies*, 13, 1, pp. 29-42.

Bloch, A. and Levy. C. (eds.) (1999) *Refugees, Citizenship and Social Policy in Europe*, Basingstoke: Macmillan.

BME Housing Project (2003) *BME Housing Project feasibility study: final report*, Cardiff: National Assembly for Wales.

Bowes, A., Dar, N. and Sim, D. (1998) *'Too white, too rough, and too many problems': a study of Pakistani housing in Britain*, Housing Policy and Practice Unit Research Report No. 3, Stirling: Department of Applied Social Science, University of Stirling.

Brownill, S. and Darke, J. (1998) *'Rich mix': inclusive strategies for urban regeneration*, Bristol: The Policy Press.

Burnett, J. (2004) 'Community, cohesion and the state', *Race & Class*, 45, 3, pp. 1-18.

Burney, E. (1967) *Housing on trial: a study of immigrants and local government*, IRR, London: Oxford University Press.

Burayidi, M. (2003) 'The multicultural city as planners' enigma', *Planning Theory and Practice*, 4, 3, pp. 259-273.

Cabinet Office (2000) *Minority ethnic issues in social exclusion and neighbourhood renewal: a guide to the work of the Social Exclusion Unit and the Policy Action Teams so far*, London: Crown copyright.

Cantle, T. (2004) 'Think Tank', *The Guardian*, 11th August 2004.

Carter, M. and El-Hassan, A. (2003) *Between NASS and a hard place*, London: hact.

Castles, S. and Miller, M. (1998) *The age of migration: international population movements in the modern world,* 2nd edition, London: The Guilford Press.

Chahal, K. (2003) *Racist harassment support projects: their role, impact and potential*, York: Joseph Rowntree Foundation.

Chahal, K. (2004) 'Experiencing ethnicity: discrimination and service provision', *Foundations*, York: Joseph Rowntree Foundation, September.

Chahal, K. and Julienne, L. (1999) *'We can't all be white!': racist victimisation in the UK*, York: Joseph Rowntree Foundation.

Chamba, R., Ahmad, W., Hirst, M., Lawton, D. and Beresford, B. (1999) *On the edge: minority ethnic families caring for a severely disabled child*, Bristol: Policy Press.

Chan, C.K., Bowpitt, G., Cole, B., Somerville, P. and Chen, J.Y. (2004) *The UK Chinese people: diversity and unmet needs*, Nottingham: Division of Social Work, Social Policy and Human Services, Nottingham Trent University.

Chaney, P. (2004) 'The post-devolution equality agenda: the case of the Welsh Assembly's statutory duty to promote equality of opportunity', *Policy & Politics*, 21, 1, pp. 63-77.

Chartered Institute of Housing [CIH] (2003) *Providing a Safe Haven - Housing Asylum Seekers and Refugees*, CIH Policy Paper, London: Chartered Institute of Housing.

Clayton, O. and Watson, W. (1996) 'Introduction', in Clayton, O. (ed.) *An American dilemma revisited*, New York: Russell Sage Foundation, pp. xxiii-xxix.

Cohen, S. (2001) *Immigration controls, the family and the welfare state*, London: Jessica Kingsley.

Cole, I. and Robinson, D. (2003) *Somali housing experiences in England*, Sheffield: CRESR, Sheffield Hallam University.

Commission for Racial Equality [CRE] (1984) *Race and council housing in Hackney:* report of a formal investigation, London: CRE.

CRE (1984a) *Abbey National Building Society*, Report of a formal investigation, London: CRE.

CRE (1985) *Walsall Metropolitan Borough Council: practices and policies of housing allocation*, Report of a formal investigation, London: CRE.

CRE (1985a) *Race and mortgage lending*, Report of formal investigation, London: CRE.

CRE (1985b) *Review of the Race Relations Act 1976: proposals for change*, London: CRE.

CRE (1987) *Living in terror: a report on racial violence and harassment in housing*, London: CRE.

CRE (1988) *Homelessness and discrimination*, Report of a formal investigation into the London Borough of Tower Hamlets, London: CRE.

CRE (1988a) *Racial discrimination in a London estate agency*, Report of a formal investigation, London: CRE.

CRE (1990) *Putting your house in order: estate agents and equal opportunity policies*, London: CRE.

CRE (1990a) *Racial discrimination in an Oldham estate agency*, Report of a formal investigation, London: CRE.

CRE (1990b) *'Sorry it's gone'*, London: CRE.

CRE (1999) *Auditing for equality: auditing councils' performance against the CRE's Standard for Local Government*, London: CRE.

CRE (2000) *Strengthening the Race Relations Act: the Race Relations (Amendment) Act 2000*, London: CRE, December. (Explanatory summary.)

CRE (2002) *Code of Practice on the Duty to Promote Race Equality,* London: CRE.

Community Cohesion Independent Review Team (led by Ted Cantle) (2001) *Community Cohesion: A Report of the Independent Review Team,* London: Home Office.

Community Cohesion Panel (2004) *The end of parallel lives?,* The Report of the Community Cohesion Panel, London: Home Office.

Comrie, J. (2004) 'African-Caribbean elders and their housing experiences', *Research Findings*, School of Sociology and Social Policy, Leeds: University of Leeds.

Crawley, H. (2003) 'Presumed Guilty', *The Guardian*, 22nd January.

Darden, J. (2004) 'Black access to suburban housing in America's most racially segregated metropolitan area: Detroit', paper for ISA conference on *Adequate and affordable housing for all*, Toronto.

Department of the Environment, Transport and the Regions (DETR), The Housing Corporation, and the National Assembly for Wales (2001) *Tackling racial harassment: code of practice for social landlords*, Housing Research Summary 148, London: DETR.

Department for Transport, Local Government and the Regions (DTLR) (2001) *Addressing the housing needs of black and minority ethnic people*, a DTLR (Housing Directorate) Action Plan, London: DTLR.

Dines, M. (1973) 'Cool Reception', *New Community*, 2 (4), pp. 380-383.

Dwyer, P. and Brown, D. (2004) *Meeting basic needs? Exploring the welfare strategies of forced migrants*, Summary of Findings from an ESRC-funded study, Leeds: University of Leeds.

Emerson, M., Yancey, G. and Chai, K. (2001) 'Does race matter in residential segregation? Exploring the preferences of white Americans', *American Sociological Review*, 66, 6, pp. 922-935.

Forrest, R. and Kearns, A. (1999) *Joined-up places? Social cohesion and neighbourhood regeneration*, York: Joseph Rowntree Foundation.

Fotheringham, D. and Perry, J. (2003) *Offering communities real choice – lettings and community cohesion*, Briefing Paper, Coventry: CIH.

Furbey, R. and Macey, M. (2005) 'Religion and urban regeneration: a place for faith?', *Policy & Politics*, 33, 1, pp. 95-116.

Gidley, G., Harrison, M. and Robinson, D. (1999) *Housing black and minority ethnic people in Sheffield*, Sheffield: CRESR, Sheffield Hallam University.

Gidley, G., Harrison, M. and Tomlins, R. (2002) 'The housing needs of black and minority ethnic groups', in Somerville, P. and Steele, A. (eds.), *'Race', housing and social exclusion*, London: Jessica Kingsley, pp. 61-76.

Giffinger, R. and Reeger, U. (1997) 'Turks in Austria: backgrounds, geographical distribution and housing conditions', in Özüekren, S. and Van Kempen, R. (eds.), *Turks in European cities: housing and urban segregation*, Utrecht: ERCOMER, pp. 41-66.

Gill, F. (2002) 'The diverse experiences of black and minority ethnic women in relation to housing and social exclusion', in Somerville, P. and Steele, A. (eds.), *'Race', housing and social exclusion*, London: Jessica Kingsley, pp. 159-177.

Goetz, E. (2002) 'Forced relocation vs voluntary mobility: the effects of dispersal programmes on households', *Housing Studies*, 17, 1, pp. 107-123.

Gupta, R. (2004) 'Fobbed off? Too right', *Roof*, September/October, p. 14.

HACAS Chapman Hendy (2002) *Beyond bricks and mortar: bringing regeneration into stock transfer*, Coventry: CIH.

Hansen, R. and King, D. (2000) 'Illiberalism and the New Politics of Asylum: Liberalism's Dark Side', *The Political Quarterly*, 7 (4), pp. 396-403.

Harrison, M. (1995) *Housing, 'race', social policy and empowerment*, CRER Research in Ethnic Relations Series, Aldershot: Avebury.

Harrison, M. (1998) 'Minority ethnic housing associations and local housing strategies: an uncertain future?', *Local Government Studies*, 24, 1, pp. 74-89.

Harrison, M. (1999) 'Theorising homelessness and "race"', in Kennett, P. and Marsh, A. (eds.), *Homelessness: exploring the new terrain*, Bristol: The Policy Press, pp. 101-121.

Harrison, M. (2002) 'Black and minority ethnic housing associations', in Somerville, P. and Steele, A. (eds.), *'Race', housing and social exclusion*, London: Jessica Kingsley, pp. 114-129.

Harrison, M. and Davies, J. (1995) *Constructing equality: housing associations and minority ethnic contractors*, Bristol: SAUS Publications.

Harrison, M. with Davis, C. (2001) *Housing, social policy and difference: disability, ethnicity, gender and housing*, Bristol: Policy Press.

Harrison, M. and Law, I. (1997) 'Needs and empowerment in minority ethnic housing: some issues of definition and local strategy', *Policy & Politics*, 25, 3, pp. 285-298.

Harrison, M. with Phillips, D. (2003) *Housing and black and minority ethnic communities: review of the evidence base*, London: Office of the Deputy Prime Minister.

Harrison, M. and Stevens, L. (1981) *Ethnic minorities and the availability of mortgages*, Department of Social Policy and Administration, Social Policy Research Monograph 5, Leeds: University of Leeds.

Harrison, M., Karmani, A., Law, I., Phillips, D. and Ravetz, A. (1996) *Black and minority ethnic housing associations: an evaluation of the Housing Corporation's black and minority ethnic housing association strategies, Source Research 16*, London: The Housing Corporation.

Hastings, A. (2003) 'Strategic, multilevel neighbourhood regeneration: an outward-looking approach at last ?', in Imrie, R. and Raco, M. (eds.), *Urban renaissance: New Labour, community and urban policy*, Bristol: The Policy Press, pp. 85-100

Hawtin, M., Kettle, J., and Moran, C., with Crossley, R. (1999) *Housing integration and resident participation: evaluation of a project to help integrate black and ethnic minority tenants*, York: JRF.

Hayter, T. (2000) *Open borders: the case against immigration controls*, London: Pluto Press.

Henderson, J. and Karn, V. (1987) *Race, class and state housing: inequality and the allocation of public housing in Britain*, Aldershot: Gower.

Hetherington, P. and Weaver, M. (2004) 'Razed expectations' and 'renovation vs the bulldozer', *Society Guardian*, 10th March.

Hickman, M. and Walter, B. (1997) *Discrimination and the Irish community in Britain*: A report of research undertaken for the Commission for Racial Equality, London: CRE.

Hill, C. (1967), *How colour prejudiced is Britain?*, London: Panther Books.

Hollifield, J. and Zuk, G. (1998) 'Immigrants, markets and rights', in Kurthen, H., Fijalkowski, J. and Wagner, G. (eds.), *Immigration, citizenship, and the welfare state in Germany and the United States: Part B, welfare policies and immigrants' citizenship*, Stamford: JAI Press, pp. 67-87.

Home Office (Secretary of State for the Home Department) (1975) *Racial Discrimination*, Cmnd. 6234, London: HMSO.

Home Office (1998) *Fairer, Faster, Firmer – A Modern Approach to Immigration and Asylum*, London: Home Office.

Home Office (2000) *Connecting communities: race equality support programmes*, Communities Funding Team, London: Home Office.

Home Office (2000a) *Full and equal citizens: a strategy for the integration of refugees into the UK*, London: Home Office.

Home Office (2000b) *Code of Practice on Reporting and Recording Racist Incidents*, London: Home Office.

Home Office (2001) *Ethnic Minorities' Experience of Crime and Policing: findings from the 2000 British Crime Survey*, Home Office Findings 146, London: Home Office.

Home Office (2002) *Secure Borders, Safe Haven: Integration with Diversity in Modern Britain*, London: Home Office.

Home Office (2004) *Strength in Diversity: Towards a Community Cohesion and Race Equality Strategy*, London: Home Office Communication Directorate.

Home Office (2004a) *Integration matters: a national strategy for refugee integration; a draft for consultation* (Home Office Website).

Housing Corporation (1998) *Black and Minority Ethnic Housing Policy*, London: The Housing Corporation.

Housing Corporation (2001) *The Black and Minority Ethnic Housing Policy Progress Report*, London: The Housing Corporation, July.

Housing Corporation (2001a) *Black and Minority Ethnic Registered Social Landlords: Sector Study 4,* London: The Housing Corporation.

Housing Corporation (2002) *A review of housing association race equality strategies: Sector Study 12*, London: The Housing Corporation.

Housing Corporation (2003) *The Changing Circumstances of Women Headed Households, 1992-2002: Sector Study 23,* London: The Housing Corporation.

Housing Corporation (2003a) *Black and minority ethnic housing associations: the challenge of growth and viability, Source Research Report 69*, London: The Housing Corporation.

Housing Corporation (2003b) *Equality and diversity: policy and strategies*, London: The Housing Corporation.

Housing Corporation (2004) *Muslim housing experiences, Source Research 70*, London: The Housing Corporation.

Housing Corporation (2004a) *Muslim housing experiences, Sector Study 34*, London: The Housing Corporation.

Imrie, R. and Raco, M. (eds.) (2003) *New Labour, community and urban policy*, Bristol: The Policy Press.

Joly, D. (1997) *Refugees in Europe: the hostile new agenda*, London: Minority Rights Group.

JRF (2000) 'Ethnic diversity, neighbourhoods and housing', *Foundations*, January, York: JRF.

JRF (2000a) 'Action being taken to tackle racial harassment', *Findings*, November, York: JRF.

JRF (2002) 'Black and minority ethnic organisations' experience of local compacts', *Findings*, January, York, JRF.

JRF (2003) 'Home-ownership and poverty in Britain', *Findings*, January, York:JRF.

JRF (2003a) 'Supporting and empowering victims of racist harassment', *Findings*, July, York: JRF.

JRF (2003b) 'Engaging faith communities in urban regeneration', *Findings*, March, York, JRF.

JRF (2004) 'Black voluntary and community sector funding, civic engagement and capacity-building', *Findings*, February, York, JRF.

JRF (2004a) 'Black and minority ethnic older people's views on research findings', *Findings*, May, York: JRF.

JRF (2004b) 'The changing role of Audit Commission inspection of local government', *Findings*, November, York: JRF.

Julienne, L. (2001) *The root to my tree: examining the experience of Positive Action Training in Housing*, Ruislip: L8J Publications.

Kalra, V. (2003) 'Police lore and community disorder: diversity in the criminal justice system', in Mason, D. (ed.) *Explaining ethnic differences: changing patterns of disadvantage in Britain*, Bristol: The Policy Press, pp. 139-152.

Karn, V. (1997) '"Ethnic penalties" and racial discrimination in education, employment and housing: conclusions and policy implications', in Karn, V. (ed.), *Ethnicity in the 1991 Census; Volume 4, Employment, education and housing among the ethnic minority populations of Britain*, London: The Stationery Office, pp. 265-290.

Karn, V. (ed.) (1997a) *Ethnicity in the 1991 Census; Volume 4, Employment, education and housing among the ethnic minority populations of Britain*, London: The Stationery Office

Karn, V., Mian, S., Brown, M., and Dale, A. (1999) *Tradition, change and diversity: understanding the housing needs of minority ethnic groups in Manchester, Source Research 37*, London: The Housing Corporation.

Karn, V. and Phillips, D. (1998) 'Race and ethnicity in housing: a diversity of experience', in Blackstone, T., Parekh, B. and Sanders, P. (eds.), *Race relations in Britain: a developing agenda*, London: Routledge, pp. 128-157.

Kearns, A. (2002) 'Housing disadvantage in the inner city: the needs and preferences of ethnic minorities in sub-standard housing', in Somerville, P. and Steele, A. (eds.), *'Race', housing and social exclusion*, London: Jessica Kingsley, pp. 245-267.

Kearns, A. (2003) 'Social capital, regeneration and urban policy', in Imrie, R. and Raco, M. (eds.), *Urban renaissance: New Labour, community and urban policy*, Bristol: The Policy Press, pp. 37-60.

Kvistad, G. (1998) 'Membership without politics? The social and political rights of foreigners in Germany', in Kurthen, H., Fijalkowski, J. and Wagner, G. (eds.), *Immigration, citizenship, and the welfare state in Germany and the United States: Part B, welfare policies and immigrants' citizenship*, Stamford: JAI Press, pp 141-157.

Lakey, J. (1997) 'Neighbourhoods and housing', in Modood, T. and Berthoud, R., with Lakey, J., Nazroo, J., Smith, P., Virdee, S. and Beishon, S., *Ethnic minorities in Britain: diversity and disadvantage*, London: Policy Studies Institute, pp. 184-223.

Law, I (1996) *Racism, ethnicity and social policy*, London: Prentice Hall/Harvester Wheatsheaf.

Law, I. (2004) 'Chinese action research project: household needs, community organisations and public services', *Research Findings*, Centre for Ethnicity and Racism Studies, Leeds: University of Leeds.

Law, I., Davies, J., Phillips, D. and Harrison, M. (1996) *Equity and difference: racial and ethnic inequalities in housing needs and housing investment in Leeds*, 'Race' and Public Policy Research Unit, Leeds: School of Sociology and Social Policy, University of Leeds.

Lees, L. (2003) 'Visions of "urban renaissance": the Urban Task Force and the Urban White Paper', in Imrie, R. and Raco, M. (eds.), *Urban renaissance: New Labour, community and urban policy*, Bristol: The Policy Press, pp. 61-82.

Lemos, G. (2000) *Racial harassment: action on the ground*, published for the Joseph Rowntree Foundation, London: Lemos & Crane.

Lemos & Crane (for The Housing Corporation) (undated) *Black and minority ethnic registered social landlords*, Sector Study 4, London: The Housing Corporation.

Local Government Association (LGA), with the ODPM, Home Office, CRE and Inter Faith Network for the UK (2002; updated 2nd April 2004), *Guidance on Community Cohesion*, London: LGA.

Loney, N. (2003) 'Subsisting on silence', *Regeneration & Renewal*, 24th January, pp. 18-19.

London Race and Housing Forum (1981) *Racial harassment on local authority housing estates*, London: Commission for Racial Equality.

Lupton, M. and Perry, J. (2004) *The Future of BME Housing Associations*, Coventry: CIH.

Macpherson, W. (1999) *The Stephen Lawrence inquiry: Report of an inquiry*, by Sir William Macpherson advised by T. Cook, J. Sentamu and R. Stone, Cm 4262-I, London: The Stationery Office.

Martin, G. and J. Watkinson (2003) *Rebalancing Communities: Introducing Mixed Incomes into Existing Rented Housing Estates*. York: Joseph Rowntree Foundation.

Mason, D. (2003) 'Introduction', in Mason, D. (ed.) *Explaining ethnic differences: changing patterns of disadvantage in Britain*, Bristol: The Policy Press, pp. 1-8.

Matthias, J. (2001) *The bIGPicture: meeting the needs of black and minority ethnic communities*, London: The Housing Corporation.

Ministerial Group on Public Order and Community Cohesion (2001) *Building cohesive communities*, Report, London: Home Office

Modood, T. (1997) 'Employment', in Modood, T. and Berthoud, R., with Lakey, J., Nazroo, J., Smith, P., Virdee, S. and Beishon, S., *Ethnic minorities in Britain: diversity and disadvantage*, London: Policy Studies Institute, pp. 83-149.

Morris, L. (2002) *Managing migration: civic stratification and migrants' rights*, London: Routledge.

Mullins, D., Beider, H. and Rowlands, R., and edited by Niner, P. (2004) *Empowering communities, improving housing: involving black and minority ethnic tenants and communities*, London: ODPM.

Mullins, D. and Pawson, H. (2005) ' "The land that time forgot": reforming access to social housing in England', *Policy & Politics*, 33, 2, pp. 205-230.

Musterd, S. (2003) 'Segregation and integration: a contested relationship', *Journal of Ethnic and Migration Studies*, 29, 4, pp. 623-641.

National Housing Federation (NHF), Commission for Racial Equality, Federation of Black Housing Organisations and The Housing Corporation (2001) *Race and housing inquiry: Challenge Report 2001*, London: NHF.

NHF, Race and Housing Inquiry (2002) *Race Equality Code of Practice for Housing Associations*. London: NHF.

Nazroo, J. (2001) *Ethnicity, class and health*, London: Policy Studies Institute.

Niner, P. (2004) 'Accommodating nomadism? An examination of accommodation options for gypsies and travellers in England', *Housing Studies*, 19, 2, pp. 141-159.

O'Hara, M. (2004) 'Opinion: plans to end segregated public housing in Belfast are doomed', *The Guardian*, 14th April.

Oshodi, T. (2002) 'A masterplan for Greenwich or for the community?', *Black Housing*, 121, January/March, p. 20.

Ouseley, H. (2001), *Community pride not prejudice: making diversity work in Bradford*, Bradford: Bradford Vision.

Ouseley, H. (2004) 'Forget this phoney debate, we need to confront racism', *The Guardian*, 10th April.

Page, D. (1993) *Building for communities: a study of new housing association estates*, York: Joseph Rowntree Foundation.

Parrillo, V. (1998) 'The strangers among us: societal perceptions, pressures and policy', in Kurthen, H., Fijalkowski, J. and Wagner, G. (eds.), *Immigration, citizenship, and the welfare state in Germany and the United States: Part B, welfare policies and immigrants' citizenship*, Stamford: JAI Press, pp. 47-66.

Pawson, H. (2004) 'Perpetuating polarized neighbourhoods? Analysing rehousing outcomes in the English housing association sector', *European Journal of Housing Policy*, 4, 1, pp. 77-106.

Peach, C. and Byron, M. (1993) 'Caribbean tenants in council housing: "race", class and gender', *New Community*, 19, 3, pp. 407-423.

Pearl, M. and Zetter, R. (2002) 'From refuge to exclusion: housing as an instrument of social exclusion for refugees and asylum seekers in the UK', in Somerville, P. and Steele, A. (eds.), *'Race', housing and social exclusion*, London: Jessica Kingsley.

Penoyre and Prasad Architects, with Audley English Associates, Matrix Feminist Architectural Co-op, Elsie Owusu Architects, and Safe Neighbourhoods Unit (1993) *Accommodating Diversity; the design of housing for minority ethnic, religious and cultural groups*, London: National Federation of Housing Associations and North Housing Trust.

Phillips, D. (1986) *What price equality?*, GLC Housing Research and Policy Report No. 9, London: Greater London Council.

Phillips, D. (1993) *Report on the Housing Preferences of Black and White Applicants for Housing in the London Borough of Lewisham*. Report submitted to the London Borough of Lewisham Housing Department.

Phillips, D. (1996) 'Appendix 2: an overview of the housing needs of black and minority ethnic households; census analysis', in Harrison, M., Karmani, A., Law, I., Phillips, D. and Ravetz, A., *Black and minority ethnic housing associations: an evaluation of the Housing Corporation's black and minority ethnic housing association strategies*, London: The Housing Corporation, pp. 50-65.

Phillips, D. (forthcoming) 'Parallel lives? Challenging discourses of British Muslim self-segregation', *Environment and Planning D: Society and Space*.

Phillips, D. and Harrison, M. (2000) *Access to Social Rented Housing: Findings from the Bradford Focus Groups*. Unpublished report to Bradford Metropolitan District Council.

Phillips, D., Ratcliffe, P. and Davis, C. (2003) *Asian Mobility in Leeds and Bradford; Key Findings.* Http://www.geog.leeds.ac.uk/projects/mobility.

Phillips, D. and Unsworth, R. (2002) 'Widening locational choices for minority ethnic groups in the social rented sector', in Somerville, P. and Steele, A. (eds.), *'Race', housing and social exclusion*, London: Jessica Kingsley, pp. 77-93.

Platt, L. and Noble, M. (1999) *Race, place and poverty*, York: Joseph Rowntree Foundation.

Povey, S. (2004) 'On the road again', *Roof*, November/December, p. 33.

Radia, K. (1996) *Ignored, silenced, neglected: housing and mental health care needs of Asian people in the London Boroughs of Brent, Ealing, Harrow and Tower Hamlets*, York: JRF.

Rahman, K.U. (2004), 'Network of Muslim housing professionals formed', *Black Housing*, 132, February/March, p. 8.

Rai, D. and Thiara, R. (1997) *Re-defining spaces: the needs of black women and children in refuge support services and black workers in women's aid*, Bristol: Women's Aid Federation of England.

Ratcliffe, P. (1992) 'Renewal, regeneration and "race": issues in urban policy', *New Community*, 18, 3, pp. 387-400.

Ratcliffe, P. (1996) *'Race' and housing in Bradford*, Bradford: Bradford Housing Forum.

Ratcliffe, P. (1997) '"Race", ethnicity and housing differentials in Britain', in Karn, V. (ed.), *Ethnicity in the 1991 Census; Volume 4, Employment, education and housing among the ethnic minority populations of Britain*, London: The Stationery Office, pp. 130-146.

Ratcliffe, P. (2004) *Race, ethnicity and difference: imagining the inclusive society*, Maidenhead: Open University Press.

Ratcliffe, P., with Harrison, M., Hogg, R., Line, B., Phillips, D. and Tomlins, R., and with Action Plan by Power, A. (2001) *Breaking down the barriers; improving Asian access to social rented housing*, Coventry: CIH, on behalf of Bradford MDC, Bradford Housing Forum, The Housing Corporation, and FBHO.

Refugee Council (2002) 'Refugees in today's world', *Refugee Council Briefing*, Internet reference: http://www.refugeecouncil.org.uk.

Refugee Council (2004) 'Asylum and Immigration Bill 2003: key issues and concerns', *Refugee Council Briefing*, Internet reference: http://www.refugeecouncil.org.uk.

Refugee Council (2004a) *Hungry and homeless: the impact of the withdrawal of state support on asylum seekers, refugee communities and the voluntary sector*, London: Refugee Council.

Robinson, D. (2003) *Delivering housing services to support community cohesion: a scoping paper for the Chartered Institute of Housing*, Sheffield: CRESR, Sheffield Hallam University.

Robinson, D. (2004) 'Communities and cohesion: what's housing got to do with it?', paper for *Housing Studies Association Conference*, Sheffield Hallam University, April.

Robinson, D., Coward, S., Fordham, T., Green, S. and Reeve, K. (2004) *How housing management can contribute to community cohesion: a research report*, Coventry: CIH and the Housing Corporation

Robinson, D., Iqbal, B. and Harrison, M. (2002) *A question of investment: from funding bids to black and minority ethnic housing opportunities*, London: The Housing Corporation.

Robinson, V. (2003) 'Defining the problem', in Robinson, V., Andersson, R. and Musterd, S. (eds.), *Spreading the 'burden'? A review of policies to disperse asylum seekers and refugees*, Bristol: The Policy Press, pp. 3-24.

Robinson, V. (2003a) 'Dispersal policies in the UK', in Robinson, V., Andersson, R. and Musterd, S. (eds.), *Spreading the 'burden'? A review of policies to disperse asylum seekers and refugees*, Bristol: The Policy Press, pp. 103-148.

Robinson, V. and Hale, S. (1989) *The geography of Vietnamese secondary migration in the UK*, Research Paper in Ethnic Relations No.10, Warwick: Centre for Research in Ethnic Relations.

Rodriguez, N. (1995) 'The real "new world order": the globalization of racial and ethnic relations in the late twentieth century', in Smith, M. and Feagin, J. (eds.), *The bubbling cauldron*, London: University of Minnesota Press, pp. 211-225.

Sales, R. (2002) 'Migration policy in Europe: contradictions and continuities', in Sykes, R., Bochel, C. and Ellison, N. (eds.), *Social Policy Review 14* , Bristol: The Policy Press, pp. 151-170.

Sarre, P., Phillips, D. and Skellington, R. (1989) *Ethnic minority housing: explanations and policies*, Aldershot: Avebury.

Scott, A., Pearce, D. and Goldblatt, P. (2001) 'The sizes and characteristics of the minority ethnic populations of Great Britain - latest estimates', *Population Trends*, 105, Autumn, pp. 6-15.

Secretaries of State for Trade and Industry and Constitutional Affairs (2004) *Fairness For All: A New Commission for Equality and Human Rights*, Cm 6185, London: The Stationery Office.

Shah, P. A. (2000) *Refugees, race and the legal concept of asylum in Britain*, London: Cavendish Publishing.

Siedlecka, J. (2004) 'Homelessness strategies: identifying need among minority communities', What Works 31, *Roof*, January/February, pp. 29-32.

Simpson, A. (1981) *Stacking the decks: a study of race, inequality and council housing in Nottingham*, Nottingham: Nottingham and District Community Relations Council.

Simpson, L. (2004) 'Statistics of racial segregation: measures, evidence and policy', *Urban Studies*, 41, 3, pp. 661-681.

Smith, S. (1989) *The politics of 'race' and residence*, Cambridge: Polity Press.

Smith, M. and Feagin, J. (1995) 'Putting "race" in its place' in Smith, M. and Feagin, J. (eds.), *The bubbling cauldron*, London: University of Minnesota Press, pp. 3-27.

Social Exclusion Unit (1998) *Bringing Britain together: a national strategy for neighbourhood renewal*, Report by the Social Exclusion Unit, Cmnd 4045, London: The Stationery Office.

Social Exclusion Unit (2000) *National strategy for neighbourhood renewal: a framework for consultation*, Report, London: Cabinet Office.

Sodhi, D. and Steele, A. (2000) *Contracts of exclusion: a study of black and minority ethnic outputs from registered social landlords contracting power*, London/Salford: London Equal Opportunities Federation and Salford Housing and Urban Studies Unit, University of Salford.

Sodhi, D., Johal, S., Britain, E. and Steele, A. (2001) *The diverse needs of black and minority ethnic communities: an annotated bibliography of housing and related needs studies*, Manchester: Ahmed Iqbal Ullah Race Relations Archive.

Sodhi, D., Johal, S. and Steele, A. (2001a) *The diverse needs of black and minority ethnic communities: an annotated bibliography of housing and related needs studies and initiatives to promote diversity*, Manchester: Ahmed Iqbal Ullah Race Relations Archive, 2nd edition.

Somerville, P. and Steele, A. (eds.) (2002) *'Race', housing and social exclusion*, London: Jessica Kingsley.

Somerville, P., Sodhi, D. and Steele, A. (2000) *A question of diversity: black and minority ethnic staff in the RSL sector*, Source Research 43, London: The Housing Corporation.

Steele, A. (2002) 'Black youth homelessness', in Somerville, P. and Steele, A. (eds.), *'Race', housing and social exclusion*, London: Jessica Kingsley, pp. 178-191.

Stewart, M. (1994) 'Between Whitehall and town hall: the realignment of urban regeneration policy in England', *Policy & Politics*, 22, 2, pp.133-145.

Temple, B. and Steele, A. (2004) 'Injustices of engagement: issues in housing needs assessments with minority ethnic communities', *Housing Studies*, 19, 4, pp. 541-556.

Terry, R. and Joseph, D. (1998) *Effective and protected housing investment*, York: Joseph Rowntree Foundation.

Tomlins, R. (2003) *BME housing project research*, Leicester: De Montfort University.

Tomlins, R., with Brown, T., Duncan, J., Harrison, M., Johnson, M., Line, B., Owen, D., Phillips, D. and Ratcliffe, P. (2001) *A question of delivery: an evaluation of how RSLs meet the needs of black and minority ethnic communities, Source Research 50*, London: The Housing Corporation.

Van Kempen, R. and Özüekren, S. (1997) 'Introduction', in Özüekren, S. and Van Kempen, R. (eds.), *Turks in European cities: housing and urban segregation*, Utrecht: ERCOMER, pp. 1-11.

Waterman, S. (2003) *The Jews of Leeds in 2001: portrait of a community*, JPR Report 4, London: Institute for Jewish Policy Research.

Webster, C. (1997) 'The construction of British "Asian" criminality', *International Journal of the Sociology of Law*, 25, pp. 65-86.

Werbner, P. (1990) *The migration process*, New York: Berg.

Wilson, R. (2001) *Dispersed: a study of services for asylum seekers in West Yorkshire December 1999 – March 2001*, York: Joseph Rowntree Charitable Trust.

Winant, H. (1995) 'Dictatorship, democracy, and difference: the historical construction of racial identity', in Smith, M. and Feagin, J. (eds.), *The bubbling cauldron*, London: University of Minnesota Press, pp. 31-49.

Yinger, J. (1995) *Closed doors, opportunities lost: the continuing costs of housing discrimination*, New York: Russell Sage Foundation.

Zetter, R and Pearl, M (1999) *Managing to Survive: Asylum seekers, refugees and access to social housing*, The Policy Press: Bristol.

Index

Notes:
1. The index covers the main text but not the preface or the bibliography.
2. Acts of parliament are only included if they are referred to more than once in the text.
3. Proper names (e.g. of organisations) are generally only included if they are referred to more than once in the main text. Names of government departments are omitted.